ST KATHERINE'S HOSPITAL, LEDBURY
LEDBURY
*c*1230-1547

ST KATHERINE'S HOSPITAL, LEDBURY
*c*1230-1547

by
Joe Hillaby

Ledbury and District Society Trust Ltd
in collaboration with
Logaston Press
2003

LOGASTON PRESS
Little Logaston, Logaston,
Woonton, Almeley, Herefordshire HR3 6QH

First published by Ledbury and District Society Trust Ltd
in collaboration with Logaston Press 2003
Copyright © Joe Hillaby 2003

ISBN 1 904396 12 7

Set in Baskerville & Times by Logaston Press
and printed in Great Britain by
Bell & Bain Ltd. Glasgow

Cover illustrations:
Front: *St Katherine's: Composite female saint c1340, chapel east window*
Rear: *See Table 7, p123*

For Caroline
who made it all possible

Then shall the King say unto them on his right hand, Come, ye blessed of my Father, inherit the kingdom prepared for you from the foundation of the world: For I was an hungered and ye gave me meat: I was thirsty, and ye gave me drink: I was a stranger and ye took me in: Naked, and ye clothed me: I was sick, and ye visited me ... Verily I say unto you, Inasmuch as ye have done it unto one of the least of these my brethren ye have done it unto me.

Matthew 25: 34-40

Contents

List of Tables

Maps

Acknowledgements

The history of St Katherine's *c*1230-1547 is based on the remarkable collection of deeds, court rolls, rentals, accounts etc in the archives of the Dean and Chapter of Hereford cathedral. Anybody working on this material in the new cathedral library is privileged indeed. For one who had to study the *Red Book* of the bishops of Hereford decades ago, in the forbidding circumstances of a small, ill-lit room in the offices of the Church Commissioners on the side of the Thames at Mill Bank, or in a similar and freezing cold room in one of the most famous of English country houses, the space, light and calm of the new library are very much appreciated.

So also are the warmth and helpfulness of the staff. Joan Williams, Cathedral Librarian, and Rosalind Caird, Cathedral Archivist, have done much to lighten work on what, at times, has proved the daunting task of examining the medieval records of St Katherine's. Mention should also be made of the contributions of Marion Roberts and the late Meryl Jancey, who in their time at the library jointly embarked on producing an abstract of the most important part of the St Katherine's collection, the 'Register of the Venerable Man John Elton', who served as Master for 32 years, 1515-47. This Cartulary is particularly rich in material from the date of foundation to the re-organisation of the hospital administration by Dean John Prophet. Only those who have used the Register can appreciate the value of the work which Marion and Meryl undertook.

Anyone who has cause to refer to the endnotes will realise that the completion of this book would have been impossible without access to major libraries. If there is to be adequate interpretation of the rich material in the St Katherine's records, it has to be placed in context. This means extending one's search far wider than the numerous studies of the records and archaeology of other English medieval hospitals. It has to be placed in the wider, religious, social and economic history of the period. Loan facilities at the libraries of the University of Bristol, University College, London, and the London Library, with its remarkable full runs of English archaeological and county journals, have made this possible.

The Society's thanks go to the Dean of Hereford, the Very Rev Michael Tavinor, for writing the Preface. As 65th successor to Dean Thomas de Bosbury, d1230, who undertook, on behalf of the Chapter, to 'keep, maintain and defend the rights and possessions' of Bishop Hugh Foliot's foundation, this Preface reflects the remarkable continuity which is such a distinct characteristic of the history of St Katherine's. It was Dean and Chapter who were 'to dispose of all in the said house according to their own will without contradiction of any man'. However, it has to be said that the second volume of this *History* will show that this was not always to be the case.

This book owes much to the friendship and help of many people. Firstly, it was the late Sylvia Robinson of Bank Cottage, Ledbury, who more than three decades ago aroused my enthusiasm for the history of St Katherine's. It was Sylvia who found the late 16th-century panel with the portrait of the founder, Hugh Foliot, in the centre and the inscription at either side which recorded the contemporary Anglican view of the 'Church of Rome'. This she had restored and placed on the north wall of the chapel to secure it from further adventures. A group visit to St Katherine's led by Sylvia Robinson was a memorable, and amusing, occasion which, as I learned, few ever forgot. In more recent years Mary Hawtin, from her vantage point in St Katherine's, has kept her watchful eye on the chapel.

There has been valuable assistance from Alan Vince on the medieval tiles, and Richard Marks on the stained glass, both of whom were taken on pilgrimages to the chapel for detailed inspection of its treasures but the opinions expressed are mine. A joint visit to the roof space above the Mansion House was made with Dave Baxter, Herefordshire Council Conservation Officer and a friend of long standing, who is doing much to ensure that the full significance of the building is being thoroughly explored and recorded. I have had many wide-ranging and enjoyable conversations with the Rev Ian Gibbs of Munslow on matters concerning the medieval church. The enthusiasm of Peter Garnet and Alan Starkey is well known to members from the displays on the history of the town that have been mounted by the Society, and to the many groups from kindred societies who visit the town. It has now found a further outlet in promoting the publication of this volume. Last, but by no means least, a note of thanks and congratulations to Andy Johnson, the Logaston Press, for producing a second splendid volume dealing with the history of Ledbury and its district. His very personal attention ensures that his publications bear the individual stamp of their authors.

Preface

Ledbury has a special place in my affections when I think of the diocese of Hereford, for it was at Ledbury that I reached the half-way stage of my walk from Tewkesbury to Hereford in May 2002. The walk was meant to be a pilgrimage, linking two ministries, and it proved to be a project helping me to meet a good number of fellow pilgrims—I called at every church on the way, leaving a prayer card in each, and was accompanied on the way by clergy through whose parishes I passed.

Ledbury proved a welcome pause on the journey as I renewed my strength and enjoyed the hospitality of the Rector and the community.

On that pilgrimage, I discovered the important links between Ledbury and Hereford, not least in the work of St Katherine's Hospital, of which the Dean and Chapter of Hereford have been guardians for so many centuries. These links are still warmly preserved and the Chapter consider it an important part of their ministry to have care of this ancient foundation, supported as they are by the Master and his team.

In St Katherine's Hospital, many themes are gathered together—care of body and soul, prayer and pilgrimage, and we are indebted to Joe Hillaby for giving us such a comprehensive guide to the ways in which these themes played an important part in the pre-Reformation history of the foundation.

I pray that the links between Hereford and Ledbury may grow stronger and that St Katherine's may continue to play its part in the care and nurture of the community of Ledbury.

The Very Rev Michael Tavinor
The Deanery
Hereford

Introduction

The Ledbury and District Society was founded in 1973 to encourage public interest and involvement in the protection of the heritage of Ledbury and its district. This book, it is hoped, will contribute to both objectives.

St Katherine's has always had strong links with the district served by the town. At foundation it was given the churches of Weston, Yarkhill and Kempley. It may be thought that Kempley, in Gloucestershire, has little contact with Ledbury. In writing this book I have learned otherwise. Visiting Mr Kenneth Brooke of Friars Court to view and photograph his 15th-century cruck-framed barn, I found that he had an intimate knowledge of those now farming the lands mentioned in the early chapters of this book: Netherton, Massington, Ockeridge, Orlham etc. Why? Because they had all been members of Ledbury Young Farmers.

St Katherine's had a wide range of lands in Eastnor. Its extensive collection of 13th- and early 14th-century deeds provides a mass of information, otherwise unobtainable, on the place-names of the area, enabling us to build up a picture of its richly varied economy and landscape prior to the Black Death in 1349. The hospital was granted other lands across the Malverns, at Berrow. Here also the shire boundary counted, and still counts, for little. In 1288 at least three of Ledbury's burgesses had the surname *Berwe* and in the 18th century Ledbury was Berrow's post town. Now its postcode is HR8 and Brian Haynes and his neighbours of Whiteleaved Oak still frequent Ledbury's shops and markets each week. St Katherine's history is also inextricably bound up with Ashperton or Stretton due to the major role the Grandison family played as patrons.

Foliot founded St Katherine's *c*1230 as a place of succour for the poor and infirm and as a chantry chapel. Here a chaplain was to offer up daily prayers for the repose of Foliot's soul and those of other benefactors. Other chaplaincies were founded by local people. By 1360 there were six, making it effectively a college of chantry priests. The 775th anniversary of foundation is only a year away. Three-quarters of a millennium is a proud achievement for any institution. In this case it is primarily due to the supervisory role of the Dean and Chapter of Hereford cathedral, to whom the founder, Hugh Foliot, entrusted his hospital.

It is from their records that we know so much about St Katherine's and its district in the 13th and 14th centuries. A 1316 inventory shows that the hospital's estates now extended to 1,100 acres. By 1364 the total was 1,600. The inventory provides valuable details of St Katherine's different farms, or granges, and a vivid picture of life in the precinct, hall and chapel, with its services, books and vestments and, most remarkable of all, a list of the relics which it held, including parts of the True Cross and the cross of St Andrew. In the years 1330-40 the hospital flourished under the patronage of the de

Grandisons, whose family lands lay close to Neuchâtel but whose earliest English estates lay about Stretton and Ashperton. Hall and chapel underwent a major programme of reconstruction, providing very high quality stained glass for the chapel. Only vestiges survive in the east window but these are sufficient to indicate its strong family resemblance to the glass in the Latin chapel at Christ Church cathedral, Oxford, described as 'some of the most important glass of the second quarter of the 14th century'. The fine timber roof of the hall, with its beautifully cusped wind braces, belongs to the same period.

St Katherine's was deeply affected by the Black Death, 1349. It led to the collapse of its demesne economy. Instead of farming much of its own lands, these were now leased out to laymen. Instead of agricultural produce for home consumption, the master enjoyed a much enhanced cash income, with all its blandishments. Ledbury parishioners revealed the dire crisis which the hospital now faced at an episcopal visitation in 1398. John Prophet who, between 1392 and 1416, served both Richard II and Henry IV in the Royal Council and later as Keeper of the Privy Seal, combined these duties with the deanship of Hereford cathedral. It was his reform ordinances which carried St Katherine's successfully through to the reign of Elizabeth I.

The 15th century witnessed the building of the H-shaped half-timbered Master's House, until recently the surgery. Now undergoing specialist examination, the major part still lies embedded in the existing brick structure, on the south side amounting to little more than a brick skin. Its remarkable roof trusses are still visible to those with the courage and suitable clothing to get into the roof space. The book includes the first photographs to be published of this roof, with its most interesting spere truss dividing the great open hall from the screens passage and service wing to the east. The Master's House 'is an extremely rare building ... possibly the only surviving (medieval) example of a purpose-built master's house left in this country'.

The chapel's late medieval tiles are also of great interest. They belong to a group of which the most famous examples are the 3,800 tiles by the high altar at St David's cathedral where originally there were 13,340 such tiles, yet the group is named from the house of William Canynges in Bristol where the first series, now in the British Museum, came to light. These have been described as 'the most impressive products of the Malvern school' (of tilers) in the Museum's collection. Only some 500 of these tiles remain at St Katherine's, but they are especially important for they are in better condition than those at St David's or London.

The terminal date of the book is 1547, the year that parliament abolished chantries. Unlike many hospitals, St Katherine's weathered this storm also. It had been founded not only to provide the poor and infirm with 'rest, warmth, cleanliness and adequate diet' but also for its chaplains to offer up daily prayers for the souls of its founder and benefactors, in which all would participate. This was not the only way in which its role was diminished. Its concern now was, for the most part, care for the bodies rather than the souls of those it had been founded to serve. A further volume will, it is planned, take the story of St Katherine's to our own day.

1   Foundation

Ledbury's hospital of St Katherine was founded by Bishop Hugh Foliot (1219-34). He was probably related to two earlier bishops of Hereford, Gilbert Foliot (1139-63), a famous scholar and later bishop of London, and Robert Foliot (1174-86). Bishop Hugh describes the hospital's role in two charters. In the first he declares that he built the hospital dedicated to God and the blessed Katherine for 'the support of pilgrims (or wayfarers) and the poor', a formula more appropriate to a large institution on a major route. Although undated this charter cannot be later than 1231 for it was confirmed by Dean Thomas of Bosbury, who died in September of that year, with his Hereford chapter. As the second charter bears the date March 1233, foundation can hardly have been much earlier than 1231.

Foliot's second charter refers not to pilgrims or wayfarers but to the 'poor and weak lying therein'. Subsequent endowments specify 'the poor and needy', only occasionally 'the poor and infirm', underlining the fact that St Katherine's was, in modern parlance, an almshouse not hospital.[1] Like other medieval hospitals it sought to provide 'rest, warmth, cleanliness and an adequate diet'. The use of herbs and blood-letting were common practice but, even if thought appropriate, few hospitals could afford the skills of a professional physician. In 1290 bishop Swinfield paid Master John Gyreberd 6s 8d and his assistant 6d for attendance at Ledbury on 2 March. A physician of national repute could claim about £6 for a week.[2] Fundamentally, until the dissolution of the chantry chapels in 1547, St Katherine's was dedicated to the salvation of souls, not bodies.

Foliot's Motives

The charters indicate that Foliot's motives were twofold. Primarily the hospital chapel was to be a chantry where chaplains would sing masses and say prayers, in perpetuity, for the well-being and good estate of the bishop whilst alive and for the swift passage of his soul through purgatory, as also for his predecessors and successors. In purgatory, unlike hell, the soul was purified through temporary suffering. The church believed that 'the intercessions of the faithful, that is the saying of masses and prayers, giving alms and other works of piety', would help to relieve its passage through purgatory. As the prayers of the poor were held to be especially efficacious, a hospital offered a distinct advantage over the conventional chantry. Few, if any, of the inmates were literate so they participated through recitation of the Lord's Prayer (*Paternoster*), Hail Mary (*Ave Maria*), possibly the Creed, and later often the full Rosary. Not only did this reduce the danger of the chaplains neglecting their duties but, as with masses, the greater the number of prayers the greater, it was believed, their efficacy. As an incentive for its future good government, which was to rest in the hands of dean and chapter, Foliot provided that masses and prayers should also be said for the canons of Hereford; and that a trental, a daily mass for 30 days, should be sung on the death of each canon. Ecclesiastical authority did not recognise any service outside the parish church, except with the consent of its rectors. Thus a licence for the celebration of divine service in the chapel was granted by Hugh's brother, Thomas Foliot, and Philip de Braose, rectors or portionists, of Ledbury parish church. If, as Bishop Hugh hoped, the hospital would in time support two chaplains, the second was to pray for the souls of the living, and also all benefactors as an incentive for further local endowments.[3]

Foliot's aspiration was fulfilled before his death in 1234 when William *de Alkerugge*, Ockeridge, the second largest landowner in Ledbury manor, assigned certain tenements 'for the maintenance of an honest and young chaplain' to celebrate mass on Sundays forever for his own soul and that of his wife. The deed was inspected by the bishop and witnessed by his brother, Thomas, as cathedral treasurer.[4] Other benefactors were to be drawn by the same deep belief in prayers of intercession. Further chaplaincies were founded. By 1364 there is evidence of at least five chaplains and the chantry continued to attract endowments. As late as 1407 Margery Wynd granted fourteen acres of wood at Tyrells Frith, Little Marcle, for the maintenance of the master and 'certain chaplains to celebrate divine service daily'. This she directed should be 'according to the primeval foundation'; 'the support of certain poor persons' was secondary.[5]

Secondly, Foliot regarded his foundation as a work of charity. As Archbishop Langton reminded the citizens of Hereford in 1226, in an attempt to secure their support for the newly-founded hospital of St Ethelbert, 'alms-giving should not be reckoned of little account amongst other works of charity ... It behoves us by works of mercy to anticipate the final harvest, to sow on earth that which, if God grant it, we ought to gather in Heaven. He who sows in blessings will of blessings also reap eternal life.' From Matthew 25:31-46, who describes how the Good Shepherd would divide his sheep from the goats, the church derived its concept of the Six Corporal Acts of Mercy: to feed the hungry, give drink to the thirsty, harbour the stranger, clothe the naked, visit the sick and minister to prisoners (Fig 1.1). For the bishop above all, as shepherd of his flock, it was incumbent to be, in the words of Job, 'the father of the poor, eyes to the blind, feet to the lame'. When Robert de Bethune, most saintly of Hereford's

Fig 1.1 All Saints, York. The Six Corporal Acts of Mercy: Feeding the Hungry

bishops (1131-48), came to his palace at Ledbury, where Richard de Capella, his predecessor, had founded a small borough, he found a multitude of the poor lying before the gates. Consequently he maintained in each of his manor houses a number of paupers, providing 'a daily ration and the requisite clothes and shoes throughout the year'. Foliot's foundation of St Katherine's may thus represent the flowering of an institution already more than a century old. However, it has to be borne in mind that Foliot was motivated as much by the spiritual benefits that would accrue for himself from the religious life of the *familia*, the community who served the poor, as by charity, concern for the relief of the poor.[6]

Endowment

If the foundation charter is taken at face value, endowment by the bishop was meagre indeed, three burgages in his borough of Ledbury providing an annual income of 3s. One and a half burgages he bought from John fitz Gersant, the property monger of the district. Another burgage is of great interest for it is described as 'in New Street', indicating that development of that, the last of Ledbury's medieval streets, had taken place prior to 1230. In addition a half burgage was bought from Margaret, the daughter of Gilbert Franceis.[7] Although not mentioned, Foliot's grant included the site, the construction of the hospital itself and its ancillary buildings.

The hospital site originally occupied almost two-thirds of the western frontage of the market place founded by de Capella. This raises a fundamental issue in relation to the topography of the early borough, for burgage plots in the market place would have been at a considerable premium. For Foliot to have disposed of existing burgages to make way for the hospital would, in the middle ages, have been an impossible task but, more significantly, an unnecessary one. As St Katherine's was not a commercial institution, it had no need of a market frontage. Its purpose would have been better served away from the noise and smell of the market place. The only satisfactory explanation is that this was the original site of the episcopal palace which served also as the administrative centre and home farm for his extensive estates in the locality. Indeed a building on the hospital's Bye Street frontage was still called the Bishop's Palace in the early 20th century. The foundation of St Katherine's on this site enabled Foliot to re-establish himself in a more congenial location away from the hubbub of the town centre.[8]

Foliot had a partner in his enterprise, for lay endowments played a major part in sustaining medieval hospitals. Just as he had sought ecclesiastical guarantors, the dean and chapter, so also he sought lay protection, and with it financial support. Greatest of the barons of the southern march was Walter II de Lacy. From strongholds at Ludlow (Fig 1.3b),

Fig 1.2 Kempley, St. Mary's: Fresco of c1120 thought to represent Hugh I de Lacy

Fig 1.3a Weobley Castle, the original head of the Lacy lordship

Weobley (Fig 1.3a), Castle Frome and Longtown in Ewias Lacy his family had played a crucial role in local politics since 1075. Walter had been sheriff of the county during the critical years of Henry II's minority, 1216-23. As patron of Hamo of Hereford he could call on the resources of one of the wealthiest Jewish financiers of the era. His English manors, assessed at fifty-one and a quarter knights' fees, had a particular concentration in the Frome valley, centred on Castle Frome.[9] In Wales he was lord of Ewias (Fig 13c). More important, in Ireland he ruled the whole of the ancient kingdom of Meath from his castle at Trim, the most powerful in Ireland (Fig 1.3d). De Lacy's political, as much as his material, support was an essential element for

Fig 1.3b Ludlow Castle, head of Walter II de Lacy's English Lordship

Fig 1.3c Longtown Castle in the de Lacy marcher Lordship of Ewias Lacy

Foliot in the success of his enterprise. No layman could, apparently, provide firmer guarantees—as well as important endowments.[10]

To St Katherine's Walter granted the churches, that is the advowsons, the right to appoint a vicar and to enjoy some of the tithes and glebe, of Weston (Beggard) and Yarkhill, valued in 1291 at £4 and £5 6s 8d per annum respectively, as well as the manor of Yarkhill. For this manor he had given Simon de Clifford rents of £30, half in Holme Lacy, the remainder in his lordship of Meath. St Katherine's was also granted the church of Kempley with 'certain tenements and fields'. This church was in all probability begun *c*1120 by Hugh I de Lacy, son of Walter I, founder of the family. One of the two contemporary frescoes of 'pilgrims' in the chancel is thought to be Hugh I (Fig 1.2). The advowson of the church, with 'the tenements and fields', now belonged to Geoffrey de

Fig 1.3d Trim Castle, head of Walter II's Lordship of Meath

Longchamp of Wilton Castle near Ross, but evidence suggests the real donor was his wife, Isabel, who had family links with the de Lacys.[11]

There is no evidence that de Lacy was a beneficiary of the prayers offered up at St Katherine's. He could rely on many other institutions to intercede for his soul. In Ewias Walter and his father, Hugh, funded the lavish rebuilding of the Augustinian priory of St John the Baptist at Llanthony. Also in Ewias, high up on the edge of the Black Mountains at Craswall, Walter founded in about

Fig 1.4 Christ Church Cathedral, Oxford: St Katherine with Wheel and Sword

1223 the second English house of Grandmontine hermit monks, the 'Bonshommes', renowned for their generosity to the poor. At Ludlow he was associated with the foundation c1221, under the shadow of his great castle, of Peter Undergod's hospital of St John the Baptist by Teme bridge. At Aconbury, in 1218-23, he supported his wife, Margaret, in her foundation of the house of Augustinian canonesses, with its hospital for the sick and the poor. At Hereford, 'across the Wye towards Eign', the leper house of St Thomas was established in 1221 by a member of his entourage, William fitz Warin.[12] In Ireland he founded cells of Llanthony Prima and was a benefactor of the abbeys of St Thomas's, Dublin, Fore and Bective. At Beybeg he established white monks and at Ballymore Loughsewdy black nuns. For the annalist of the ancient abbey of Clonmacnoise Walter was the 'bountifullest foreigner in steeds, attire and gold that ever came to Erin'. In terms of Lacy family political support, however, Foliot miscalculated; Walter died without male heirs, blind and with most of his English lands mortgaged to Jewish financiers.[13]

Dedication

The hospital's dedication represents Foliot's personal devotion to St Katherine of Alexandria. Although held to be a 4th-century martyr, there is no evidence of her cult until the 9th century, at Sinai. According to the *Golden Legend* she was of royal birth, not only learned but of 'incredible beauty'. Arguing by allegory and metaphor, logical and mystical inference, she enquired of the emperor Maxentius why he vainly gathered crowds to worship the stupidity of idols, urging him instead to acknowledge the Creator. Unable to overcome her in debate, Maxentius sent for 50 of his masters of logic and rhetoric, only for them to be converted by Katherine. In fury he ordered them to be thrown into the flames and Katherine to be incarcerated, without food, for 12 days. Finding that she had been fed by an angel, and that she had also converted his empress, Maxentius ordered the preparation of the famous wheel—in fact a pair, armed with swords and sharp nails, moving in contrary directions—only to see it destroyed by an angel. He thus resorted to a simple expedient, execution by the sword. Hence Katherine's two medieval attributes, the wheel and the sword (Fig 1.4). Angels carried her body to the top of Mount Sinai where her tomb was discovered in the 9th century and her shrine can still be seen.[14]

In the west Katherine's cult arose from the translation of a relic from Sinai to Rouen by the mid 11th century. According to legend a monk spent seven years serving her cult on Sinai, praying incessantly that he might be worthy of a relic. Suddenly one of her fingers fell off. This he took back to his abbey of la Trinité whence her cult spread rapidly to England. By 1100 a miracle play based on her life was being performed at Dunstable and in 1148 Matilda, King Stephen's queen, founded a royal hospital in the saint's honour close by the Tower of London. If the evidence of English stained glass and wall paintings can be trusted, by the 15th century she was the most popular of our female saints. The reason is simple. At the moment of her execution, it is said, a voice was heard to declare: 'Heaven's gates are open to you and those who will celebrate your passion with devout minds'. Such divine assurance that her intercession would be effective undoubtedly explains her great appeal.[15]

Foliot founded another chantry to Katherine in the Romanesque double chapel built between palace and cathedral by bishop Robert de Losinga, 1079-95. This was divided into upper and lower chapels. It is not clear in which Foliot's chantry was to be found, as Stukeley refers to the upper as 'St Catherine's Chappel' in his drawing but as 'St Magdalen's' in his text (Figs 1.5a-c). As at Ledbury, chaplains were to say prayers, in perpetuity, for the repose of Foliot's soul and those of his predecessors and successors. Here again, as control was placed in the hands of dean and chapter, they were included amongst the beneficiaries. St Katherine thus continued to be honoured at Hereford, and in 1255 the Savoyard Bishop Aquablanca dedicated a hospital to her at his home town of Aigueblanche, where services continued to be performed according to the Hereford Use.[16]

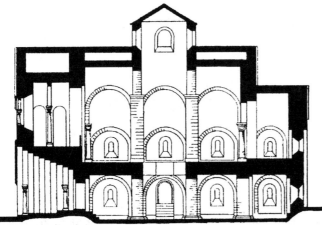

Fig 1.5 Bishop's Palace Chapel. Hereford
a Top: Upper Chapel prior to demolition by Bishop Egerton
c1738. W. Stukeley
b Centre: Longitudinal section looking north, west portal to left,
sanctuary to right. N. Drinkwater
c Lower: In 1989, showing north wall of upper and lower chapels

Dean and Chapter as Guardians

By his second charter, of 1233, Foliot had conferred the guardianship of St Katherine's on the dean and chapter. They were to 'keep, maintain and defend its rights and possessions', to ensure that 'all goods which belonged, or should thereafter belong, to the hospital were to be applied only to the use of the poor and weak lying in the hospital'; and 'to dispose of all in the said house according to their own will forever and without the contradiction of any man'. The dean and chapter were to nominate chaplains and ensure that the chapel's goods and possessions were used only for the benefit of those ministering there and, on the death or departure of any of the lay brethren, who assisted the master in the running of the hospital, they were to fill the vacancy. The charter makes no reference to the appointment of the master, but this responsibility they assumed. A document of 1354 suggests that until Dean Prophet issued his Ordinances of 1398 the master was usually selected from the ranks of the brethren. Of the almsfolk what very little we know comes from a late source. They were thirteen in number.[17]

The dangers that were to face St Katherine's were fully anticipated by Foliot. At the end of his charter he publicly and solemnly excommunicated all who should at any time presume to subtract, diminish or misapply the hospital's possessions and estates contrary to its terms. In what eventually proved to be a vain attempt to ensure that these essential duties were fulfilled, he granted the dean and chapter an annual fee of 40s for which they were to inspect his foundation each year. Their failure to perform these duties with adequate rigour led on occasions to severe crises, which threatened the institution's very existence. In consequence the story of St Katherine's is a microcosm of the vicissitudes of the history of dean and chapter over almost eight centuries. To this day Foliot's second charter has continued to play the major role in the history of St Katherine's. It informed the judgment of the Exchequer Court in 1580 and again in 1819. The trust conferred on dean and chapter is one they still exercise today.[18]

Although supervision was the responsibility of dean and chapter, in practice government lay with master and brethren. To them land and rents were granted, and it was they who effected all purchases, leases and exchanges. Many leases are described as with 'the consent' or even the 'unanimous consent' of the brethren. On occasions they were joined by the sisters, also members of the *familia*. The hospital's seal was the formal expression of this corporate legal identity. Two extant 13th-century impressions depict

Fig 1.6 Seal of St Katherine's Hospital

the west front of a major church with St Katherine seated and Bishop Hugh in supplication below (Fig 1.6). The common seal from which they were taken was kept in a little ivory box in the sacristy, 'under the keys of the master and brethren of the house'. Presentations to the churches at Weston, Yarkhill and Kempley were also made by the 'warden, and the brothers' who presented, amongst others, Hugh the priest to Weston in 1305, but by 1388 the brethren were being excluded from such formal transactions by the master. By the 16th century master and brethren were again acting as a corporation sole. The Exchequer Court determined in 1580 that they were usurping the authority of dean and chapter and thus in breach of Foliot's trust and acting illegally.[19]

Such a division of authority between the founder's trustees and the master, acting with or without his brethren, was characteristic of many medieval hospitals. Despite its pitfalls it was the best that could be achieved at the time. As threats to the hospital in the medieval period came principally from negligent or corrupt masters, it was only when dean and chapter fulfilled their monitorial role effectively that the well-being of St Katherine's was assured. Detailed reforms in 1398 by John Prophet, the greatest of Hereford's medieval deans, went some way to resolve such long-standing difficulties.

Eventually the Exchequer Court became the ultimate guarantor of St Katherine's constitution. In 1580, after a legal battle of more than a decade in the Star Chamber and Exchequer Courts, the dean and chapter, led by the redoubtable canon Edward Cowper, Archdeacon of Hereford, successfully resisted Queen Elizabeth's attempt to terminate Foliot's 350-year-old trust. In 1797 it was the attorney general who instituted proceedings against Dean Nathan Wetherell, the chapter and the Master, Canon James Birt. A further, even longer, legal battle led in 1819 to a revised constitution being issued by the Exchequer Court, in which ultimate financial control was placed in the hands of the bishop, and to the building of the almshouses as we see them today, a process only completed in 1866. The fourth and final scheme of reform was provided by the Charity Commissioners in 1962 when the original jurisdiction, in Foliot's words 'without contradiction of any man', was restored to dean and chapter.

2   The Hospital Buildings: Evidence of the Inventory

The ideals and thus organisation, architecture and nomenclature of the early English medieval hospital were monastic in origin and based on the principle of the common life. Not surprisingly many contemporaries 'found it impossible to distinguish between certain hospitals and small houses of religious'.[20] The plan of the medieval hospital was derived from the monastic infirmary where not only sick but also aged monks, those who had been professed 50 years, were cared for. This consisted of a large open hall, with beds down each side, and a chapel at the eastern end. In the greater Benedictine houses such halls were large, with double aisles. At Ely the hall was 105 feet x 44 feet; at Canterbury and Gloucester five columns and arches of the arcades remain as well as vestiges of the small infirmary cloister. The monastic infirmary also had its own kitchen. Some of the greater hospitals could afford to follow the monastic layout and a few even had a double court-yard plan. For most, however, this was beyond their resources. Nevertheless the need for such ancillary facilities as kitchen, buttery, washhouse, herb garden and separate accommodation for master, brethren and sisters remained, however random the layout in practice.

The Hospital Plan

Although based on the monastic infirmary, hospitals differed widely in size and design, but hall and chapel were the heart of all such institutions. The simplest and most common design was an open hall where the eastern bay, or bays, served as a chapel. Where the hall lay north-south the chapel had to be attached at right angles to permit the altar to face east. Larger halls could have aisles on

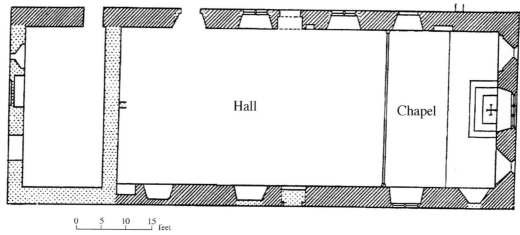

Fig 2.1 Plan of St Katherine's Chapel and Hall

either side, accommodating beds and providing clerestory lighting, a plan seen locally at St John the Evangelist, Cirencester, founded by Henry II about a century before St Katherine's. A variant permitted total segregation of the sexes, an open hall with a double pitched roof supported by a single arcade down the centre and twin eastern chapels, as at St Nicholas, Salisbury, almost contemporary with Ledbury.[21]

St Katherine's is of the basic open-hall design (Fig 2.1). The division between hall and chapel, now blocked by a timber partition, was originally marked by the timber truss still to be seen. The large multipurpose infirmary hall will have had beds down the side walls, leaving a generous space in the centre for the activities of the day and where at meal times trestle tables could be set up, as can be seen at Beaune in Burgundy today (Fig 2.2). The hall was open to the roof. Reference to fire dogs in the hall in an inventory of 1316 suggests a fire was an early feature. Today there are the remains of a later fireplace in the centre of the south wall, but no signs of a projecting chimney stack such as on the east side of the Master's House. Smoke was carried up a flue built into the wall and out of a vent at the top.

For the Royal Commission both hall and chapel, with its three eastern windows, 'appear to have been rebuilt c1330-40'. Pevsner concurs: 'Chapel and hospital, in one, built early in the 14th century, of red stone.'

Fig 2.2 Grande Salle des Pauvres, Hôtel-Dieu, Beaune, from the chapel end

Fig 2.3a St Katherine's: East front with two 13th-century lancets and central 14th-century Decorated window of three lights

12

The two outer lancets, however, were not part of the 14th-century rebuilding programme but of Foliot's east end of *c*1230. His design was a triplet of lancets with its central window taller than the outer pair. The evidence for this is clear. A larger, Decorated window was inserted *c*1330-40 into the original unified Early English design for the east end (Fig 2.3a). Below the northern jamb one can still see part of the head and sill of the left-hand side of an aumbry, a cupboard built into the wall for the safekeeping of the altar vessels. As usual, this had been built to the left of and close to the altar, but it had to be blocked up and a new aumbry built in the north wall when the Decorated window was constructed (See Figs 8.5a&b). Its predecessor, the Early English central window, was thus considerably narrower, a lancet. Designs similar to the original triplet but more elaborate in form can be seen at the east end of the choir of Hereford cathedral, *c*1220 (Fig 2.3b), and of the chapel at St Leonard's, York, *c*1235 (Fig 2.3c).

The hall, with its chapel, is essentially of the same two periods: an original building of *c*1230 and a reconstruction of *c*1330-40. From this date the timber roof, the doorways and most of the windows. The original windows, in both chapel and hall, were lancets of which a well-preserved example can be seen in the south wall of the chapel. The fact that hall and chapel were lit by windows on the south as well as the north shows that the building was freestanding. Development of the hospital's market-place frontage to the south of the chapel came after reconstruction in 1330-40.

The truss between the chapel and infirmary hall is quite different from those in the hall for its function was similar to that of the chancel arch of a parish church. It divided chapel from hall and clergy from laity, a division further emphasised by a timber screen below, similar to that of the

Fig 2.3b Hereford cathedral, east end of choir

Fig 2.3c York, St Leonard's, east end of chapel

chancel screen of parish churches (Fig 2.4a). At Ludlow, where the chapel arch of Undergod's hospital is incorporated in the end wall of a later house, it is of stone rather than wood (Fig 2.4b). At St Katherine's the truss consists of a pair of five-sided wall posts with capitals of wood from which springs a pair of braces holding a tie-beam, above which a further pair form a segmental arch (Fig 2.5). This tie-beam served an important liturgical as well as structural purpose, for it carried the Rood, Christ crucified, with the Virgin on His right and St John on His left, with candles on the beam for illumination. At the hospital's own church of St Mary's at Kempley the 12th-century triangular painted background to a sculpted Rood and a fresco of St John on Christ's left can still be seen, but the accompanying Virgin has been lost.(Fig 2.6).

Immediately behind, on a wooden tympanum, would have been the Doom, the Last Judgment. These differed in detail but the overall theme, as the late Dooms at St Thomas's, Salisbury, Staningfield and Wenhaston in Suffolk and South Leigh, Oxon show, is always clear-cut. At the top in the centre was Christ as Judge, seated on a rainbow, displaying His wounds (Fig 2.7). On either side the Virgin and St John interceded for humanity. Below, the last trump is sounded and the graves give up the souls of the dead (shown naked), some wearing crowns, mitres and cardinals' hats to emphasise that none are exempt from this day of judgment. In many cases the artist appears to have taken a delight in portraying such figures being dispatched to join the damned. Another feature in which the artists seemed to have revelled is the portrayal of the archangel

Fig 2.4a St Katherine's: Timber Partition now covering site of rood, tympanum and chapel archway below

Fig 2.4b Ludlow: Chapel arch of St John's Hospital

Michael weighing the souls, a scene vividly depicted in the stained glass of the east window at Eaton Bishop (Fig 2.8). Often demons are portrayed attempting to tip the scales by hanging on to one side. At St Mary's, Kempley a 15th-century wall painting on the splay of one of the nave's north windows shows Michael weighing a naked soul in the scales and the Virgin on his left as at Eaton Bishop (Fig 2.8). Less frequently the Virgin is shown placing her rosary on the scales by the soul of a person assiduous in devotion to her.

On Christ's right the blessed are greeted by angels and, passing St Peter, the gate keeper, gain admittance to the heavenly mansion, shown as a medieval walled town. On Christ's left the damned are thrust into the maw of hell by an array of devils. To many the distinction between the permanence of hell and the temporary nature of purgatory may well have become blurred by such scenes. At the early 15th-century *Hôtel Dieu* at Beaune in Burgundy this scene is portrayed in Roger van der Weyden's masterpiece, *The Polyptych of the Last Judgment*. At Ledbury the bed-ridden could look through the screen, beneath the Rood, into the chapel with its stone altar and candles, lighting up the images of the Virgin, St Katherine and others, to participate in the services, especially the recitation of intercessory prayers for the founder and all benefactors. It will have been this

Fig 2.5 St Katherine's: Chapel arch, timber capital

Fig 2.6 St Mary's, Kempley: Painted background to sculpted Rood and St John

15

Eaton Bishop: Fig 2.7 Christ as Judge   *Fig 2.8 St Michael weighs a Soul*

sight of Christ crucified, with the Virgin and St John as their advocates, which provided them with the hope of salvation.

As in the monastery, daily life within the medieval hospital was lived according to a *Rule*. For most this meant the rule of the Augustinian canons which offered greater flexibility for those who worked with the needy. At Ledbury an inventory of 1316 tells us that the 'Rule of the house' was written into a book of psalms kept in the sacristy. Of its precise terms we are ignorant but common factors in the rules observed by other houses, such as St Mary Magdalene's leper hospital at Dudstone in Gloucester, St Mary's, Chichester, and St Leonard's, York, one of the largest of all English hospitals, indicate the main provisions. All entering St Katherine's as members of its religious community would have had to swear an oath of poverty, chastity and obedience and adherence to the common life. Other important provisions related to observance of the divine office, the saying of the canonical hours, and the wearing of a distinctive dress.[22]

Throughout the year the day was divided into equal 'hours' of light and dark, indicated by the sundial. Matins, the night office, was followed by lauds, the first of the seven day 'hours'. The offices of the first, third, sixth and ninth hours would follow through the day which ended with vespers and compline. This was accompanied at Chichester and elsewhere by prayers for the pope, archbishop, bishop of the diocese, dean and chapter of the cathedral, all prelates of the church, the king and

16

queen, and for the founder and all those named benefactors, living and dead, who had granted fixed rents. It was the chaplains who said masses for the founder and benefactors, but all members of the community in priests' orders had to say private masses after lauds.

The illiterate poor had in their own small way an important role to play. At Dudstone, unable to participate in the hours, they were required to learn by heart the Lord's Prayer, Hail Mary and Apostles' Creed. They had to say 24 Paternosters in place of matins, seven instead of vespers and five for each of the other hours. Special services were held on the great moveable feasts of the Christian year, Easter and Pentecost, the immoveable feasts of the Nativity and Epiphany and the anniversaries of the major saints of the calendar. Most important of these, on 25 November, was the feast of their patron, Katherine of Alexandria, a celebration suppressed by the Holy See as recently as 1969.

The 1316 Inventory

An inventory of 'all the goods, moveable and immoveable, chattels, books, charters, charges, instruments, relics and other ecclesiastical ornaments belonging to the Hospital' was drawn up on Brother Philip de Chaddesley's entry to office as Master in January 1316. It is neatly divided into 12 sections. Appropriately, the first three deal with objects relating to the religious life of the community: service books; vessels and ornaments for use at the altar; and relics. These are followed by 'writings', that is property deeds (4); lands and rents of the estates (5); and 'utensils and tables' (6). Sections 7 to 10 deal with husbandry at Ledbury and Eastnor and the outlying granges of Kempley, Weston and Yarkhill. The last two sections detail sums outstanding (Appendix 1).[23]

Books

As all books were hand written and on parchment, they were costly items. Ecclesiastical legislation shows that many parishes had the greatest difficulty in affording even the most basic service books. Thus the first section of the inventory lists the hospital's nineteen volumes. These are of great interest as the major source as to the order and form of the religious life of the community. All but one were liturgical, used throughout the year for the mass or divine office. Their range reflects the complexity of these services, due in no small part to the fact that the texts, music and ritual differed for each day of the week and were more elaborate on Sundays. In addition there were individual services for the many festivals. Further complexity was due to the fact that Easter Sunday is a moveable feast. The commemoration of the Resurrection, determined by the paschal full moon, can fall anywhere between 21 March and 25 April. Their liturgical collection guided the community through all these variables.

Two *missals* or mass books, with ceremonial directions, provided all that was necessary to be said or sung for mass throughout the year. The mass was in two parts, the Ordinary which remained constant and the Proper in which the text changed from day to day. The *canon of the mass*, fixed and unchanging, was that part of the mass at which the celebrant silently uttered the words of Jesus at the last supper, elevated the host, and ended by chanting the final words aloud. Although the priest was required to know it by heart, he had to have the text before him to ensure he made no mistake. This was followed, before communion, by the Lord's Prayer and the kiss of peace. As the pages of the *canon* were used every day, this section of the missal, subject to such heavy wear, became tired and eventually unreadable. Hence the need for this separate copy of the *canon*. Indeed, after the introduction of the printed missal the *canon* was sometimes printed, not on paper, as was the rest of the book, but on vellum, to give much greater durability.

Three *tropers* provided the fixed texts of such parts of the mass as *Kyrie*, *Gloria*, *Sanctus* and *Agnus* which were set to music and sung. They possibly contained polyphonic settings of parts of the Ordinary and of the Office chants but especially the sequences, the prolongation of the Alleluia to give the deacon time to reach the pulpit to chant the gospel. One 'much used and unbound' *troper* might, it has been suggested, indicate a degree of musical experimentation at St Katherine's. There were also three *graduals*, books of plainsong with words and music of the *antiphons*, choral refrains, usually from the Bible, forming responses sung before and after the psalms and canticles. As they were normally sung on the steps of ambo or altar, their collection took its name from the Latin for steps, *gradus*. There were two separate books of *antiphons*.

The *psalter*, of which there were three, was a basic text for the divine office, the saying of prayers at fixed hours of the day and night, included the recitation of the psalms with the intent of saying the full course through the week. Longer psalms were divided into sections, whilst the shorter were coupled. The first office, prime, included the *martyrology*, a calendar naming the saints, both martyrs and confessors of the faith, under their feast days. A passage from the appropriate *Life* for the day was then read, followed by a chapter from St Katherine's own *Rule* or *Statutes*, which was written into the first of the three psalters. Next came the 'chapter' meeting. The other two psalters illustrate the continuing efforts to bring together the different books used in the office, of which the end result was to be the *breviary*. The second psalter contained a hymnary, its hymns arranged according to the liturgical year, and part of an antiphoner. The third included not only the hymnary but also services for the various saints' days, bound together, to which the clerk significantly added, 'without notes'. The *ordinal* informed the priest of the office to be recited at the various times of the church year. The next item, a *portiphorium*, portable *breviary*, indicates the large size of the normal service books. For the master's personal use, it contained in one volume the various psalms, hymns and lessons which priests and clerics in major orders were obliged to recite daily. If not quite a pocket book, it could be carried by the master for use on his travels, pursuing the business of the house or otherwise. The final item was 'one book of (Norman-)French which begins "*Coment sapientes*"'. These are probably the *incipit*, the opening words, of a commentary on the search for wisdom: human, the principles of virtuous living, and divine, not only the books of the Old Testament but also the Word made incarnate, Christ Himself.[24]

Vestments etc

Details of the vestments, ornaments and furnishings provided in the second section of the inventory enable us to appreciate the richness of services held in the chapel. Vestments were listed in accordance with the occasion (Fig 2.9). First came solemn festivals, when the *chasuble* (A), the outermost garment worn by a priest during the celebration of mass, was made of brocade, a rich fabric with a raised pattern, often embellished with silver or gold thread. The *alb* (B), a long white linen garment, was worn under the chasuble. Its *apparels* (C), small pieces of ornamental embroidery, on the front at the base and on the cuffs,

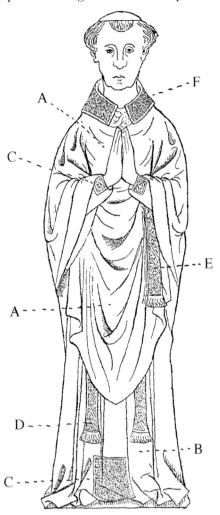

Fig 2.9 Priest in Mass Vestments
A Chasuble; B Alb; C Apparels of the alb; D Stole; E Manipee; F Amice

18

were of silk; the *stole* (D), a narrow ornamental band worn around the neck, the ends of which hung down beyond the chasuble, was 'of rich material', as was the *maniple* (E), another ornamental band, worn over the left arm. The *amice* (F) of decorated linen cloth, worn around the neck, was on these occasions embroidered with gold. In addition there was a *tunic*, the liturgical outer garment worn by deacons, of striped silk. There was a Sunday chasuble and alb with apparels, the chasuble being of 'cloth of Tars', a rich oriental fabric, possibly from Tarsus or Tabriz. The four weekday chasubles and albs were of fustian. For the brothers, who evidently assisted at services on occasions, there were four surplices. The list ends with reference to two rochets, surplice-like vestments of linen worn by clerics, including those of minor orders, and even sacristans. The quality and range of the vestments stand in contrast to the 'three surplices and a rochet' which, ten years earlier, Archbishop Winchelsey had ruled were the basic requirements for every parish church, a standard which frequently proved to be the exception rather than the rule.

As to ornaments etc, the two chalices and the patens were of silver gilt, but the three cruets in which the wine and water were brought to the altar were of pewter. For the altar there were nine embroidered cloths, and for the celebrants's use three towels. Two chests were used to house the books and ecclesiastical vestments. Statues of the Blessed Virgin and St Katherine are referred to in a number of deeds. Thus Adam de Strete granted an annual rent of 5d. and 1d. respectively to keep candles burning before them. As late as 1508/9 the lordship of Cradley was still providing a one-pound wax candle annually to burn before the image of St Katherine, a sight to comfort the inmates through the long nights. The list of the most treasured of all the community's possessions, its relics, will be considered in Chapter 7.[25]

Two Communities?
Whilst the plan of hall and chapel is quite straightforward, the overall layout of the hospital site, now occupied by the car park and surrounded on the west by the remains of its mid-18th-century brick wall, is highly problematic. Section 6 of the inventory, 'utensils and tables', provides a valuable glimpse of some of the precinct buildings, and of the more mundane life of the hospital. The inventory lists the contents of the hall in the same way it lists the contents of other communal facilities, suggesting meals were taken communally by master, brethren, sisters and almsfolk. There were four trestle tables, much favoured for their greater flexibility as compared with the so-called dormant or sleeping tables, together with two long and three short benches. Here also were a bench cover of pales, that is striped material, plates and cutlery. Reference to a pair of andirons, fire-dogs, with a cauldron and basin for washing, confirms the existence of a fireplace in the hall. Provision of warm water for washing hands was certainly a luxury not enjoyed by monks who had to use the lavatorium, a stone basin with cold running water, in the cloister or let into the wall by the refectory entrance. In addition to a large jug and six wooden cups, probably for master and brethren, there were eighteen silver spoons, a pewter saltcellar, six tablecloths and four towels.

The two daily communal meals were eaten in silence, accompanied by appropriate prayers and readings. At St Mary's, Chichester 'if a priest is present let him publicly say the benediction and each brother say the Lord's Prayer in private. If no priest is present let each make the sign of the cross over the bread and say *In Nomine Patris*. After the meal let each lift up his hands and return thanks to God and say *Paternoster*. Let them eat in silence and without murmuring, whatever is placed before them, providing that what is prepared shall be sufficient for nature and not addressed to the taste'. Master and brethren slept separate from the poor and infirm, in a dormitory with six beds, suggesting a complement of five brethren, but there were only four surplices in the chapel. Each wore a uniform, the one large and two small chests in the dormitory containing double sets of clothing. At St Mark's, Bristol, however, 'master, chaplains and brethren who wear the habit' ate and slept together 'in one house, the refectory'. The communal washhouse empha-

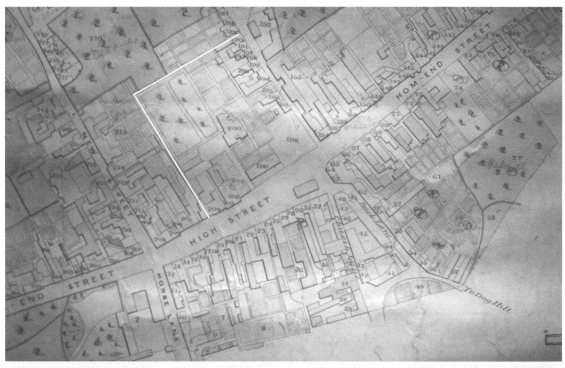

St Katherine's: Fig 2.10a Top: Map of precinct; Fig 2.10b Lower: Aerial view of precinct
In both cases the edge of the precinct not bounded by roads is marked by a white line

sises this sense of two communities. Its large trough was divided, one part for *familia*, master and brethren, the other for *hospitalis*, the poor and needy'.[26]

The service area, including kitchen, larder, pantry and cellar with brewhouse, served the needs of the whole community. The kitchen for safety reasons would have been a separate structure. It was equipped with a lead cauldron, six posnets, small metal pots with a handle and three feet, used for boiling, two mortars and pestles, a stone salt mill and nine small measures. Although the inventory was drawn up at the end of January, the larder was well supplied, with four ox carcasses and twenty salted bacons. There was also a cellar with a brewhouse, which contained four large bins for malt, fourteen barrels and two casks, whilst there was a 12-gallon bronze ale measure in the kitchen. The table for bread-making was kept in the washhouse with the communal trough.

The inventory provides no clue as to the layout of these buildings within the precinct. It may be that they were situated around a cloister or quandrangle, with the chapel and hall forming the southern range, as at St Helen's, the Great Hospital, Norwich founded by the bishop only a few years later than St Katherine's. Here the master and chaplains' quarters were the northern range. St Nicholas, Salisbury, founded *c*1230 and another episcopal foundation, also had a building to accommodate the *familia* to the north and probably a cloister-type layout similar to that at Norwich. If this had been the case at St Katherine's, the Great Gate would then have been on the east side of the cloister, with kitchen and allied buildings to the west, close to the infirmary hall where the community ate.[27]

No reference is made to the chaplains' or sisters' accommodation, nor to that of the servants and farmhands who lived in. The former probably lived in their own quarters within the precinct, whilst the latter were, no doubt, accommodated in the farm buildings which formed the western part of the hospital complex, as shown in the 1584-95 accounts.[28]

The Authority of the Master

Without firm leadership to ensure strict adherence to their Rule, internal dissension was bound to arise.[29] The master was frequently termed *custos*, on occasions procurator, preceptor or prior. Such evidence as there is suggests that until the later 14th century it was from the chaplains that many were drawn. Brother William, also referred to as a chaplain, appears in two early leases, of 1239 and 1242.[30] Seven other, undated, charters in which he is named as beneficiary confirm that he was the first master, because their witnesses were drawn from the group of local worthies who supported St Katherine's in its early years. These included Alan de *Walintone* (Wellington), William de *Aukerugge* (Ockeridge),Walter *Camerarius* (Chamberlain), William Caperun, Osbert Marshall, John fitz Gersant, William de Paris, John de Solers and Masters Robert and later Hugh de Furches.[31]

The role of the other members of the *familia*, the brothers and sisters, was varied. Some would be counterparts of the *conversi*, the lay brethren of a Cistercian monastery. At Ospringe in Kent, where they were called 'obedientiaries' or 'custodians', they were allocated specific responsibilities, the brethren taking charge of the cellar with its stores, of the running of the brewhouse and bakehouse, larder and garden, whilst the sisters had nursing and domestic roles. There is evidence at Ledbury that literate brethren assisted the master with the administration of the hospital's estates. Thus the manorial accounts for 1333 were drawn up by Brother Roger. Early rules show that the sexes were kept firmly apart, except at work and prayer. The mid-12th-century statutes of St Mary Magdalene's at Dudstone enact that men and women were not to go into each others' quarters, nor 'be found together in cellar, larder, orchard or field, under mealtime penalty for forty days'.[32]

The regulations of St Mary's, Chichester give the oath of admission and other details. 'I will in all things be faithful to the house and observe to the utmost the rules established. I will observe towards myself chastity, towards my superiors obedience and will hold no property of my own ...'.

Their hair was then cut and the kiss of admission given. Henceforth they were addressed as brother or sister. As to daily life, they were to 'pray continually, or be engaged in work, that the devil may not find them with nothing to do. When the seven canonical hours are said daily brothers and sisters who are ignorant of them say every week day, at each hour, the Lord's Prayer seven times, with the *Gloria Patri*, except at matins, when they must repeat 50 *Paternosters*. On feast days they must say 15 *Paternosters* each hour, at matins 100 and every day 150 *Ave Marias*. For a brother or sister who has died, let them say 150 *Paternosters*. Let whoso knows it say the Psalter. None must omit things enjoined as penance because of prayers.'

The Great Court

Both hospital and estate buildings were enclosed within a great court, some 300 by 330 feet, the area today marked out by the car park (Figs 2.10a&b). The buildings of the home farm, which were within this precinct, are described in chapter 4. The principal access was through the 'Great Gate' or 'the Gatehouse' as it is referred to on occasions. Such gatehouses were a marked feature not only of monastic precincts but also of many hospitals. At Ospringe a chamber 8' by 8' formed the upper storey. At St Katherine's the early 19th-century stone gateposts immediately north of the chapel— deprived of their iron gates for salvage during World War II—indicate the site of the Great Gate (Fig 2.11).

Fresh water was ducted from Coneygree Wood in the Bishop's Park, for the parish register records in 1592 that 'whole(some) water was conveyed in new (renewed) lead from the Coninger unto the High Crosse and there to the Hospital gate or conduit there'. The latrines and waste may have been flushed into the culverted stream which came down from the Upper Hall; a section of this stone culvert is still visible under the old grammar school in Church Lane. Over the Lower Cross and down Bye Street it flowed as an open drain or kennel. From the borough's earliest days 'the disgusting habit of slaughtering animals in the public highway' meant that the kennel ran with blood and the noisome effluent 'from so many privies and slaughtering rooms'. Development of burgage plots along the market place and Bye Street frontages would have shielded St Katherine's from some of this. St Mark's, Bristol, had piped water from Brandon Hill and drains leading to the river Avon, *c*1240.[33]

A number of mostly large hospitals, such as St Katherine's-by-the-Tower and St Mary Spital, London, St Thomas, Southwark, and St Bartholomew's, Bristol, had rights of sepulture. Burial became the seventh corporal act of mercy. The Maison Dieu at Ospringe was conceded burial rights by the abbot of St Augustine's, Canterbury in 1245.[34] There is no evidence that St Katherine's had such rights to its own cemetery. Indeed, the earliest parish register records the burial of two members of the community in the parochial churchyard.[35]

Fig 2.11 St Katherine's: 'The Great Gate' or 'Gatehouse' today

22

3 The Growth of an Estate: the Evidence of Deeds

In 1328, when the dean and chapter sought Edward III's inspection and confirmation of Foliot's foundation charter, seven sets of deeds were appended. These represent the hospital's most treasured acquisitions to that date, other than the lands St Katherine's acquired with the churches of Weston, Yarkhill and Kempley at foundation, which are discussed in Chapter 6. The cathedral's extensive collection of St Katherine's medieval deeds enables us to trace the processes by which these and other estates were acquired. Some of the deeds are originals, but many are copies, transcribed by John Elton, Master 1515-47, who brought together a wide range of material, not only deeds but also court rolls and rentals, into a cartulary which he describes as his '*Register*'. This is made up of three separately paginated series of records, the deeds forming the third part, of 170 pages.[36]

The deeds relate not only to lands in the open fields of Ledbury foreign, that part of the parish outside the limits of the borough, and Eastnor, but other important properties about Chase End at Berrow, just across the Malverns in Worcestershire, at the Hyde in Cradley, at Malmespool Mill, and burgages in Ledbury market place and Widemarsh Street, Hereford. Although all but one are decorously described as donations, some are not quite as altruistic as at first sight they appear, for St Katherine's had to spend more than £100 in legal fees defending its title to a number of these lands.[37]

A number of the deeds inspected in 1328 specify the amount of land granted, but the acre was not the precise measurement we know today. In origin, the basis of land measurement was the quantity that could be ploughed in a certain time. The carucate, hide or ploughland, for example, which consisted of four virgates or yardlands, represented the land an eight-oxen plough team could till in a year, but this would depend on the nature of the soil. Thus carucates, virgates and acres were all customary measures. The statute acre of 4,840 square yards was first introduced by Edward I in 1277 but this made slow progress. It had to be reintroduced by Edward III in 1357, and re-enacted by Henry VIII in 1532.

Locally the hide, ploughland or carucate varied considerably. In 1240 the Worcester priory register posed the question, 'How many acres make a virgate in various places?' In Worcestershire and Warwickshire the virgate was commonly between 25 and 30 acres, but in the St Katherine's manors it was uniformly 60. When comparisons are made with other estates care has thus to be exercised. A court roll of 1332 notes that 'one virgate of land in Weston contains 60 acres and one noke is one quarter of a virgate', and at Kempley the 1497 court roll records that 'one noke contains fifteen acres and thus is a quarter part of one virgate'. Thus on the St Katherine's lands the noke was 15 acres, the virgate 60 and the carucate 240 acres, a standard probably adopted from the neighbouring estates of the bishop.[38] Even at the end of the 18th century the precise area of the acres referred to in St Katherine's records was perceived as a problem, although probably an overestimated problem. In a dispute with Lord Somers over lands in Eastnor, the master was advised by his surveyor that 'This difficulty, the kind of acre (customary or computed), and if computed the size of the acre, seems to be the point to be adjusted first'.

1. Gersant's Grant and the Eastnor lands

The first of the seven sets of deeds confirmed in 1328 relates to the lands granted by John fitz Gersant, a prominent member of that group of local worthies whose names appear so frequently in the early charters. He was very active in the local land market. As Foliot mentioned in his first charter, Gersant was the man from whom he had purchased the one and a half burgages in Ledbury which formed part of St Katherine's initial endowment. From Gersant St Katherine's received lands which, taken together, were of major importance. The 1316 inventory refers to 44 of Gersants 'writings', almost a fifth of the total of 237 deeds in the hospital's collection.[39] This reflects the fact that he granted not major holdings, of virgates and half-virgates, but a large number of widely dispersed selions, the long and narrow, individually ploughed strips, in Ledbury foreign and Eastnor.

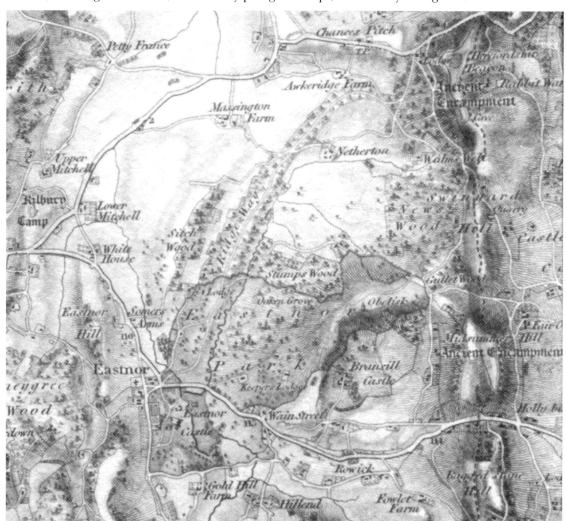

Map 1: 1831 OS, Eastnor Lands

24

The selion was the base unit of the open fields, its shape and size depending on the lie of the land. For example, about 1240, for 15s, Roger *de Northington* granted Geoffrey *de Cruce* of Ledbury three acres of land, viz one acre of four selions with two headlands, the second acre of seven selions and the third of nine. The headland was an area at the end of the furlong, a series of selions, which could not be ploughed for lack of turning space for an oxen team. As a result it was often left as pasture. Butts were short or subdivided strips and gores were triangular or irregularly shaped pieces of land at a furlong's end. The furlong's direction was normally such as to allow excess rainwater to drain off the ridges into the furrows and thence to the stream or sitch at the valley bottom.

The hospital's deeds provide a vivid picture of the open fields in that large wedge of land between the Ledbury-Malvern and Ledbury-Tewkesbury roads. This includes half of Eastnor parish and the Ledbury townships of Netherton, Massington and Ockeridge lying to the north, in that strip of the parish which extends to the county boundary on the Malvern ridge about British Camp (Map 1). The landscape of this area is dominated by a series of four wooded ridges dividing four valleys. Moving from east to west, these are firstly the southwest hook of highland from the Malverns above Gullet Wood which includes Bircher Wood, Ashen Fields Coppice, Oaken Grove and Tinkers Grove; secondly the Ridgeway; thirdly Sitch Wood; and finally the high land about Eastnor hill and Frith Wood.[40] The sides of the valleys had, to varying degrees, been cleared of woodland, to create arable fields, but the remaining areas, of more (rough pasture) and woodland etc, were also of considerable importance to the varied farming economy of the area.

Fig 3.1 Brankeswellesiche

This area was drained by four streams or sitches: Bronsil Sitch, the Glynch or Court Brook, the Sitch and the Withybrook. Although the streams are not named, their courses can be followed on the Ordnance Survey 1:25,000 Explorer map. The term 'sitch' is found not only in place-names, such as Sitch Wood pasture, meadow and coppice, but also in a surname. Roger le Doublesiche appears in an undated St Katherine's deed relating to the sale of land in Netherton township, between the highway, presumably the Ridgeway, and the Glynch Brook.[41]

The most easterly of Eastnor's open fields were at Bronsil. The early form of the name is *Brankeswelle*, meaning the spring of Branoc, a Welsh personal name.[42] From both sides of the valley rainwater from its furrows fed into *Brankeswellesiche* (Fig 3.1). This stream rises at the edge of Castle Coppice. Today, after flowing past Bronsil Cottages, being diverted to feed the castle moat on the way, it crosses the Eastnor-Hollybush road to join the Glynch brook flowing from Eastnor lake just south of Wayend Street. The Glynch, the second stream, is recorded in a charter of 963 relating to the stretch downstream, beyond Eastnor, as Clenchers Brook, the name coming from the Welsh *glan*, 'pure, clean'. In a mid-14th-century deed this is 'the river called *Glenche*'. Confusingly, its upper course was also known as the Court brook from the 'Old Courtes' of Castleditch. It rises at Walm's Well in News or Newes Wood, still pronounced by locals 'Newers' Wood, just below Clutters Cave (Figs 3.2, 3.3, 3.6). It then flows west to serve the furlongs about Netherton where it turns south through the present deer park, to enter Eastnor lake. A small tributary, rising in Bircher Wood below Peacock Villa, flows northwest, forming Eastnor's northern boundary with Ledbury, and joins the Glynch above the duck pool. The third watercourse, a mere rill, the Sitch, serves the narrow valley between the Ridgeway and Sitch Wood, joining the last of the four streams, the Withybrook, just north of Eastnor village.[43] In St Katherine's medieval deeds the latter is described merely as 'rivulet' or 'the waters' but in an Ockeridge terrier or land survey of 1621 it is Withybrook, whilst Great

Fig 3.2 Clutter's Cave

Fig 3.3 Walm's Well

Withyfield is described as being north of the open field known as Horsecroft. It rises by Ockeridge and flows southward past Massington and then, following the railway, into the valley between Sitch Wood and Eastnor Hill. Like the Glynch in the deer park, it retains its alders and in the middle ages will have had a long narrow meadow following its lower reach. Horsecroft was situated on either side of this Withybrook, between Sitch Wood and what is now White House Farm, and Withycroft Field lay to the north (Fig 3.4). Joined by the Sitch, the brook then flows into Eastnor Lake.

The Eastnor and Ledbury deeds provide a rich harvest of place-names, not only for fields, furlongs and strips but also for woods and woodland clearances. There are no St Katherine's court rolls for this area, but 16th-century terriers help to build up a clearer picture of the distribution of the hospital's lands in Eastnor and Ledbury parish to the north. The place-names on tithe maps are often regarded as valuable indicators of medieval settlement but, for Eastnor and Ledbury, there is almost no correspondence with those in the deeds and terriers. Apart from woodlands, such as Bircher and Sitch woods, the only names in common are Horsecroft Field, numbered 177 and 178 on the tithe map, and Withybrook Field, 192, and the overall area in both cases is greatly contracted.

Gersant's principal grant consisted of 94 selions, 12 butts, a grove of one and a half acres and 13d in rent, in eighteen distinct parcels. In Eastnor there were: in *Brankeswallfelde* two parcels, of four and five selions, in different parts of the same furlong and a further four selions, on the other side of the stream, *Brankeswallesiche*, extending to *Brankeswalle* itself; in Horsecroft field seven selions in the upper furlong, eight and ten in the lower furlong, 'with the meadow, pasture and more which lie at the head of 41 selions in the same field and extend to the neighbouring rivulet', the Withybrook; a further seven selions between the highway, evidently between what is now White House Farm and Roger Oates, formerly the Somers Arms Temperance Hotel, and the fishpond (close to the Sitch brook), together with the 'hay' of Horsecroft as far as the brook; and one butt

Fig 3.4 Horsecroft Field from the west showing Withy Brook

27

between the 'hayment' of Horsecroft and the brook; and at *Goram* 12 butts. In Ledbury foreign he granted eight selions in the lower furlong of *Little Wydecroft*, extending to *Wydecroftesbroke*, with four in the upper, and four at *Helmeresbryge*, between the brook and the highway to Ledbury; in Great Wydecroft eight, nine and four selions in the upper furlong, again extending to the highway, and five selions in the lower furlong; at *Redewythie* another seven furlongs; and in *Edricsgrove* one and half acres of woodland.

Details of Gersant's grants are found in two charters. In the first he explains that he gave these lands for his 'own soul and those of his ancestors', but the second records the 'consideration' paid by Brother William, the Master: 46 silver marks, £30 13s 4d, with one seam or packload of corn, based on the London quarter of eight bushels as established by Magna Carta.[44] Another five selions 'under Brankeswalle' went to St Katherine's with 2d a year to be paid 'for candles at the feast of St Michael in the church of St Peter at Ledbury'. Eventually John granted all his lands and rents to Brother William, for eighteen years. In return he was to receive a corrody, a daily allowance for himself, his wife and maid of 'two white loaves and three of wheat quality, each weighing two pounds, pottage, two gallons of good ale as drunk in the *familia* and one as drunk in the *hospitalis* and was to have, without contradiction, fruit of the garden' (and orchard?), a prominent feature of hospital precincts.[45] Such provision suggests a desire to spend his last years at ease in a trouble-free old age rather than a yearning to die in the odour of sanctity.

Given the dispersed nature of the selions being granted by Gersant and others, the masters were anxious, wherever possible, to exchange strips to permit consolidation and so form enclosures - for arable, pasture and meadow. To this end Brother William bought five selions and one butt in Wheatcroft from Alice, widow of Roger of *Northington*, for 7s.[46] Shortly afterwards, in another exchange, Roger *de Piribrok* granted an acre of arable in Weston, lying in *Craswell*, between the hospital's lands on both sides. In Kempley, Walter *de Accenebury* exchanged a meadow, lying between that of the hospital and the arable of the lord of the manor, Reginald de Grey, for two pieces of land belonging to the hospital, one called *Calverparruc* and the other in *Brodefeld*, both adjacent to his own holdings. Also in Kempley, at a date unknown, master and brethren exchanged certain lands in *Oldeworthin* at *Wodewallepul*.[47]

2. Ockeridge

Here William *de Alkerugge* held 240 acres of the bishop by military tenure. Ockeridge, with Massington, was in Ledbury foreign, between Chances Pitch and the Ridgeway, by the head of the Withybrook. William's grant was to provide for 'the maintenance of an honest and young chaplain to celebrate mass in the said hospital for his own soul, that of his wife, Margery, and his ancestors and successors forever on Sundays and the solemn feasts'. The deed was inspected and corroborated by the bishop himself who died in August 1234, thus giving a terminal date. The witnesses included not only Adam of Ledbury, steward of St Katherine's, who was evidently responsible for the establishment of the hospital prior to William's appointment as first master, but also Foliot's brother, Thomas, as cathedral treasurer, and Adam of Shrewsbury, now the bishop's steward. Of all seven sets of deeds confirmed in 1328 this is the most straightforward, providing a vivid picture of the different types of land found at the time in this part of the Malverns. William granted 60 selions, three butts, three acres of arable, some hay land and a small wood: in *Peseden* field ten selions and two acres; in *Westfelde* fourteen selions along and ten 'below' one of the 'ways', service routes; at *Twyseledway* thirteen selions; 'under the more (rough pasture) of Robert de *Mughale*' another thirteen selions and three butts with ditches; 'next the way called *Estgeft*' a further acre of arable. Other items were the 'grove by the more as far as the lane to Alured the Baker's hayment', 'half of *Holeya* with the hayment adjoining' and la *Heyrudyng*. This was in Richard Falconer's more, by 'the Old Ditch', extending as far as *Heyrudyng well*, *Rudying* being cleared land, from *rude* or *rede*, the local form of the Middle English *ride*, a clearing.[48]

La Heyrudyng is well-documented. In the first comprehensive survey of the St Katherine's estates, drawn up for the Exchequer Court by the bishop and dean of Worcester in 1580, a pasture 'called Ruddings, by estimation six acres' is associated with another 'called Newsfeilds alias News Wood, by estimation 50 acres'. Two centuries later, between 1785 and 1813, the Ruddings and News Wood were the subjects of a 28-year dispute between St Katherine's and the Eastnor

Fig 3.5 Shire Ditch

estate. In the 1813 act which resolved this dispute these were 'Ruddings, pasture, 8 acres' and 'Newe Wood and Field, coppicing, 53 acres'. News Wood is still coppiced by the estate. The location of the Ruddings, as close to News Wood, enables 'the Old Ditch' of William of Ockeridge's deed to be identified.

Given Ockeridge's site and the two references to 'more', in this context rough upland pasture, it was either the ditch of the southern enlargement of British Camp or the Shire Ditch, the Red Earls Dyke (Fig 3.5), for both are within the bounds of Ledbury parish whilst the camp itself is in

Fig 3.6 Newes Wood

Colwall parish. It may be argued that, as Foliot, who corroborated this deed, died in 1234, it could not be the Shire Ditch for that was not built until after the confrontation between Bishop Thomas Cantilupe and the Red Earl, Gilbert de Clare, in 1287. However English Heritage's recent Malvern Hills Archaeological Survey has shown that this part of the Shire Ditch underlies, and thus predates, the counterscarp of Midsummer Hill Iron-Age hill fort. As the closer to News Wood, therefore, this seems more likely to be the 'Old Ditch'.[49]

A second grant by William de Ockeridge paid due regard to both of the hospital's functions: 'for the well being of my soul and the soul of Margery, my wife, and for the sustenance of the poor in the hospital of St Katherine'. It consisted of an assart with ditch and close within a certain more, previously the marriage portion of his daughter, Margaret, and a messuage in *Aukerug* with three acres of arable, bought from Hugh the Clerk.[50]

3. The Berrow, Worcestershire

Berrow, on the eastern slope of the Malverns, lies wholly within Malvern Chase, held in the 13th century by the de Clare earls of Gloucester. Roger *de la Berche*, who had succeeded his father, Robert, as lord of the manor prior to 1226, granted St Katherine's by an undated deed yearly rents in Berrow totalling 26s 10^{1}/$_{2}$d and three hens. Geoffrey *de Berwe*, a member of the family, was the wealthiest resident of the manor in the 1280 Worcestershire lay subsidy rolls, but by the early 15th century the manor had passed by marriage to the Ruyhales of Birtsmorton.[51]

As the lands were on the far side of the Malverns, in Worcestershire, Roger's grant requires some explanation. In the Anglo-Saxon era Berrow and Pendock were closely associated with Overbury, east of the Severn under Bredon Hill (Fig 3.7). Although deep in the 'wilderness' of Malvern, they were important to Overbury as rough summer pasture. In 875 Pendock, including Berrow, had been given to the church of Worcester and the bounds of *le Berwe* are described in a charter of 972. Although a later fabrication, its author had first-hand knowledge of the area, for he describes the northern bounds as following the *pyrt* brook from a col of the Malverns known as

Fig 3.7 Berrow, looking east to the Cotswolds

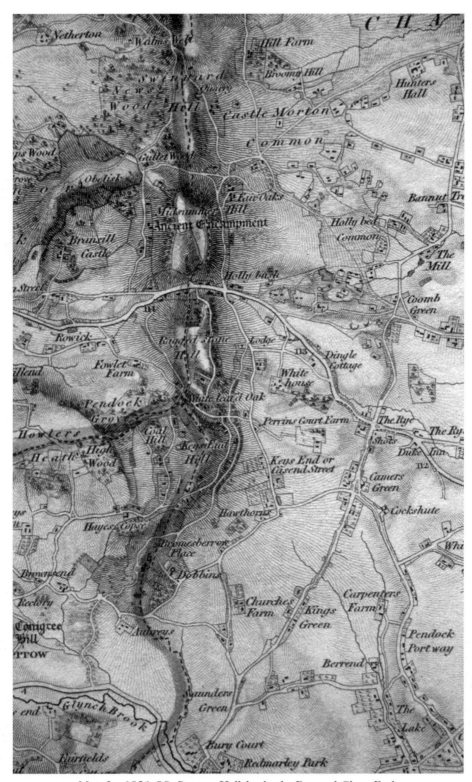

Map 2: 1831 OS, Berrow, Hollybush, the Rye and Chase End

'winter coombe', in Hollybush, as far as the Rye, where now the Ledbury-Tewkesbury, A438, crosses the Gloucester-Malvern, B4208, road (Map 2).[52] In 1086, with 'woodland one league long and one wide', Overbury, including Pendock and Berrow, still belonged to Worcester cathedral. Pendock achieved parochial status but Berrow, despite settlement growth, remained a mere chapelry of the cathedral. Nevertheless even in the 13th century Roger *de Berche* looked, not to Worcester, but to Ledbury. He was not the only one. The *Red Book*, a detailed survey of the rents and other revenues due from the episcopal estates *c*1288, records three Ledbury burgesses called *Berwe*: Philip in the Homend, Geoffrey in *Bysshopestrete* and John with one and a half burgages as well as his market stall or booth. Even in the 18th century Ledbury was Berrow's post town.[53]

Roger's rents came from six parcels of land for which John Carpenter paid 10s 3d, Walter de Bosco 6s, Elured *Pertrych* 3s 1^1/2d, William Cheret 1s, Walter Mase 3s and John Pygace 3s 6d and three hens. With these six parcels went the services, homage, issues and demands from both lands and tenants. Medieval and 16th-century court rolls and leases, discussed in Chapter 6, indicate that these lands lay about Chase End (*Keys End*) and its vicinity.[54]

4. The Hyde, Cradley

The largest and one of the earliest of the grants, apparently a gift, was made by John de Stanford. This was rent of £1 12s 6d from four tenancies, some 160 acres in all, in the Cradley township of Hyde, where the source of the Leadon is only a few yards below Hidelow Farm. The little stream forms the parochial boundary between Acton Beauchamp on the north and Cradley and Evesbatch to the south (Map 3). There Walter, son of William, and Richard le Freman each held one virgate, some 60 acres, paying 12s a year with homage and usual services. Walter le Freman also held half a virgate, 30 acres, for which the rent was 6s whilst Seward de Yselford held ten acres at 2s 6d. The tenants of the larger holdings paid just under 2^1/2d an acre whilst Seward paid 3d. In the bishop of Worcester's 1580 survey the Hyde is assessed at three yardlands, that is 180 acres. In the early 19th century it was surveyed with more precision, as Hidelow and Copley Farms, at 175 acres. The two farms, still to be seen on the high ground a quarter of a mile south of Acton Green on the Ridgeway Cross to Bromyard road, remained in the hospital's hands until virtually the end of the 20th century.

John de Stanford confirmed his grant by two charters. Both refer to the same properties and have the same impressive list of witnesses, including Walter de Bannebury and Adam of Shrewsbury, both of whom had served Foliot as steward. With St Katherine's, Adam was a major beneficiary of Foliot's will of 1234.[55] In the first charter John grants the rents to 'the venerable Father Hugh Foliot or to whomsoever he assigns it'. The circumstances of the grant are then explained. This was no gift. It was made in return for Foliot's repayment of £18 13s 4d which John owed to the great Jewish financier, Hamo of Hereford, and Manasser, his father-in-law. John was parting with these Cradley lands—at 11^1/2 years' purchase. As Hamo died in 1231 it confirms that the charter can be dated to the period of St Katherine's foundation. John's second charter makes no reference to Foliot. The lands are granted instead to 'God, the hospital of Ledbury under Malvern and the Rectors of the same serving and maintaining the poor'. Furthermore both the sale and its circumstances are masked, for the lands, we are told, were granted 'for the salvation of the soul of John de Stanford, his wife and ancestors and successors ... in pure and perpetual alms'. John evidently sought whatever merit he could from a transaction which was essentially debt repayment.[56]

Other evidence confirms that Foliot was engaged in the rapidly growing traffic in estates encumbered by debt. At least one of the rents providing an endowment for Foliot's other chantry, at the Hereford palace chapel, also came from Hamo. This is not surprising for Foliot's neighbours, the monks of Worcester and the Beauchamps, hereditary sheriffs of Worcester, had already blazed the same trail.[57] In a society based on and highly retentive of land, such encumbered estates provided an opportunity for developing ecclesiastical institutions to satisfy at least some of their avid investment needs, as the great Cistercian houses of the north had already shown. Thus, Reginald, first master of St Ethelbert's almshouses in Hereford, by paying Leuca de Wormeton's debts to the Hereford Jewry, obtained a lease on six acres of her dower lands.[58]

John de Stanford made a further grant at the Hyde, of a 6s rent on another half a virgate. Again the witness list provides clues as to the date. It includes Stephen Thornbury, Dean of Hereford 1234x1236 until 1250, and Richard de

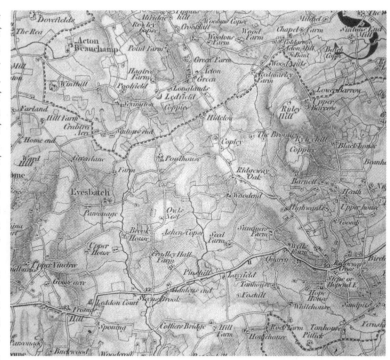

Map 3: 1831 OS, The Hyde, Cradley

Gravesend, Treasurer of the cathedral from c1237 to 1253. In this year he was elected Dean of Lincoln where he played a major role in the ritual child murder accusation levied against the Jews of that town in 1255. Stanford's second deed was thus signed between 1237 and 1250. This was not the end of the story. After John's death Matilda, his widow, evidently far from convinced that his two grants had indeed been made 'for the salvation of her soul', brought an action against the master of St Katherine's before the Justices of the King's Bench at Westminster. She claimed as her dower, by custom of the manor, one-third of the total rent of the 38s 6d granted to the hospital by her late husband. When John, her eldest son, was prevailed upon to give evidence against her, she was obliged 'to warrant and make satisfaction so that she can never make any suit against the master for the said third and for the greater security of this she has put her seal to these writings'.[59]

5. Malmespool Mill

Peter de Donnington, who held 120 acres of the bishop, like William of Ockeridge by military tenure, gave St Katherine's a ten-year lease on his Malmespool water mill for £13 6s 8d in 1261. This he did out of his 'great necessity'. Shortly afterwards, for £21 6s. 4d, he granted it in perpetuity, 'with mores, pastures and all other things pertaining to hold freely and quietly in peace for ever'. Yet in 1291 the hospital had to pay his son, John, £3 for relaxation of all his rights and claims in the mill, together with 'all those lands and tenements which, with his brothers and sisters, he had bought of his father'. The witnesses included such leading figures in Ledbury society as Robert de Furches, the bishop's bailiff between 1283, or perhaps 1286, and 1299, John de Solers who held half a knight's fee at the *Hasele* and William Esegar, a member of whose family was later to grant Orlham farm to St Katherine's.[60] In 1299 Peter's widow, Martha, 'in her great indigency', had to mortgage ten selions in *Overhaufeld*. Where such grants were made 'out of great necessity' St Katherine's, like other ecclesiastical institutions, was acquiring gaged land, as at the Hyde, Cradley, in return for discharging debt. Whether this was an act of charity, 'the freeing of Christians from Jewish money-lenders', or just good sharp business practice depends on the terms of the deal. The evidence suggests Malmespool Mill was clearly in the latter category. The mill, with its lands, which lay just off the Ledbury-Gloucester road near Dunbridge, remained in the hospital's hands until purchased, for use as a feeder, by the promoters of the Gloucester to Hereford canal, completed as far as Ledbury in 1798.[61]

6 and 7. Weston-juxta-Yarkhill and Hereford City

Simon de Weston granted the hospital one and a half virgates, 90 acres, of arable, six acres of meadow and 7s rent in 'Weston-juxta-Yarkhill' (Map 5). The deed can be dated to the late 13th century as the witness list again includes the bishop's bailiff, Robert de Furches. As Simon issued a writ against master and brethren in the King's Bench, Westminster, it would appear that his grant was made under circumstances similar to that of John de Gersant, already discussed, with two quite distinct charters, one probably referring to a grant 'in pure and simple alms' for the benefit of his soul, the other referring to 'a consideration'. It was in terms of the latter that master, brethren and sisters had to come to an accommodation with Simon for the assignment of all his rights in the contested lands, at a cost of £13 6s 8d. This was a matter of purchase, as also in the cases of John de Stanford and Peter de Donnington.[62]

The seventh and final grant is something of a mystery. In her free widowhood Matilda Puch gave 'certain lands in the Market Place and *Wydemaires*, Widemarsh, in the town of Hereford with the houses built thereon'. The property is referred to in St Katherine's bailiff's accounts for 1360 when John and Sibill Monyword of Hereford were paying an annual rent of 4s. The Monywords have been described as the best documented of all English middlemen marketing wool. A John Monyword was member of parliament for the city in 1322, Richard in 1326 and another John in 1384. These properties were not included in the comprehensive survey of the hospital's assets in 1580, nor has any further reference been found to them.[63]

To secure their possession of most of these lands—the fitz Gersant lands, the Hyde at Cradley, Malmespool Mill and Simon de Weston's grant—the hospital had to pay at least £100 6s 4d in legal fees. Given the meagreness of the original endowment, how was such a large sum raised? Foliot's foundation charter records that, whilst de Lacy and Longchamp gave three churches, the bishop himself had endowed it with merely three burgages in Ledbury, bringing in just 3s 8d per annum. Foliot's will is not extant but from other sources it is known that he left his successor, Ralph de Maidstone (1234-39), £26 for restocking the episcopal estates. This came to be established as a custom when Ralph left seed corn and farm stock to his own successor. Most of the money realised on the sale of Foliot's personal property went however to St Katherine's, Ledbury, St Katherine's chapel by the cathedral and the augmentation of Adam de Shrewsbury's prebend.[64] It was probably this legacy which enabled the early masters to speculate in the local land market and meet these fees.

Smaller Holdings

The 1316 inventory shows that, in addition to the seven major grants confirmed by Edward III *c*1231, numerous small grants of lands and rents had been received, some of no more than a selion or 1d in rent. It refers to 260 'writings' in seven large deed boxes and one chest in the sacristy. One deed box contained copies of Foliot's two charters, a papal bull and twenty letters of indulgence granted by various bishops, which provided partial remission of the penalty for forgiven sin to people assisting the hospital in its good works. These indulgences will, no doubt, have attracted many of St Katherine's small gifts. Not all were of lands or rents. Thus Robert *le Wafre*'s father promised in perpetuity one *cronocum* (four bushels) of corn annually from his mill at Leadon Frome. This was probably near or on the site of Dodd's Mill on the Leadon, just within the boundary of Bosbury parish, where the *Red Book* refers to William the Miller holding a mill and nine acres of customary land at an annual rent of 25s. The corn was probably intended for use as dole bread, out-relief, for regular distribution to the poor at large at the hospital gates.[65]

These 260 'writings' were a miscellaneous collection of legal documents relating to the hospital's properties: not only grants but deeds, such as relaxations and quitclaims in their support, and leases made by the master and brethren of hospital lands. The inventory was intended to serve as a checklist. Thus at Kempley it refers to eight 'writings' and two feet of fines, final agreements before a court on disputes relating to land, rents etc. For Weston, Yarkhill, the Hyde at Cradley and Berrow there were eighteen such 'writings', for Eastnor twenty-two.

The 68 'deeds and writings' for Ledbury borough and foreign, with 44 more for Gersant's former tenements there, are a distinct group. Many identify places within the foreign with greater precision and thus throw a welcome light on its settlement pattern at the opening of the 14th century: 23 related to *Storchintone*, that is Siddington; 20 for *Donyntone*, Donnington; 24 for *Awrugg*, Ockeridge, *Masnoton*, Massington and *Colewelle*, the last evidently a reference to *Holemedue*, Holemeadow, just beyond Ledbury parish boundary to the north of Ockeridge, which Philip Ruddoc, who held 240 acres by military tenure of the bishop in his Colwall manor, had granted to the hospital in 1242. Finally there were eight 'writings' for tenements in *Walyntone*, Wellington, and another at Eastnor (Map 6).

All these Ledbury parish place-names, except Ockeridge, have the ending -ington: Netherton, which in early forms was *Northynton* and *Nordintune*, and Siddington, also *Suchyntone* and *Suthintone*, were 'settlements in the north and south of the estate'. On the other hand Donnington, *Dunynton*, *Donyngton* and Massington, *Mansinton*, *Masissinton* carry personal names as *Dunna's* and *Mæssa's* estates, whilst Wellington, *Walinton*, may be *Weola's* estate. Ockeridge, *Aukruge* or *Alkruge* is 'Alca's ridge'. Peter de Donnington, John de Massington, Alan de Wellington and William de Ockeridge were all tenants by military tenure of the bishop, holding from 120 to 360 acres of land. It is not surprising, therefore, that they were all were members of that group of local worthies who appeared so frequently as witnesses in the early St Katherine's deeds. Furthermore in other deeds Ockeridge, Netherton and the unidentified *Elmeton*, like Berrow, are all called 'townships', that is sub-divisions of the parish, with a distinct identity as agricultural communities and status in law with clearly defined duties, if not rights. The township was, for example, responsible for raising the hue and cry and following the trail of stolen stock.[66]

Such place-names are evidence of an early dispersed settlement pattern in Ledbury foreign. This explains why, instead of the three or four open fields which served parishes elsewhere, there was a complex range in the 13th- and 14th-century St Katherine's deeds for the area. Township fields were characteristic of a number of large Herefordshire manors, such as Much Marcle. They are especially clear on the buries, the sub-divisions of the great manor of Leominster, where for example Stockton bury included the townships of Stockton itself, Kimbolton, Middleton and Hamnish. The same pattern can be found at the buries of Ivington, Luston and Stoke Prior. At Marden the townships were even more numerous: Marden itself, Wisteston, Fromington, the Vauld, the Venn and the Vern.[67]

Rents from the borough and foreign in 1316 cannot be disentangled for the inventory gives only a combined total. This is despite the fundamental distinction between the rural villein tenure of the foreign and the burgage tenure of the borough. In the early 1120s, when the borough was founded, the original manor, as described in Domesday book, was divided into two. The denzein, the borough or area within, was detached from the foreign, the area without. 'Town air', it was said, 'makes free', and all burgesses who held land of the bishop were free of those services due to the lord in the countryside. They were free to move anywhere they wished, and to marry and to leave property to whomsoever they wished.

The growth of St Katherine's urban holding during its first half century can be established with precision from the *Red Book*. To Foliot's original endowment of two and a half burgages a further six and a half burgages had been added. The *Red Book* lists the original endowment of one and a half burgages, plus two curtilages, in New Street, half a burgage in the Homend and another in Bishop (Bye) Street. A further section lists property without attribution to any street: six burgages, four market stalls, *selde*, and a vacant place as belonging to the hospital. These may refer to market development in either Middletown, that is High Street, or Bye Street, in all probability both. Certainly later leases refer to property in the Butchers Row and on St Katherine's High Street frontage. In addition a 'Margaret of the hospital', possibly one of the sisters, held a half burgage plot in New Street.

4 The Granges:
Kempley, Weston and Yarkhill

According to the inventory St Katherine's annual income totalled £43 18s 4d in 1316 and its total land holding was 1137 acres. Revenue from its three churches, which provided 45% of this total, £17 17s, will be discussed in a later chapter. The remainder was derived from two sources: its demesne lands, its rural estates, which were cultivated directly and rents and other payments from its tenants, free and villein. Details of the value of these demesne lands and the tenement rents are given in Table 1.

Table 1: St Katherine's Manorial Values, January 1316 (HD&CA 1658a)

	Demesne Lands				Tenement Rents				Church			Total			
	£	s	d	%	£	s	d	%	£	s	d	£	s	d	%
Ledbury/ Eastnor	4	6	2	51	4	2	0[1]	49				11	14	2[2]	21
Kempley	4	14	6	86		15	6	14	8	0	0	14	5	6[3]	34
Weston	3	5	2	90		7	0	10	4	10	4[4]	8	2	6	20
Yarkhill		10	0	37		17	0	63	5	6	8	6	13	8	17
Cradley[5]					1	18	6	100				1	18	6	5
Berrow					1	4	0	100				1	4	0	3
Total	12	15	10		9	4	0		17	17	0	43	18	4[2&3]	

[1] incl 16s for mill; [2] incl £3 6s rent of assize; [3] incl 15s 6d rent of assize; [4] incl 10s 4d fines; [5] The Hyde

The framework through which the hospital's demesne lands were worked was the grange, each with its own barn and other agricultural facilities. The grange, with its range of farm buildings, is not to be confused with the manor, the administrative unit which had its own court, discussed in Chapter 6 (Table 2). The term 'grange' is derived from the classical Latin *granarium*, a granary. By the 12th century, however, St Paul's cathedral deeds refer to barns as either *grangia* or *orrea* and a similar interchangeability is found in St Katherine's records. A barn is *grangia* at the Hyde, Cradley in 1316 but *orrea* at Kempley in the 1448 court rolls. The distinction between the use of the term grange as barn and ecclesiastical estate is made clear by a deed of the French abbey of Ourscamp in 1156, referring to *orreum grangie de Warnaviller*, the barn within the grange of Warnavillers.[68]

Table 2: St Katherine's Churches, Granges and Manors

	Ledbury/Eastnor	Kempley	Weston	Yarkhill	Hyde, Cradley	Berrow
Church		+	+	+		
Grange	+	+	+	+		
Manor	+	+	—— + ——		+	+

At its four granges of Kempley, Weston, Yarkhill and Ledbury with Eastnor St Katherine's retained a range of lands to be cultivated as demesne. Other lands, held by tenants, either freemen or villeins, provided rents. The villeins, who held their land by custom of the manor, are usually referred to as customary tenants or *nativi* in the hospital records. The hospital's demesne was farmed either by services due in kind from its villein tenants or by the paid labour of those with little or no land of their own. The records suggest St Katherine's was relying increasingly on the use of paid labour. Indeed, the obligation for villeins to perform regular week work, as opposed to seasonal work, is not found in any St Katherine's court rolls. By 1316 court rolls show that more services were gradually being commuted to money rents. Services and dues which could be required by the hospital as lord from its customary tenants included not only boon work but numerous payments such as relief, a fine for entry into a holding; aids, due on special occasions; and heriot, the legal responsibility of an heir to pay the deceased's best beast or chattels before succeeding to the lands. Before he could wed, the villein had to have his lord's licence, a privilege for which again payment was normally due. A freeman could marry whom he wished. The fundamental distinction, however, between the villein and freeman was legal in that the latter could call on the royal courts to adjudicate in any dispute concerning his rights to the land. Thus both John de Stanford's widow, Matilda, and Simon de Weston took their disputes with the master and brethren over land to the crown courts at Westminster. However the distinction between free and servile tenure was becoming blurred for numerous men were already holding both free and customary lands.

The inventory shows that, some 85 years after foundation, master and brethren had amassed 606 acres of demesne land for which it gives an annual value of £12 15s 10d, apparently excluding the value of villein services and fines. Tenement rents brought in a further annual income of £9 4s, giving a total from these sources of £21 19s 10d (Table 1). Details from the *Red Book* enable this to be compared with Bishop Richard Swinfield's income from his neighbouring manors: £66 5s 8d yearly from Ledbury foreign, in rents, services and demesne, was exceptional; the £25 18s 2d from Eastnor much closer to his manorial average of just over £30. As it also had 531 acres of tenanted land, St Katherine's total holding amounted to 1,137 acres.[69]

Only Kempley, Weston, Yarkhill and Ledbury with Eastnor, with their demesne lands, were managed as granges. At the Hyde and Berrow all lands were held on lease, for John de Stanford and Roger de la Berwe had granted merely rents. The ratio of demesne to leased land varied widely in terms of value: 90% was demesne at Weston; 86% at Kempley; 51% at Ledbury with Eastnor; and 37% at Yarkhill. Ledbury, farmed with Eastnor, and Kempley, each with over 200 acres of demesne, were extensive granges. Weston and Yarkhill each had its own grange but, being small, were linked by a single manorial court, at Weston. At the heart of each grange was a range of farm buildings, at Ledbury about a large courtyard, but at Yarkhill merely a barn.

The inventory provides details of the acreage and value of the demesne at the four granges in terms of arable, meadow, pasture, more, that is rough pasture, and underwood. It thus gives a clear

Table 3: St Katherine's Demesne, Values in January 1316 (HD&CA 1658a)

Manor	Arable			Meadow			Pasture			More/Underwood			Total			
	Acres	val d.	total £ s. d.	Acres	val s. d.	total s. d.	Acres	val d.	total s. d.	Acres	val d.	total s. d.	Acres	%	value £ s. d.	%
Ledbury/	180	4	3 0 8	9.5	1 0	9 6	31	4	10 4	5 u&m	4	1 8	229.5	38	4 6 2	34
Eastnor										4 u	12	4 0				
Kempley	247.5	4	4 2 6	10	1 0	10 0				3.5 m	7	2 0	261	43	4 14 6	37
Weston	96.5	6	2 8 3	7	2 0	14 0	1.5	18	2 3	2 m		?	107	18	3 5 2	25
Yarkhill	3	(6)	1 6	1	1 6	1 6	5?		7 0				9?	1	10 0	4
Total	527		£9 12 11	27.5		£1 15 0	37.5		19s 7d	14.5		7s 8d	606.5		£12 15 10	
%	87%			4.5%			6%			2.4%						

Acres x *val(ue)* = total   *m: moor; u: underwood*

38

picture of the husbandry practised at each (Table 3). The contents of the barns, and thus the principal crops and crop rotation, can also be identified (Table 4). Differences in landscape and situation were exploited to the full. At Kempley, where all but 13½ of the 261 acres were demesne, cereal production was dominant, but elsewhere animal husbandry played a significant part. Weston and Yarkhill on the banks of the Frome specialised in dairying whilst at Ledbury and Eastnor, with their woodlands, the emphasis was on sheep and pigs. By specialisation at the granges, St Katherine's was able to meet most of its food requirements from its own demesne.

Table 4: Arable Production (in loads)
Contents of the St Katherine's Barns, January 1316
(HD&CA 1658a)

Manor	Wheat	Oats	+ Peas/Beans	= Total
Ledbury	12	8	6	14
Kempley	20	12	6	18
Weston	16	10	10	20
Yarkhill	12	3	3	6
Total	60	33	25	58

One would assume, from merely 12 loads of wheat and eight of oats in the Ledbury barns, as compared for example to the 16 and ten at the much smaller grange at Weston, that stock at Ledbury was consumed first, the contents of the other barns then being brought in as required, in carts with wheels fettered with iron. However, caution has to be exercised in coming to other conclusions from barn contents. This was no ordinary year. The winter the inventory was taken witnessed the onset of the Great Famine. During the catastrophically bad harvests of 1315 and 1316, when extraordinarily heavy rain in the late summer affected both the ripening and harvesting of the grain, wheat reached the giddy level of 16s 8d a quarter, an all-time medieval high for two consecutive years. The barn contents, therefore, are not indicative of what would be left in January after a normal harvest.[70]

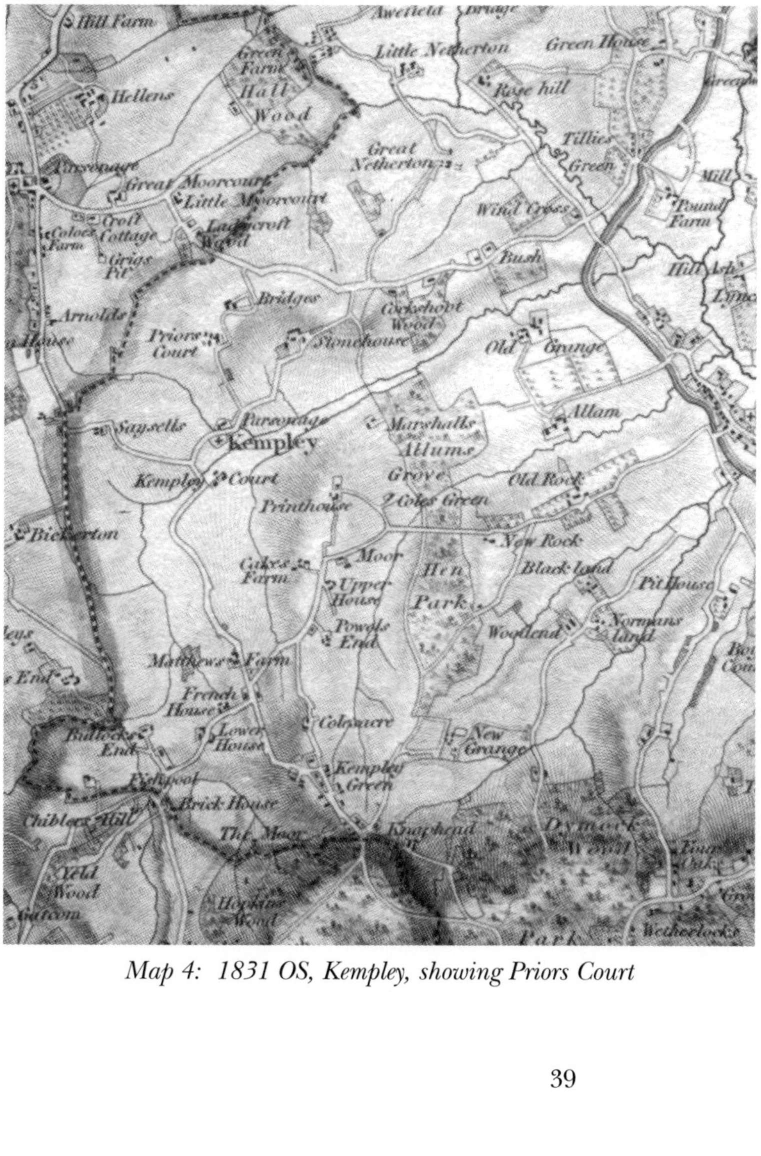

Kempley Grange

The largest and most valuable of the demesne holdings was Freres Court, later known as Priors and now Friars Court, Kempley (Map 4). The 'certain tenements and lands' given, with the church, by Geoffrey de Longchamp of Wilton and Isabel de Miners, his wife, amounted to 261 acres worth £4 14s 6d. This compares favourably with the 229½ acres valued at £4 6s 2d

Map 4: 1831 OS, Kempley, showing Priors Court

at Ledbury with Eastnor. At Kempley the demesne accounted for 86% of annual manorial income, as compared to 51% at Ledbury and Eastnor. Receipts from rents provided only 15s 6d, 14% of the annual manorial income, whereas at Ledbury with Eastnor they were £4 2s, 49% (Table 1).

Here 247$^{1}/_{2}$ acres, 95% of the demesne, was arable. There was no pasture, only 10 acres of meadow, worth 10s, and 3$^{1}/_{2}$of more, worth 2s (Table 3). There were no cattle, sheep or pigs. The contents of the barn—20 loads of wheat, 12 of oats and six of peas and beans—show how the arable was exploited (Table 4). As at Ledbury, Weston and Yarkhill, there was winter-sown wheat, spring-sown oats and legumes, and then the land lay fallow. The combination of winter- and spring-sown crops enabled the sowing season, the period of intense activity in terms of ploughing and sowing, to be broken up, thus reducing the demand for labour on both demesne and villein holdings at these peak periods.

The ox remained the favoured plough beast for the heavy soils of the area. The inventory lists 12 oxen and two ploughs at Ledbury with Eastnor and at Kempley. There the arable was thus worked by two plough teams. Weston and Yarkhill had but one between them. There is no indication as to which of the three varieties of plough was used. The wheel plough gave a constant depth but could get bogged down in wet conditions. A 'foot' of iron or wood, which took the place of wheels, gave its name to the foot plough. The swing plough dispensed with the foot but required a skilled ploughman to achieve a quality comparable to that of the wheeled variety.[71]

Elsewhere, over most of eastern England and much of the Midlands including south Worcestershire, by the end of the 13th century the horse was the preferred draught animal. Yet Walter of Henley, in his *Hosebondrie*, written in French about this time, puts the case for the ox force-fully. It cost only 3s 4d a year, as opposed to 13s 6d for the horse. At the end of its active life, as the carcasses in St Katherine's larder indicate, 'with ten pennyworth of grass' the ox was fit for consumption—whereas the horse 'hathe nothing but his skynne'.[72]

Kempley grange had two heavy carts. Each had two wheels, fettered with iron. Drawn by oxen, it could carry over 2,200 lbs, the short ton. Known as the *plaustrum*, it was the predecessor of the wain, but with wheels unfettered it was the *plaustrum nudum*. The *plaustrum* would have been used to transfer the contents of the Kempley barns to Ledbury as the hospital's supplies from the home grange were consumed. There was also a lighter two-wheeled cart, a *careta*, drawn by either a single horse or two in tandem. The sides were of light wicker or rails and it had but half the capacity of the *plaustrum*. According to Fitzherbert's *Husbandry* the heavy cart was constructed mostly of oak, the lighter of ash. Both could be extended to the front or rear by the use of ladders held in place by ropes attached to wooden pegs on the sides. Two such 'ropes for the heavy cart' are mentioned in the Ledbury entries. The inventory refers to two distinctive types of harness. The oxen drawing heavy cart, the *plaustrum*, had yokes over their shoulders attached to a central pole. For the light cart,

Fig 4.1 Kempley: Friars Court, 15th-century barn

*Fig 4.2a & b Kempley: Friars Court, Pair of crucks (left) and detail of spur at wall plate level (right)
in 15th-century barn*

careta, pulled by a horse or horses, a collar with hames, two curved bars which held the traces, was attached by hooks and chains to side shafts. The inventory shows two horses at Kempley. As to other implements only two iron hoes, two shovels, two bills and a mattock are listed.[73]

The barn in which the harvest was stored would have been of the conventional design, with either three bays and one set of doors or six bays with two sets. It was apparently of the former type for a large timber-framed barn still standing at Friars Court, Kempley, as the grange is now called, consists of six bays of which the three on the south side, with a tie-beam roof structure, are 17th-century additions (Fig 4.1). On the north side however there are three 15th-century bays. This bay is still flanked by its two pairs of vast original crucks (Fig 4.2a). The collar-beams have been removed from both trusses but three of the original four cruck spurs are still in place (Fig 4.2b). Projecting from the cruck blades, these spurs carry the wall plate. The walls beneath are composed of square timber panelling. There are doors on either side of the central, threshing, bay, that on the field side being considerably higher than its counterpart on the farmyard side. Its pair of high, wide doors permitted the access of laden carts to unload the sheaves for storage in the bays on either side. Once emptied they could pass through the lower doorway to the cart shed in the yard.

By the time this three-bay barn was built, the lands of the grange were no longer worked as demesne. In consequence of the Black Death of 1349 all St Katherine's demesne was being leased out by the end of that century. However its predecessor will have been of a similar design. In a terrier of 1615 Edwyn's, another of St Katherine's Kempley properties, is described as 'a four-bay farmhouse, tiled, with two barns of three bays and an ox house and mill, each of one bay'. Tiling being specified for the farmhouse, one assumes all the others were thatched.[74]

Over the winter months a team of men was faced with the back-breaking task of threshing the grain with hand flails on the stone flagged floor of the central bay. Its tall doors provided adequate light on even the darkest of winter days. As threshing progressed the straw was stored in one of the outer bays, to be used as fodder or bedding material for the animals. Winnowing, removing the chaff from the grain by tossing it in the air, also took place in the central bay. Such taxing work of both threshing and winnowing was accompanied by the provision of ample small beer.

41

Michaelmas, 29 September, represented both the end and the beginning of the year: with the harvest home, demesne and tenants' animals were let loose on the stubble, but they were removed when the annual cycle recommenced with the sowing of the autumn grain, wheat, and its harrowing, to keep the birds from the seed. This would have been completed, at the earliest, by Hallowmas, All Saints Day, 1 November; at the latest by Martinmas, 11 November from which day responsibility for protecting the winter grain rested with the hayward. At Candlemas, 2 February, the animals would be driven from the rest of the arable so that ploughing could begin for the spring-sown crops of oats, peas and beans. All being well, the seed would be in the ground by the feast of the Annunciation, Lady Day, 25 March. Easter, like Christmas and Whitsun, was a week of holidays. Harvest began at Lammas, 1 August, *hlaf maesse* or loaf mass, so-called from the bread baked from the first ripe corn.

Weston Grange

Although forming one manor, Weston and Yarkhill apparently operated as separate granges. Called Weston-juxta-Yarkhill or Weston-by-Yarkhill to distinguish it from Weston-under-Penyard, it was, as the name declares, the settlement, *ton*, west of Yarkhill. The antiquity and importance of the latter is brought out by a charter of 805x11 in which Coenwulf, King of Mercia, in exchange for ten *manentes*, hides, at 'Geardcylle in the land of the *Magonsetum*', granted Archbishop Wulfred lands in Kent, at Estry and Lympne. Domesday book shows that by 1086 the roles of the two settlements had been reversed. Weston was now rated at six hides and Yarkhill at two. In 1545 it was still 'Weston Nighe Yorckhill' and in the Valor Ecclesiasticus of 1558 it is 'Weston super Fromey'. Only later did Weston begin to dissociate itself from Yarkhill to become Beggars Weston (Map 5).[75]

The inventory lists the Weston demesne holding as 96½ acres of arable, seven acres of meadow, one and a half acres of pasture and two acres of more (Table 3). These represent the 90

Map 5: 1831 OS, Yarkhill and Weston, showing Friars Court

acres of arable, six of meadow and three of more which St Katherine's had received from Simon de Weston. Probably an acre of more had been improved to provide a further acre of much needed meadow land. The high value of Weston's lands is remarkable. At Ledbury with Eastnor and at Kempley arable was worth 4d an acre. Similar valuations are found on the episcopal manors of Ledbury foreign, Eastnor and Bosbury; at Colwall, which included Coddington, it was only 3d and at Upton Bishop, near Ross, a mere 2d an acre. At 6d an acre, the Weston and Yarkhill demesne arable was 50% higher than the norm for the Ledbury area, a reflection of the great productivity of these low-lying lands on the banks of the Frome.

There were six oxen and a plough, with harness; a carthorse, with harness; and another cart bound with iron. The only other farm implements listed are an iron mattock, a large pick with a blade on one end for breaking up soil and cutting roots etc, and a sieve. Pride of place amongst the farm buildings around the, probably cobbled, grange yard would have been taken by the barn, in this district of wood, no doubt. In January it still contained the remainder of the autumn's harvest and grain tithes: sixteen loads of wheat, ten of oats and ten of peas and beans, by estimation (Table 4). Nearby, probably facing south to benefit from the winter sun, would be the 'sheere' with six stalls for the oxen and a stable for the horse.

Although there were almost 100 acres of arable, the inventory of animals shows that dairying was concentrated on these two Fromeside manors. A dairy formed a major part of the grange complex at Weston. The herd included a bull, ten cows, eight bullocks, six heifers and seven calves; this, it has to be remembered, was in January, when livestock numbers were at their lowest. Stock that could not be overwintered through lack of winter keep was fattened in summer to be slaughtered for meat in the autumn. Here the hay was carefully 'stored in sacks', not open wagon-loads as at Ledbury. These sacks were evidently stored elsewhere, in or close to the byre or shippen, for they were not included with the grain and pulse in the inventory of the barn's contents. At Ledbury and the Kempley grange there is no mention of cattle. Herein lies Weston, and Yarkhill's, special contribution to the hospital's economy.

The inventory provides the explanation. Weston and Yarkhill's meadow was valued even higher than the pasture for the middle ages knew nothing of sowing grass seed like corn. Hay was thus a valuable commodity. It was harvested only where it grew naturally, by rivers and streams and other wet places. Such was its value in providing winter provender that it was well worth the effort to convert marshy land to meadow. Generally, as at Ledbury and Kempley, an acre of meadow, at 1s, was equivalent to three acres of arable, but the Yarkhill meadows were worth 1s 6d an acre and those at Weston 2s an acre, twice as much (Table 3). This reflects their high productivity, attributable to their position on the north bank of the Frome where flooding, by raising the temperature of the land in spring, induced early growth, with the probability of a second mowing. Indeed the Weston meadows are identified in Domesday Book as meadow for oxen. Nevertheless, the total amount of meadow in the demesne here was only seven acres, so the appropriated churches at Weston and Yarkhill must also have played an important role in the provision of hay. Generally regarded as small tithes, hay belonged to the vicar but at these two parishes it was successfully claimed by St Katherine's as rector. In addition the hospital could call upon the glebe meadow of the two churches.

Pasture at Weston was 1s 6d an acre, four and a half times more valuable than that at Ledbury. The acreage of pasture at Yarkhill is unknown, but it was worth 7s. Applying the Weston valuation this represents a further five acres for the hospital's herd on the rich grasslands of the lower Frome. As with meadow, the additional value of the pasture can be attributed to flooding, raising the temperature level of the soil. With early growth it enabled the herd to be moved out of the byre at an early stage, reducing the quantity of hay required and advancing milk production. To augment the pasture there was 'more', in this context 'a low, flat level of former marshland, reclaimed and drained'. At Yarkhill the acreage of pasture cannot be read but on the 1804 Enclosure Award for Weston and Yarkhill stretches of land in the flood plain of the Frome are still referred to as Upper and Lower Mores and even Moory Meadow. In the 16th century the great flood plains of the Lugg about Leominster, formerly more, had become renowned as fattening grounds, 'the fertility of which are comparable with Nilus'.

The annual cycle of the common meadows was dominated by Candlemas, the festival of the Purification of the Virgin celebrated with candles on 2 February, and Lammas Day, 1 August. At Candlemas the meadow was closed to allow the growth of hay. On St John's day, 24 June, the feast of the solstice, it was opened for the hay to be cut by all with meadow rights. As the court rolls show, this was the time when the hospital required mowing service from its tenants. Lammas marked the end of the hay harvest. Once the hay was removed from the meadows they were thrown open to all with grazing rights. This was by stint, the customary number of animals allowed according to the size of each commoner's holding. For the annual cycle of the pastures May Day and Martinmas were the important dates. The pastures were thrown open on 1 May for the bull, cows, bullocks, heifers and calves, overwintered in the Weston byre, and closed on 11 November.

The importance of the cattle was as a dairy herd. Walter of Henley estimated that three well-fed cows should give one stone of cheese and four pounds of butter between May and Michaelmas. The inclusion of a cheese mould, bronze measure and trestle table at Weston, but at no other, grange confirms its specialist dairy function. What little milk there was in winter fetched three times more than in summer. A *Ralph le Couhurde* of Weston is mentioned in 1325 when he leased a messuage with croft in 'the more' for which 2s per annum, service of one man to lift hay for a day, suit of court and the other customs were due. He was one of the leading figures of the hospital's estates. Walter of Henley describes the cowherd's duties. He must have 'fine bulls and large, well-matched, near the cows to mate when they will'. Each night he must 'lie with the cows' in the fold.[76]

Four Weston leases were renewed at a manorial court held within a month of the inventory being drawn up. All four included service of lifting hay at *Weteney* meadow. Next year the court rolls refer to an 'illegal watercourse', suggesting an attempt to create water meadows. A court roll of 1380 shows that, despite the general collapse of land values as a consequence of the massive depopulation caused by the Black Death, land here actually increased in value. An acre of meadow at *Coferney*, Covender Meadow on the 1804 enclosure map, at the confluence of the Lodon and the Frome in Yarkhill, commanded a rent of 20d, 2d more than in 1316. In addition the service of lifting hay, for two days, at *Weteneye* could still be insisted upon. Such evidence underlines the importance of these meadows in the hospital's economy. In 1629 *Weteneye* remained 'the common meadow' and here St Katherine's, through its Friars Court lands, still held seven acres. At enclosure in 1804 there remained 22 acres of common meadow at Covender of which the hospital received almost five acres; but at Witney a mere four and a half.

Yarkhill Grange

As a grange Yarkhill was less important. The demesne holding was minute, a mere nine acres: There were only three acres of arable, one of meadow and pasture worth 7s. Yarkhill nevertheless had its own barn which held 12 loads of wheat, three of oats and three of peas and beans. The diminutive area of arable in demesne suggests this was a tithe barn rather than serving as an ancillary to Weston. Full income from rents and assizes is unknown for here the edge of the inventory is missing, but rents from tenements at (Little) Hyde brought in only 17s. In addition there was a mill, valued at 16s.

5   Ledbury with Eastnor Grange

There is no reference to a grange at Eastnor, for the lands there were apparently administered jointly with those at Ledbury. This was for reasons of convenience. Eastnor's western boundary lies within half a mile of St Katherine's, and Ledbury's eastern parish boundary was as far away from the hospital as Eastnor's. From the county boundary at Clenchers Mill the Ledbury/Eastnor boundary extends, by Little Woolpits, through Hospital Wood and along the top of Coneygree Wood. By Hill and Lower Mitchell farms it strikes east, cutting across Sitch Wood and the Ridgeway to the Malverns at the northern end of Midsummer Hill. It was in this area to the east of Ledbury, between the Ledbury-Tewkesbury and Ledbury-Malvern roads, that the majority of the hospital's lands lay.

Fig 5.1 'White leved Oake he bereth white leaves'

No part of the hospital's combined Ledbury and Eastnor lands lay more than some three miles from St Katherine's, for both Ledbury's boundaries, the eastern and the western, beyond the Leadon, were the same distance away. At this time Ledbury included the whole of Wellington Heath which only became an independent ecclesiastical parish in 1840.

Much of St Katherine's property at Eastnor lay within the Ledbury Chase of the bishops of Hereford. All the eastern segment of the parish lay within its bounds, described in documents of 1277, 1394 and 1575-80. They followed the ancient diocesan, and later county, boundary along the Malvern ridge from *Baldyate*, the Wyche Gap, to *Brustenyate* or *Windyate*, Wynds Point by the Malvern Hills Hotel, *Swyneyate*, Swinesgate now Swinyard Hill above News Wood, the Gullet; *Shakellyate*, Shacklegate, in the Hollybush Gap; *Dead Orle*, the dead alder tree; to *Chaylemersh Pool*, Charmill Pool—its site established by Thomas Dingley's reference in the late 17th century to the 'greate Oake cauled the white leved Oake he bereth white leaves' (Fig.5.1). From Whiteleaved Oak, where the shires of Hereford, Worcester and Gloucester still meet, the bounds of the Chase continued to follow those of diocese and county southwest as far as

45

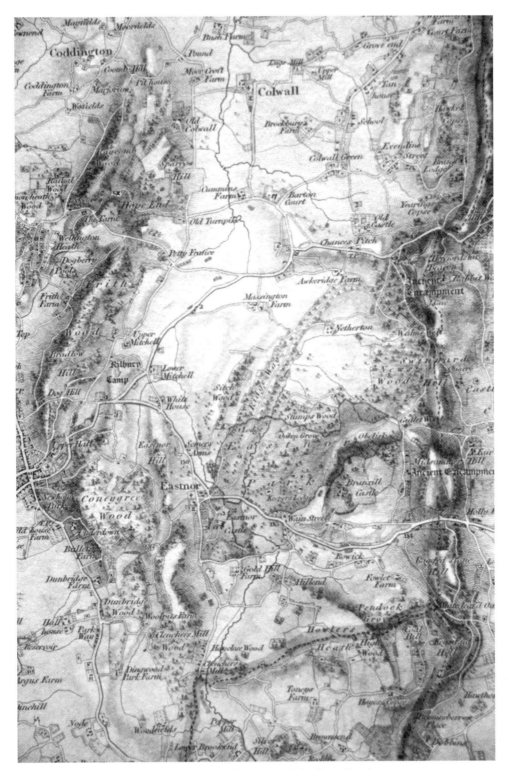

Map 6: 1831 OS, Eastnor and Ledbury Lands

Clenchfords myll, Clenchers Mill. There they turned due north to Eastnor church and then northeast by the Ridgeway to Frog Lane, Bartons Gate and *Brodleye* to the Wyche. The bishop thus had access to the chase from his palaces and parks at both Ledbury in the south and Colwall to the north (Map 6).[77]

The *Household Roll of Bishop Swinfield* illustrates the reliance placed on the chase, not only for deer but for other types of game. It describes the supervisory role of Adam Harpin, Cantilupe's and Swinfield's valet of the household and chief falconer and fowler. In June, with his helpers, he kept watch over eyries to catch the young falcons just before they left the nest. In autumn they set out to net wild partridges and other birds. Personal names, whether occupational or nickname, reflect this activity. Richard Falconer of Ockeridge appears in a number of St Katherine's deeds and, with the major local landowners, witnessed John Gersant's principal grant to the hospital. Elured *Pertrych* was one of a long line whose name, Partridge, was eventually given to their property in Berrow. A Richard *Partrich* had a burgage and a half—and his butcher's stall—in Ledbury. It has been calculated that overall half the game was poached. A park keeper, John le Blont of Ledbury, was convicted in 1276 of such a transgression on his own patch.[78]

Much of this land had long been devoted to agriculture. At Eastnor and Berrow, although still heavily wooded, particularly on the high ground, it had been settled long before the Conquest. Between 1148 and 1163 Henry confirmed the see's assarts, woodland clearances, in the chase 'under the Malverns'. Despite such evidence of woodland clearance, *c*1288 Robert Eseger with 31 other free tenants of the bishop in Ledbury foreign and William de Goldhulle with 12 others in Eastnor were still paying ancient Welsh produce rents, like honey on St Andrew's day, fish at the Annunciation and a goose at Michaelmas. Such rents are still regarded by historians, relying merely on Domesday as their evidence, as being restricted to the Welsh-speaking area west of Offa's Dyke as early as 1086. Assarts, whether carried out by the lord or tenant, were a welcome means of enhancing the former's income, but that forest land still had an important role is confirmed by the appearance of Richard Forester amongst the witnesses to the hospital's deeds. The *Red Book c*1285 shows that of the $23^{1}/_{2}$ acres of pasture in Ledbury, five were 'recent land'. In Eastnor Miles le Boteler paid £1 3s for assarts and pastures and in Cradley Peter de la Hulle, who held 120 acres by military tenure, paid 2s for his six acres of assarts. Place-names in St Katherine's court rolls etc provide evidence that this process had been taking place long before the hospital's acquisition of its Eastnor and Berrow lands. As with *La Heyrudyng*, later the Rudding, in Ockeridge, so are *Dodemonesrudyng* of 1369, 1411, 1517 and 1593 in Berrow, and a croft called *Rudyng*, 'with more adjoining', at Kempley in 1361 further examples of the use of the word as cleared land.[79]

Similarly *le Paroks* in the 1374, *parrok* and *Wyneparrok* in the 1490, and *Wyn Perocke* in the 1593 Berrow court rolls, is the diminutive form of the Old English *pearr*, a beast enclosure. This became 'a fence enclosing a small piece of ground' and later such ground 'enclosed by a fence'. This term is also found at Yarkhill in 1321 when Robert de Wytewykes, his wife and son leased a messuage and three acres of land and one *peroc* which Thomas *Partrich* had formerly held of the hospital. The Kempley rolls of *c*1326 refer to a parcel of land as *Calverparruc* and in 1370 and 1380 to two acres as *Longeparok*. The court rolls of 1484 refer to *Wodwalparrock* and in 1490 *Wyneparrok* was a croft, the rent being a mere $^{1}/_{2}$d per annum. It is this combination of woodland with more, enclosures and clearings intermixed with extensive stretches of arable in the valley bottoms, which explains the distinctive contribution of the economy of the grange which served Ledbury and Eastnor. With its sheep and pigs as well as arable, it stands in contrast to Kempley grange where 95% of the demesne was devoted to the production of grains and pulse.

The buildings which served Ledbury foreign and the Eastnor lands were in effect a home farm. They lay within the western part of the hospital enclosure. Its precinct was bounded on the east by the market place, on the north by Bishop, now Bye, Street and on the west is marked today by the remains of an 18th-century brick wall. On the south side, however, the line of the precinct is marked by a stone wall, now the north wall of the recent extension at the rear of the Feathers. It is

Fig 5.2 Ledbury. Stone Wall along South Boundary of Precinct

a very imposing piece of masonry, some 24 feet in height of which six are now below ground level, some 60 feet in length and three feet thick (Fig 5.2). As to its original purpose, if it was part of the hospital complex, it represents either part of the southern boundary wall or one wall of a substantial building.

It cannot be explained in terms of the former, a precinct wall cutting off the hurly burly of the area of the Hundred House or Booth Hall on the present Feathers site. At the large abbey at Fountains the precinct wall, which enclosed an area of some 700 acres, stands to full height on the south and west but is only 12 feet high, including the coping. Even for a town centre site the 24-foot height of St Katherine's south wall would have been wildly excessive to mark out the precinct. What of a substantial building? It was not the master and brethren's dormitory for, the inventory tells us, this had but six beds. Situated in the western home farm area of the precinct, was it part of a great barn? Local examples of such medieval ecclesiastical barns are certainly very long: in Worcestershire Bredon barn 132 feet, Middle Littleton 137 but Leigh Court a mere 100; in Gloucestershire Ashleworth is 125 feet and Frocester 191. All are stone walled, except Leigh Court, but the height of the side walls, dictated by wagon height, ranges between a mere 12 and 14 feet. Internal height, and thus capacity, was achieved by the use of great roof trusses, anchored by strong stone buttresses. The wall at St Katherine's is not, therefore, the vestige of a barn—unless it was of a unique design. Another suggestion, that it was the northern part of a great stone building, the Hundred House or Booth Hall, on what is now the Feathers site, is equally improbable, on account not only of its site, set so far back from the street, but also of its 60-foot length.

The inventory makes it clear that functionally the precinct was divided into two distinct areas. To the east were the buildings of the religious community, the hospital proper. The formal entrance from the market place was the 'Great Gatehouse'. By 1528, however, Hugh Colier was paying 2s 6d rent for 'the garden next him where the Gatehouse was'.[80] To the west, at the back of the site, was the grange which today would be called the home farm: stable, ox house, sheepfold, piggery and barn are all mentioned. These would have been around a cobbled court. Additional buildings not mentioned must have included a dairy for cheese-making from sheep's milk, a dovecote to provide an alternative to salted meat during the winter, huts for geese, ducks and chickens, and beehives. We know from the corrody granted to John fitz Gersant's family in his old age that they were to have 'fruit of the garden' which would have included herbs and vegetables.[81] In addition there will have been an orchard.

In the stable were two carthorses, with a decayed cart and nearby its harness and traces. In the shere were 12 oxen with two ploughs making up, as at Kempley, two six-oxen teams and two wagons bound with iron. Here also were two heavy carts, their wheels having iron tyres, and with their harness were a range of tools: two iron hoes, two spades, two forks, four shovels, two mattocks and two bills. A John *le Cartare* and his family are mentioned in hospital deeds of 1319 and 1323.[82]

The barn contained the usual range of grains and legumes: 12 loads of wheat, eight of oats, six of peas and beans and also four wagon loads of hay but, as noted, the contents cannot represent the annual production from the Ledbury and Eastnor lands. Although the three-bay barn leased for many years by the Ledbury and District Society Trust for its newspaper collection service at St Katherine's was built in the late 17th or early 18th century, it conforms to the traditional medieval type as still to be seen at Friars Court, Kempley, for it has the central threshing bay with storage for grain and straw on either side (Fig 5.3). The demesne's grain production was principally for internal consumption by master, brethren, servants and the poor. A small amount may have been used as out-relief, a poor dole, distributed regularly to needy people in the town; but later sources suggest this dole grain may already have been met from a specific grant or grants, such as the four bushels from Leadon mill granted by Robert le Wafre's father. If St Katherine's was following best practice, surplus grain would be sold and seed corn bought elsewhere; but for this there is no evidence.

Wheat, which thrived on the heavy loams, was the main crop at all four granges. Local evidence of seasonal variations in wheat prices can be found in Swinfield's *Roll*. At Michaelmas 1289 it cost $6^{1}/_{4}$d on the local market but by July 1290 it was 1s $0^{1}/_{2}$d a bushel. Fluctuations from year to year were dependent on weather. In the disastrous harvest of the autumn prior to the inventory the price rose for two years, to 2s 1d per bushel, the highest recorded in the medieval period. Oats, the second crop, were more tolerant of rain than barley. They were used for brewing and animal feed but oat cakes do appear in some records. Only once is barley which, in this county found favour only in the sandy soils of the south, mentioned in Swinfield's *Roll*, when it was two-thirds the price of wheat; rye not at all. Lower grade breads from mixed crops—such as maslin or muncorn, wheat and rye; beremancorn, wheat and barley; or drage, barley and oats—would not have been eaten, nor would the barley loaves which, in the 13th century, held such sway in eastern England, unless the barley or rye was brought in from outside, which is unlikely.

Much of the grain harvest was drunk. Wheat and oats could both be used in brewing but, as wheat was much the preferred grain for bread, oats predominated. At St Paul's cathedral a century

Fig 5.3 St Katherine's: 17th- or early 18th-century barn

earlier the ratio of oats to wheat and barley used in brewing was more than 4:1:1. The *cellarium* was the store place for provisions and casks of ale. The brewhouse held four large bins for malt, fourteen barrels, two casks and one tankard. At Kempley, where there was but one bronze ale measure, its capacity was not given. Ale produced was of three categories, best, strong and small, that is light, ale. In whatever form, it was consumed in vast quantities and provided the name for many of the holidays and festivities of rural life: wake ales, bride ales, church ales, lamb ales, scot ales etc.

Peas and beans were valuable spring crops which put nitrogen into the soil. They were not sown but dibbled in the fields by the women, back-breaking work. The legumes provided a welcome alternative food crop for both man and beast. Pulse generally formed the base of pottage, a vegetable soup which only rarely contained meat. There were three varieties of peas, green, white and black. Peascod was made from fresh green peas which, with white peas, were dried for winter use. They all became staples of the medieval countryman's diet and no doubt of both staff and poor at St Katherine's.

Although dairying was left to the Weston grange, animals played a major role at Ledbury with Eastnor. With no cows animal husbandry was closely related to the woodlands of the rolling hills where sheep, less demanding than cattle, could be raised on poorer land. In January there were still 120 sheep in St Katherine's folds, with *creckes*, that is the racks, mangers or cribs to hold their feed, and the hurdles, used to make pens. The flocks on the Malverns, however, could in no way rival those of the Cistercian houses of the Marches. Dore Abbey, for example, had more than 3,000 sheep on its extensive granges.

St Katherine's flock was overwintered within the precinct. in timber sheds, roofed with thatch to provide warmth. Here 'the shepherd and his dog must sleep, and not leave them to go to fairs, markets, wrestling matches, wakes or the tavern without putting a good keeper in his stead'. In January, just before lambing had begun, the flock would have been at its lowest level. In the courtyard their *creckes* would be filled with coarse hay, oat straw, pea straw and pods. Here lambing could be fully supervised and milking would be easy. Only after the lambs were weaned, at about five months, did milking cease. According to Henley, thirty sheep gave as much butter and cheese as three cows but production related to nutrition. The average could be a litre a day from which cheese was made, with bread, a staple of the medieval diet.[83] Like the bishop's flock, their numbers may have been augmented by sheep from the Welsh mountains. Thus in the spring of 1290 Adam Harpin, with the bishop's shepherds, bought 208 Welsh ewes at Montgomery and 103 at Bromfield markets, which they took to the sheep runs of the episcopal parks at Dingwood and Eastnor.[84]

Fig 5.4 Glynch Brook

50

About Easter the flocks would be taken out to the sheep runs in the hospital's pasture-woodland with its coarse grazing amongst the great oaks. Ewes to be sold for meat, between Easter and Michaelmas, were washed and shorn. When the meadows were opened, at Lammas, it was the older and weaker ewes which would be fattened for slaughter later in the autumn. Once the harvest was gathered the sheep could be folded at night on the stubble, within the hurdles referred to in the inventory. The dung, trodden into the ground by the flock, although poor compared with that of horse and cow, was nevertheless a treasured nutrient. The hospital's flocks thus provided meat, milk and dung, in addition to cash from wool sales.[85]

A number of shepherds appear in the St Katherine's records. Their tenements, which can be identified, indicate that the sheep's pasture-woodland grazing lay on the western slopes of the Malverns. Peter *le Burcare*, in July 1316, and Roger *le Bacarius*, in May 1318, are referred to in an exchange of lands at *Bagynhale* or *Bagginhale* in Eastnor where the head of one of the selions lay 'beyond the highway to *Brankissische*', Bronsil sitch, to the north of which the hospital held News Wood, still marked on the Ordnance Survey maps. In 1341 Gilbert de Middleton, with the consent of his brethren, granted a lease to Robert *le Schepherde*, Alice his wife and Henry, their son, of a messuage and ten selions, excepting the barn, at Netherton in Holley field extending to the (head)waters of *Gleng*, Glynch (Fig 5.4). In 1358 a John *le Shepherde* was involved in a similar transaction concerning lands at Ockeridge.[86]

Sheep have remained, until almost our own times, an important element in the economy of this area, as place-names on the 1840 Eastnor tithe map indicate, such as: Shepherds Knoll, Shepherds Park, Sheephill Croft, Meadow and Field, Sheepcot Field and two Sheep Walks. After World War II they virtually disappeared from the hills but now Malvern Hills Conservators have introduced a flock of 250 Cheviots to combat the spread of bracken due to undergrazing.

In the Ledbury courtyard there was also a large piggery, with a boar, four sows, sixteen hoggets (yearlings) and, already in January, nineteen piglets. Here they would be fed on cereal, general waste, and malt dregs from the brewing process. In the autumn they would be allowed on the stubble, under the swineherd's careful eye, and when the acorn harvest was abundant they would be fattened up in the pasture-woodland for six weeks. As the 'twenty salt bacons' still in St Katherine's larder in January remind us, most pork was for internal consumption. The hospital's Kempley tenants had to pay for the privilege of pannage, pasturage for their pigs, as is formally recorded on the court rolls. Although there are no extant rolls, similar payments would have applied at Ledbury and Eastnor.

Table 5: St Katherine's, Ledbury (1316) and Leominster Priory (1327)
Comparative Data (%)

Manor	Comparative Demesne Land Use				Comparative Demesne Arable production		
	Arable	Meadow	Pasture	Moor	Wheat	Oats	Peas/beans
St Katherine's	88%	4.4%	5.4%	2.4%	51%	28%	21%
Leominster	87%	5%	4%	4%	48%	52%	0

HD&CA 1658a Price, 150-1, 155-6, 163, 166-7

Comparisons of land use and thus demesne production can be made between the St Katherine's hospital and Leominster priory estates, in 1316 and 1327 respectively. The correspondence between the two is remarkable. Both practiced the three-season rotation of two crops and a fallow, characteristic of lowland Herefordshire, and the overall proportion of arable to pasture and meadow is very close. At St Katherine's 88% was arable, 4.4% meadow, 5.4% pasture and 2.4% more; at Leominster (excluding woodland) 87% was arable, 5% meadow, 4% pasture and 4% more (Table 5). The principal difference is that, in terms of spring crops, Leominster relied wholly on oats but at St Katherine's oats were grown with peas and beans in the ratio of 3:2. The advantages of the latter have already been described and are reflected in the steady growth of their popularity throughout the 14th century.[87]

A contract granted by Philip the Master and the brethren in 1324 records the terms of employment of a bailiff. This contract was considered sufficiently important to be confirmed by Dean Stephen de Ledbury and the chapter in their chapter house at Hereford. In return for a payment of 10s annually and one bushel of the best dried and well aired corn every week Richard Prentout promised to serve the master and brethren faithfully as bailiff 'at Kempley or Ledbury'. As substantial security for his good behaviour he paid 20 marks, £13 13s 4d. For the ultimate return of this sum master and brethren bound themselves by all their lands and possession at Kempley, Ledbury and Weston, to his distraint should it be necessary. Nationally, the surname Prentout, 'take all', is uncommon, but locally other examples can be found. The court rolls for Cradley in 1319/20 record an Adam Preintoct and for Kempley in 1361 a John Prentout, who stood pledge for 10s, suggesting that Richard was recruited locally.[88]

Other resources were unique to Ledbury with Eastnor. 'Four acres of underwood, *subboscus*,' were worth 12d per acre, equivalent to the prized hay meadows here and at Kempley. Underwood stood in marked contrast to pasture-woodland. The difference was pinpointed by the precise annual value which could be put on the one but not the other, for underwood was coppice, cropped on a regular rotation, as oak, ash, elm, lime, alder, hazel and holly all send up new growth when cut back to the stump, as the Oaken Grove, Ashen Coppice and Bircher Wood on the current OS Explorer 14 map still testify. To ensure regrowth the stools had to be fully protected. Domestic animals were rigorously excluded by banks, ditches and hedges to prevent browsing of the new shoots. Situation, tree type and probably above all demand dictated the length of the cutting cycle. The combination of 'five acres of underwood and moreland, in another place' is also mentioned in the inventory but here the land was worth merely 20d a year, 4d an acre.[89]

The products of the underwood had many and varied uses. Hazel and willow were valued for wattle-making, for fencing and in-filling for the walls of timber-framed buildings, as rods and spars for thatching, hurdles and so forth. Household and farm utensils were made from coppice wood. In many places it was invaluable for both charcoal- and lime-burning. Archaeological evidence of charcoal-burning has recently been discovered in Frith Wood and no doubt will be found in other coppice woods close at hand. Both plentiful evidence on the ground and early Ordnance Survey maps show that Ledbury with Eastnor had a large number of lime quarries, which would provide building stone as well as mortar and limewash for buildings. Evidence for the use of quicklime would be associated with kilns but these have yet to be identified.[90]

Mills were a valuable source of income. The bishop had three mills at Ledbury. In the borough a water mill was worth £2 13s 4d and a windmill £1 6s 8d. In Thomas Cantilupe's day the mill at Wygmunds tree, on the Leadon north of Beggars Ash in the foreign, had been leased for £2 13s 4d.[91] At Bosbury nearby the rent of his water mill, with nine acres of arable, was a mere £1 5s; on the manors of Eastnor, Colwall and Cradley there were none. Malmespool Mill, which St Katherine's had acquired from Peter de Donnington some 50 years earlier, was on the southern stretch of the Leadon, close to its junction with the county's boundary with Gloucestershire. In 1314/15, 'worn out and almost collapsed', it was yet worth four loads of corn, 16s a year. Its condition is not surprising for the timber working parts, sluice gates, of such mills had a limited life. Rebuilding was frequent. In rentals of 1516 and 1528 it was worth 20s. In 1581 it was 'called Malmespoles', a 'water mill, corn mill or grist mill with two parcels of land, two parcels of meadow, a green and all watercourses, fisheries and millways'.[92] In addition there was the Yarkhill mill, valued at 16s.

6 Manor Courts & Receipt Rolls: Estate Administration & Economy

St Katherine's five manors, Ledbury with Eastnor, Kempley, Weston with Yarkhill, Berrow and the Hyde at Cradley, were its units of estate administration. Each had its own court through which such matters as rent collection, personal services due to the lord and general organisation of work on the demesne were supervised. In addition the courts had an important judicial function. However they operated as enclaves within more ancient manorial units. At Ledbury and Eastnor they were within the bounds of two large episcopal manors which may well represent lands granted to the see shortly after its foundation in the late 7th century. At Kempley the antiquity of the court house of the Lacy, Longchamp and Grey lords of the manor is proclaimed by its site, just across the stream to the south of the parish church. St Katherine's court, on the other hand, was some distance away, off the main road and to the north. At Weston also St Katherine's court house was distant from both church and the original manorial court (see Map 5, p42).

There are some 80 court rolls of St Katherine's manors in the dean and chapter's archives, spanning virtually three centuries. They are among the transcripts which John Elton, Master 1515-47, brought together with the deeds etc in his '*Register*' (cartulary). The rolls form the second of three separately paginated parts. There are rolls for four of the hospital's five manors: for Berrow from 1307 to 1536; for Kempley from 1307 to 1599; for Weston from 1312 to 1536/7; and for The Hyde, Cradley, from 1316 to 1349. No early rolls survive for the manor of Ledbury with Eastnor, merely one for 1516 and a short series of rentals between 1513 and 1556.[93]

Distribution of these rolls is not wholly random. Almost half relate to the fourteen years of the mastership of Philip de Chaddesley, 1316-29. Four rolls, however, antedate his entry into office in January 1316. The two earliest record details of courts held at Kempley and Berrow on the same day, 'Tuesday before the feast of the blessed Mary Magdalene', 18 July 1307, ten days after Edward II's accession. Despite the coincidence it is unlikely that these two represent the commencement of the series. If they do, then St Katherine's was lagging a considerable way behind good practice, as found at the cathedral where the series of the dean and chapter's manorial rolls commences in 1271. Nationally the first extant court roll is for the English manors of the Norman abbey of Bec in 1246 but there are extracts from the abbey of St Albans rolls in 1227.[94]

The most informative series is for Kempley, with its large acreage of labour-intensive arable demesne. The 1307 roll is followed by a group of ten for 1316-25, during Chaddesley's mastership, but the remainder are widely scattered, ending in 1515. The longest series, of 28 rolls, is for Berrow. The first is again in 1307, with three in 1351-54, oddments for 1369, 1374 and 1411, another group of four in 1475-81, from the reign of Edward IV, and one from that of Henry VII in 1505. Finally there are seven from Henry VIII's reign, 1515-17, 1525-26, 1529 and 1536, all the work of John Elton. Weston's seventeen rolls have a distribution similar to those of Kempley, a bunch of twelve of 1312-25 during Chaddesley's mastership and then scattered to 1503. The Hyde, Cradley, has the shortest run: eleven for the years 1316-26, the other two in 1339 and 1349.

The manorial meeting place at both Weston and Kempley was known as *Frerecourt*, the brothers' court. This title first appears in a Weston rental of 1342. By 1565 it was *Freyrs Court* but six years later it was *Fryors Court*. By the time of the earliest 1" Ordnance Survey, in 1831, it had been corrupted to Friars Court. It was finally sold, after more than seven centuries in the hands of the master and brethren of St Katherine's, to J.Probert in 1959.[95] At Kempley the earliest extant record, as *Frerecourt* and *Frerecroft*, was at a manorial court held on 9 December 1484, less than a year before Richard III's death at Bosworth Field. In 1579 it was 'Friors Courte', by 1831 Priors Court, but is now Friar's Court (see Map 4, p39).[96] Within the St Katherine's precinct a similar but larger structure was, no doubt, used as the court house. With the building of the master's Mansion House in the 15th century its great hall would have served for the three-weekly courts of the Ledbury-with-Eastnor lands.

In the 1316 inventory, the Weston lands were valued at £3 5s 2d. In 1332 *Frerecourt* was in the hands of John Hunt, together with the tithes of corn of the parishes of Weston and Yarkhill, for which he paid £3 6s 8d a year. In 1565 the manor of *Freyrs courte* at Weston, 'with all its houses and buildings' as well as demesne lands, meadows and pastures of one and a half yard-lands, was leased to Henry Wotton for 99 years at the same rent, £3 6s 8d. Wotton had, however, to maintain the chancel of the church, and at his own death or that of any tenant the master was to receive a heriot of 25s 8d or the best live beast, at his choice. The adjoining garden and orchard were of one and a half acres. This remained the meeting place of the joint Weston and Yarkhill manorial court, as Wotton's lease included provision for 'the steward or other officers of the keeper and brethren to call and keep a court within the site as often as it pleases them for the profit and on behalf of the hospital'. Wotton had also to provide for 'the steward and other officers, when the court is kept there, meat and drink, competent for their degree, for dinner, and provender for their horses'. In a terrier of 1629 the court is described as of four bays, with a barn of five and a mill house of one (see Map 5, p42).[97]

At smaller manors, courts were frequently held under a prominent tree, usually an oak. At Berrow in 1581 a jury found it had been 'held and kept in a certain place, the *Keysyn* Street, under a certain elm'. Here, as so often, the place-name came from a local family. Robert Keys and Geoffrey *de la Barue* were charged the largest sums, one mark each, 13s 4d, in the Berrow subsidy roll of *c*1280. *Kesyn* was *Keysushynd* in

Fig 6.1 Chase End Street road sign

1352 and *Keysende* in 1411. Corruption to Chase End, from its position at the southwestern corner of Malvern chase, is recent, for it was still *Keys End* or *Casend* Street on the 1831 1" Ordnance Survey (Fig 6.1 & see Map 2, p31).[98]

The rolls tell us much about manorial administration and economy. The manor courts' jurisdiction was twofold. Firstly they controlled all transfers of land. The hospital's tenants, on taking up lands, whether by inheritance or lease, had to come before the manor court to swear an oath of fealty, to be faithful and loyal to their lord and justiceable by his court in body and chattels, publicly acknowledging that they held their lands of the master and brethren 'with suit of court and all services' demanded by custom of the manor. Strict maintenance of these customs, the obligations attached to tenure of land, especially the villein labour services due either in person or by cash, was essential to the continued working of the lord's demesne. Thus at Berrow in 1326 the jury presented that 'John de Wodeley has alienated one acre of land to James Haliday'. For this James was distrained, his property seized by an officer of the court. Whether by inheritance, surrender, grant anew, exchange or alienation, all such transfers had to be conducted through the manor court, the terms and conditions being publicly acknowledged in open court and recorded on the roll by the clerk. Likewise escheats, reversions to the lord, tenants' deaths, widows' dowers and marriage of villeins' children all came within the purview of the court. Secondly the court was responsible for the overall administration, not only of the common fields but also of pastures, meadows, mores and wastes. The latter included stinting, the regulation of both the time and the number of animals to be admitted, the maintenance of common ways and the prevention and remedying of nuisances and abuses.

The courts met every three weeks. Thus at Cradley in 1316 John son of Richard acknowledged suit of court every three weeks, and at Kempley in the same year the court insisted that John Geffrey, a decidedly awkward character, in publicly doing fealty should acknowledge that he 'owes suit of court from three to three weeks'. Similarly at Berrow in 1326 Nicholas *de la Hulle*, after doing fealty, acknowledged suit of court every three weeks 'at reasonable summons', usually by notice on the church door. In practice this timetable was not adhered to rigidly, for three Berrow rolls in that year show that courts were held on 17 March, 10 April and 8 May, that is three weeks between the first and second courts but a four-week interval before the next. The 1321 rolls for Weston, on the other hand, show that Robert *de Wytewykes* and Thomas *Partrich* were given the privilege of attending only two courts annually, because their messuages and lands were in Yarkhill.

Attendance was obligatory for all adults who held land of the lord. The steward or bailiff of master and brethren presided. Only two are named in the rolls: Richard *atte Pathe* in 1374 and Richard *Blachede* in 1380, both at Kempley. A note at the bottom of a 1484 Kempley roll, recording the court's perquisites for that day as £2 1s 2d, adds that, as the steward was with the lord, Richard Wycherley, at the hospital, there were no expenses 'for the provision of meat and drink competent for his degree'. The steward opened the court by swearing in the jury, or honour, drawn from the tenants. Its presentments and verdicts, based on manorial custom, were recorded by the clerk. The names of those who owed suit of court were then read from the roll. Those without essoins, legitimate excuses for absence, were in the court's mercy and, as with most other offences, liable to a fine affeered or set by the court according to custom. For payment they had to find pledges from amongst their neighbours. Thus at Berrow in January 1326 Ralph *de Holeford* and Walter *Partriche* were in mercy, having failed to produce the man for whom they had stood as pledges, Thomas *de Mora*, who had been attached by the court for rent arrears as well as failure to make suit of court. At the same court Nicholas *de la Hulle* was also in mercy for he had stood pledge for Ralph who, we must assume, had also failed to appear. The court's ultimate sanction was distraint.

As well as suit of court all customary land was held with liability for heriot and relief and, except at Berrow, subject to control of wardship and marriage. Thus at Kempley in 1497 the jury presented that John Tethegy had died holding a messuage and 30 acres by copy (of the court roll), 'so falls to the lord his red bullock as heriot'. Relief, the fine made for entry into a tenancy, was generally a year's rent but at Kempley in 1317 Alice, widow of John le Holder, with John their son, gave only 12d for relief and ingress to his messuage and one acre of land, when the rent was 16d per annum. In 1484 John Tethegy and his wife, Isabelle, paid 13s 4d for entry to the messuage called *Wodwards* with 30 acres of land.

The lord, whether an individual or, as in the case of St Katherine's, a corporation, was held to be the protector of all on the manor. Acting for the lord, the court assumed full responsibility for guardianship and wards. In 1326 Agnes, widow of Robert de Holford of Berrow, was given joint guardianship of their son and heir, John, with her brother, Richard. At Weston, when Alice the widow of Simon Savage died in October 1342, John their two-year-old heir, with the messuage and two acres of arable, was 'taken into the hands of the lord'. The court had then to find someone to take John's lands and act as his guardian until he came of age. At Berrow in 1369 Hugh Blake's widow, Katherine, was given sole guardianship of their son and heir, Richard. For entry to the messuage and three acres of arable held in socage, freehold, she had to pay 16d, the equivalent of a year's rent. In addition she had to pay 14s, some ten times the rent, as heriot, in lieu of her husband's best beast or chattel. For her toft and croft, called Newtonfeld, held by customary or villein tenure, Katherine was however pardoned heriot, for she was now deemed 'a pauper'. Evidently she had been allowed to retain Hugh's plough beast as essential to her livelihood, but how she would find the 14s demanded by the master and brethren in lieu of heriot remains a mystery.

Before his daughter could marry, a customary tenant was obliged to obtain his lord's licence for which *merchet* was payable. This varied from 1s to half a mark, 6s 8d. However, in the case of one widow, evidently well endowed, £1 had to be paid before the licence was issued. At Kempley in 1316 John Geffrey was charged with marrying not only his daughter without warrant but also his sons. The outcome is not known. John, whose reputation was to last long in the folk memory—and that of the manor court—will be encountered on later occasions. Such a licence for the marriage of sons is unusual but a fine was payable if they were put to learning, that is left the manor to attend university or take holy orders, for this represented loss of service to the lord.[99]

Widowhood and dower, as well as wardship, claims of heirs and orphans, and marriage, were strictly regulated by the court, according to the custom of the manor. 'O good Lord', one medieval widow remarked, 'how is it that widows have a greater reward than married folk? How much better and more comfortable estate we widows have than ever we had in marriage.'[100] The hospital's deeds show that a widow was entitled to one third of her late husband's customary lands as dower; it was a half in a few places, such as Tardebigge and Wolverley in the neighbouring county of Worcester, elsewhere even two thirds. Dower was not dependent on motherhood and was retained even on remarriage.[101] The problems this could cause for male heirs were sometimes overcome by creating a joint tenancy. This may well explain some of those cases where the widow had to fight hard to reassert her dower rights.

Some widows were acute business women and had much greater success in pressing their claims to their dowry of one-third than John de Stanford's widow, Matilda, whose eldest son gave evidence against her when she claimed one-third of the £1 18s 6d in rents which her late husband had granted to St Katherine's.[102] Alice, widow of Roger of *Northington* (Netherton), one of that group of local worthies who supported St Katherine's in its infancy, formally renounced all her dower rights in her husband's lands, sold by John Gersant to St Katherine's. For this she succeeded in obtaining from Brother William, the first master, 20s, the equivalent of six years' income from ten acres at 4d an acre for arable. Alice had already received 7s 6d from Brother William for other dower lands—five selions and eight butts in *Wetecroft* extending to the sitch, with her parts of Horsecroft hayment, a meadow in Horsecroft and another meadow. In yet another transaction she was paid 2s for four selions in *Brankeswall* (Bronsil) field, an acre her husband had sold to Thomas Keci and all her part of 'the old mount' behind her 'court' at Netherton, evidently part of the Ridgeway immediately to the west (Figs 6.3a&b). The topography of this Bronsil area was to be transformed when the Beauchamp family built their castle here in the 15th century (Fig 6.2). John Gersant, that sharp businessman, soon learned to be wary of widows and their dowers. Not satisfied when Alice de Subdona, 'by her own wish and with the assent of her friends', released all her dower rights to three parts of 12 acres which he had bought from her eldest son, Robert, Gersant insisted that Alice, in further witness, should swear to accept the bargain, 'touching the gospels in the hand of the priest of Ledbury', and subject herself and all her goods movable and immovable to the jurisdiction of the archdeacon of Hereford.[103]

Although frequently infringed upon by their menfolk, women's rights were protected both by manor court and by common law. Wives' landed interests were carefully recorded. In 1369 the Berrow court noted that Thomas de la Hulle's claim to a messuage and 12 acres was that of Agnes his wife 'as of right', and similarly in 1411 that John Hulle's claim to three acres was also that of his wife Katherine, as 'of right', in this case recording that it was her dower from her father. Not only widows and orphans had such protection; widowers, if freemen, were able, by common law, to claim their right to a widower's free bench together with wardship of their heir or heirs. Thus the Kempley rolls for 1316 record that when Nick Rock did fealty to hold a messuage and curtilage it was 'by law of England'. Likewise at Berrow in 1354 Hugh le Blake's claim to a messuage and six acres was 'by the law of England'. Also known as the law of courtesy, it enshrined a husband's right once a child was born, even if, it was said, but 'a cry heard within four walls', to his wife's land during the whole of their life. This courtesy he retained in widowerhood and even after a further marriage or marriages.[104]

Fig 6.2 Bronsil Moat

Fig 6.3a Netherton in its setting with the Ridgeway beyond, seen from British Camp

The court rolls underline the distinctions between the economies of the granges at Kempley, Weston with Yarkhill, Berrow and the Hyde. The rolls for Kempley are the most forthcoming on the various services and payments due from tenants, whether villein or free. There is no reference to week work but, with virtually 250 acres of arable demesne, the demand for labour at harvest time would have been acute. Tenants of larger holdings however apparently enjoyed the privilege of commuting their remaining labour services. Whilst Walter Edwyn, with 12 acres of arable at an annual rent of 3s, had in 1314 to 'work in autumn for eight days', Isabella Jankynes, with a messuage and 30 acres at 6s 1d, had the option of commuting sixteen days' service to a payment of 2s. Similarly in 1316 John Geffrey owed sixteen days or 2s for a messuage and 23 acres. Autumn work was thus commensurate with the size of the holding and equivalent to one-third of the annual rent. The 1321 rolls are more specific about these services when Walter Edwyn acknowledged owing '*bynrypes*', that is boon reaping, harvest work done, originally, out of 'love' for the lord.

There is evidence of resistance to such harvest work in one of the earliest Kempley rolls. Matilda Edwyn, who held 12 acres as native, that is villein, had to show the court in October 1312 'why her sons do not owe *bynrypes* and other services as other customaries do'. The arrangement she had to accept is in the February 1316 roll. Matilda did fealty, not acknowledging liability for *bynrypes*, but instead of the usual rent of 3s for such a 12-acre holding she paid an additional 1s 5d. Her sons were evidently prepared to pay well over the going rate in order to commute their eight days of servile harvest labour. This is not the only example of such resistance. After the Black Death in 1349 the labour market was no longer so malleable.

With only ten acres of demesne meadow at Kempley, the amount of casual labour at hay-making was in no way comparable to that required for the 250 acres of grain harvest. The hospital's demand for *benemawe*, boon mowing, was thus apparently restricted to customary tenants with

Fig 6.3b Netherton Farm on the site of Alice's 'Court'

larger holdings. Commutation of mowing, but not lifting, services offered no problems. In 1316 whilst John Geffrey, with 30 acres, owed harvest work, he was able to commute his mowing service in *Wohnmedewe* to a payment of 3d, but had to 'find two men to lift the hay' whilst Matilda Edwyn, with a messuage and 12 acres, gave $1^{1}/_{2}$d for cutting the meadow and had to 'find one man to lift the same'. With a mere ten acres, control over the common meadow had to be strictly maintained. The 1307 roll provides evidence of the hayward at work. It records that Matilda Edwyn was in mercy for 'trespass made in the meadow' and for 'certain hay prostrated'. Given her status in the village society this, one must assume, was the act not of a crazed but of a wilful woman.

There is no mention in any of the St Katherine's rolls of the third of the boons, as they continued to be called. This was *benerethe*, the ploughing service. It is possible that it was included under the blanket term 'autumn works', although that would be an inadequate description of services due not only at autumn but also for the spring-sown crops of oats, beans and peas. Such boons, especially the onerous *bynrypes*, were traditionally accompanied by food and drink supplied by the lord. The menu was laid down by manorial custom but normally included soup, meat or fish, pottage, and wheat bread with cheese, all washed down with a sufficiency of ale. However many ecclesiastical lords were notoriously tight-fisted, so much so that at Ramsey abbey, Hunts, the tenants referred to harvest service in three categories: *alebedrep*, *waterbedrep* and *hungerbedrep*, meals with ale or water, the so-called wet or dry boons, but in the last case the worker had to bring his own food.

At Kempley, unlike Ledbury and Eastnor with their extensive woodlands, pannage was in short supply. As with *bynrypes*, there was resistance to payment for the lord's licence. John Geffrey, a customary tenant holding 30 acres, the man who, with his family, figures so prominently in the rolls, fought a long and determined battle over right to pannage for his pigs. In October 1312 the court gave him a date to show his deed certifying his claim to pannage. At Christmas he was in the court's mercy for failing to produce it. Matilda Edwyn was similarly charged at this court. She won her right to commute *bynrypes*, but she was obliged to pay pannage 'as other customary tenants do'. Some three years later, in February 1316, Geffrey undertook to 'give 2s for pannage and other customs', but in May was before the court again, charged once more with taking pannage unlawfully. He counter-attacked, claiming that he was acting according to a charter granted to him by John Wynyard, former master of the hospital, giving him the liberty to take pannage. He thereby forced the brethren into the embarrassing admission that 'they did not know where the said charter was but hope to have the same' available for inspection by the court at some later date. The extant rolls provide no details as to the resolution of this conflict. It was at this same May court that Geffrey faced the serious charge of marrying off his daughter, and sons, without his lord's licence. His family's resistance to servile dues continued to the third generation. In 1361 his granddaughter, Alice, daughter of Jon *Wodeward*, was presented for 'marrying without the lord's licence and not making *bynrypes*', for which transgressions she was fined 3s 4d.

Kempley villeins owed further dues to the master and brethren as lords. Both John Geffrey and Matilda Edwyn had to pay *hundredsilver*, a contribution to the administration of the hundred court, the unit of local government, at Michaelmas 1316. This was pro rata, 6d for her and 3d for him. At Michaelmas 1361 Robert Nicholes, now holding John Geffrey's lands, had to pay the same sum. *Yeldsilver*, also pro rata, was due on the unproductive animals slaughtered in late autumn. There are references to its payment on the feast of Hallowmass, All Saints, 1 November, when the cattle were driven to the byre. On a 12-acre holding in 1314 it was 9d and in 1361, on Robert Nicholes' 30 acres, 18d. Payments 'in aid of the lord' were also levied on villeins. The half-yearly accounts for 1332 refer to Isabella Jankynes paying not only 3s 1d for six months' rent and 2s for autumn works but also an 'aid' of 18d. Walter Edwyn had to pay pro rata, 9d.

The rolls show that at Kempley master and brethren had inherited a much tighter regime for their villein tenants than on their other manors. At Weston there were some 100 acres of arable in demesne yet there is not a single reference in the rolls to harvest labour service, pannage licences, *hundredsilver*, *yeldsilver* or aids for the lord, but there are frequent references to the service of 'lifting hay at *Weteney* meadow'. At a court in 1316, when four men did fealty, this was the only labour service which they had to acknowledge. In his lease to Ralph *le Couherde* of a messuage and croft in 1325 the master, Philip de Chaddesley, included the clause that Ralph was to 'find a man to lift hay for one day in *Weteney*'. The importance of the meadows is underlined by an entry in the court rolls for 1317 when Walter Brown and two others had to answer charges of making illegal water courses and banks, that is attempting to create private water meadows.

At Berrow and the Hyde, Cradley labour services were irrelevant, for the hospital had no demesne lands. At a court at the latter John le Colyer, who took over William le Colyer's messuage and nine acres in 1321, paid 12d for the latter's arrears, acknowledging the rent of 2s 6d but only heriot relief, wardship and marriage as servile obligations. As elsewhere, all matters of tenure, especially unlicensed subletting, were closely monitored. John Holeford was in mercy at Berrow in 1309 because he had failed to appear to explain to the court how he had acquired John de Blakes' holding. In 1354 Richard Maundeville did fealty to hold the messuage with curtilage he had bought from Richard Bradeford. At the Hyde, where John de Stanford had granted 38s 6d in rent, the lands were compact and leasing was administratively convenient. By the 18th century they had become, as they still are, two distinct farms, Hidelow and Copley. In contrast, at Berrow, where Roger *de la Berwe*'s gift had totalled 26s 10½d with three hens, the court rolls show the lands becoming increasingly fragmented.[105]

Juries were also required to present any tenant who allowed the lord's property to fall into disrepair. At the Hyde, Cradley in 1316 John *de Holyngwyke* was charged with breaking the walls of the lord's barn. Attending the court, he 'put himself on his neighbours who said on oath that the walls were destroyed by his wife'. They estimated the damage at 12d. As there was no demesne the barn was of no direct use to the hospital and, unlike Kempley, Weston or Yarkhill, where the churches were appropriated, it could not have served as a tithe barn. It was thus leased to Nicholas de Clopley who gave master and brethren 8s per annum. In 1497 the Kempley jury presented the messuage called *Wodwards* 'on account of the bad condition of the roof' and were ordered to 'take a view of the hedge between *Alwordyne* and Walter Baron's meadow'. At Cradley on 4 April 1339 a tenement called *Collierslond*, probably the messuage of John le Colyer recorded eighteen years earlier, was granted to William Hopper. The lord excused him from paying rent for two years 'so William could build there a sufficient house by the feast of John the Baptist', 29 August. Such house building was usually accompanied by the grant of *housebote*, literally house remedy, the right to take wood from the lord's lands for house building or repair. The 1380 roll for Weston stresses that 'no trees should be cut down—except for *housebote* and *heybote* (wood for fencing) and that only by view of the bailiff'. As late as the 1780s St Katherine's leases still included a clause restraining tenants from committing waste or cutting down any timber trees, that is those 2 feet or more in girth, or indeed any trees except for *firebote, hedgebote, ploughbote* or *wainbote*.[106]

It was not only court rolls but also a number of 14th- and 15th-century accounts and rentals which John Elton had copied into his *Register*. Like the rolls they relate only to the four manors of Kempley, Weston with Yarkhill, Berrow and the Hyde, Cradley. The earliest accounts are for all four in 1332. These are of particular interest as they were drawn up by Brother Roger, showing that some brethren were literate and numerate enough to play a major role in the administration of the hospital's estates. On the other hand, the Kempley accounts for 1374 and 1380 were the work of the bailiffs, Richard *atte Pathe* and Richard *Blachede*. In Henry VIII's reign the rentals for all the manors are brought together and now include details for Ledbury borough and foreign with Eastnor. These are the only records for this joint manor prior to the dissolution of the chantries in 1547.

The largest number of rentals are for Berrow, for 1332, 1337, 1345, 1361, 1382, 1430, 1476 and 1512. These provide an interesting example of historical inertia. Whereas rents on the three other manors were paid half-yearly, at the feast of the Annunciation, Lady Day (25 March), and Michaelmas (29 September), at Berrow they were paid thrice yearly, on the feasts of St Aldhelm (25 May), St Kenelm (17 July) and either at Martinmas (11 November) or the feast of St Andrew (30 November). The first two are local saints of the pre-Conquest era. St Aldhelm (639-709) was one of the first and most famous abbots of Malmesbury whilst Kenelm was a young Mercian king, allegedly murdered at Clent in 812x21 on the orders of his sister. His body was later translated to Winchcombe where his cult, fostered by the monks, was one of the most successful of the late Anglo-Saxon era. Two of Worcester cathedral priory's pre-Conquest calendars show that the feast days of Aldhelm and Kenelm were honoured with special services by the monks. Indeed in one calendar Kenelm's festival is picked out in capital letters. What is alleged to have been his tomb was unearthed at the east end of Winchcombe abbey in 1815 (Fig 6.4).[107] Throughout the medieval period

Fig 6.4 Supposed tomb of St Kenelm

most of Berrow remained a manor of the prior and convent of the cathedral church of Worcester. Their own accounts show the Worcester monks had abandoned these feasts, yet what must have been pre-Conquest and early post-Conquest practice continued to be observed by St Katherine's after they acquired their lands from Roger de Berrow in the early 13th century.

Accounts and rentals confirm the pattern shown in the court rolls. As elsewhere, despite frequent changes in tenure, overall income from the manors remained stable in the pre-Plague years. It was entry fines which tended to fluctuate according to the laws of supply and demand. However, the dramatic decline in population, nationally some 30-45%, at the Black Death, 1349 and subsequent outbreaks, led to the collapse of demesne farming on the hospital's estates. The circumstances are described in Chapter 10 but it is difficult to illustrate the process due to the poverty of the St Katherine's court rolls for the later 14th and the 15th century. The Berrow and a few Kempley rolls show the manor courts continued to meet. The Berrow rolls are of little assistance, for here there was no demesne, but the Kempley rolls for 1364 and 1370 show that, with this collapse, the interest of the courts was now purely financial: the collection of rents and other dues, and the assessment of entry fines when new tenancies were taken up, in other words the management of a system of land tenure which to us is recognisably leasehold.[108]

7 The Three Appropriated Churches

The churches of St John the Baptist at Weston and Yarkhill were the gift of Walter de Lacy and St Mary's at Kempley of Geoffrey de Longchamp. By the process of appropriation master and brethren became rectors, not only holding the advowsons of the three churches, the right to present their own nominees to the bishop for institution into the spiritual care of the parish, but also acquiring their full income. Institutional possession of the advowson of a parish church was anything but unusual. In Hereford diocese in 1419, for example, Wigmore abbey had 24 churches and chapels; Llanthony priory had nine and portions in three others; Monmouth priory had six and portions in five others; and Wormsley priory had five.[109]

The clergy, Thomas at Weston, Robert at Kempley and Moyses at Yarkhill, had formally to recognise St Katherine's status by payment of an annual pension of 1lb of incense 'at the fair of Hereford'. Robert, 'dean and rector' of Kempley, alone demurred. In 1234 he had to appear at the hospital and there swear on the gospels in front of an assembly of local notables including Walter de Mucegros, the bishop's butler, and Master Hugh de Lymp, his clerk, Alan *de Walintone*, William *de Alkerugge* and others that, without any demur, deceit or fraud, he would pay the pension to the master and brethren annually on the feast of St Ethelbert. This being done, Master Hugh affixed first the bishop's seal and then the seals of the witnesses. Only with the death of the three incumbents were master and brethren, as rectors, able to divert a major part of the revenue of these churches to their own uses.[110]

Perpetual Vicars

The prominent position in the foundation charter of the gift of the three churches underlines not only their importance as the hospital's earliest endowments but also the prominent role which they were to play, for some seven centuries, in securing its financial stability. In the 12th century many rectors of appropriated churches, in particular the great Benedictine abbeys, had taken so much profit that their priests, dismissable at will and therefore highly malleable, could hardly sustain themselves. Unchecked, this would have resulted in an uneducated clergy. To avert such dangers arising from 'this vicious custom', the Lateran Council of 1215 ruled that it was unlawful 'to muzzle the ox that treads the corn'. Rectors must present perpetual vicars, canonically instituted, removable only by due course of law. Such vicars were to have security of tenure and 'a sufficient proportion' of the revenues of their church, a minimum wage, in practice about £3 6s 8d. At Yarkhill, the 'sufficient proportion' was £2, with two loads of wheat and two of oats. The St Katherine's community, as rectors, had to ensure that the spiritual needs of each of the three parishes were adequately served, by ordaining such perpetual vicarages. If they failed to fill a vacancy the bishop himself would present, by lapse. At Kempley this happened on at least three occasions in the 15th century.[111]

In the matter of presentation the bishops' registers make it clear that, as with the granting of leases, the master and brethren were acting together under their corporate seal. The first recorded

Fig 7.1 Wilton Castle as built by the de Greys in the late 13th century

presentation, of Reginald of Little Hereford, deacon, to Yarkhill on 22 January 1303, refers to the patron as 'Master of Ledbury Hospital'. This was probably the contraction of a hasty clerk, for in 1305 when Hugh the priest and in 1324 when Thomas *de Molendino*, priest, were presented to Weston, the patrons are described as the 'master and brethren'—as they were in the presentations of Richard de Weston in 1349, on the death of 'Sir Roger', and of William Murie, chaplain, in 1368, on Richard's death. The first of the masters to act unilaterally was William Pykesley, who presented Michael Inge, chaplain, as Murie's successor on the latter's resignation in 1388. Pykesley's character and the significance of this change will be considered later.[112]

At Kempley there is no evidence in the bishop's registers of presentations until 1448. However, in 1259 Geoffrey de Longchamp's daughter and heiress, Maud, wife of John de Grey of Wilton Castle, challenged St Katherine's right of presentation in an action in the royal courts at Westminster (Fig 7.1). The Master, Adam de Putley, and the brethren retained their lands, conceding only 12 acres and the portion known as Netherhell, but had to pay Maud and her heirs an annual pension of 10 marks, £6 13s 4d. By 1316 the pension had become a pair of ungilt silver spurs and 1lb of pepper—a grant more appropriate to the baronial status of Maud's heir's—but three centuries later it was merely 'one pair of yron spurres, 2s'. There was a further challenge in 1280, for Bishop Cantilupe had to order Roger de Sevenake, the president of his diocesan courts, to ensure justice was done to the hospital in the matter of the presentation to Kempley church. Nevertheless Bishop Orleton's register shows the church in the hospital's hands in 1318. The first record of a presentation comes in 1448 when Bishop Spofford presented William Lammer by lapse, Richard Pede, the Master, having failed to act. In an *inquisition post mortem* of 1459 John Abrahall,

64

undertenant of the de Greys, is described as holding the advowson, yet in the same year Pede's successor, John Vaughan, presented Roger Penry, chaplain, and Thomas Balle, chaplain, in 1464. On the latter's death in 1471 and on that of Hugh Barowe, Balle's successor, in 1479, Vaughan failed to fulfil his responsibilities and presentations were made by Bishop Myllyng, by lapse. Vaughan's failings had no adverse impact on his career. On his resignation as master in 1483 Myllyng presented him to the canonry and prebend of Gorwall and, for a short time before his death in 1485, he was *custos* of the cathedral's relics.[113]

Parochial Revenue

Even after 'sufficient' provision had been made for the perpetual vicar, the rector generally continued to enjoy a considerable part of the church's revenue. This was drawn principally from its tithes and glebe lands. St Katherine's three churches certainly provided a substantial proportion of its income: in 1316, for example, 45% of its total annual resources. At Kempley the church was valued at £8, representing 59% of the manor's value; at Weston £4, 49%; and at Yarkhill £5 6s 8d, 80% (Table 1). However, as these sums are based on the papal taxation of 1291, the real value of the three churches to St Katherine's may well have been considerably higher. St Katherine's right to such rich pickings did not go unchallenged.[114]

The de Greys of Wilton were not the only parties that had to be bought off. In the mid 14th century the master and brethren came to an agreement with the prior and convent of St Guthlac's, Hereford, over the latter's claim to two parts of the greater tithes of the demesne lands at Kempley, Weston and Yarkhill. In support of the Weston claim St Guthlac's produced three charters of confirmation, by bishops Robert de Bethune (1131-48), William de Vere (1186-98) and Giles de Braose (1200-15), but Yarkhill is not referred to in any of these. The only extant evidence as to St Guthlac's claim at Yarkhill is a spurious charter, ascribed to Henry II (1154-89) but in a 15th-century hand. Nevertheless the context makes it clear that the rights claimed at all three places had in fact been part of the original endowment granted by Walter I de Lacy to St Peter's church, Hereford, in the great Norman market place, now High Town. It was whilst inspecting St Peter's tower that Walter fell to his death. In 1143 Robert de Bethune transferred Walter's endowments, and all the others belonging to St Peter's, to the new priory which he had founded outside Hereford's walls, dedicated to St Guthlac, a transfer confirmed by the first of the three charters mentioned above.

Omission of the Yarkhill tithes was probably a clerical oversight. The spurious 15th-century charter suggests the monks of St Peter's, Gloucester, the mother house of St Guthlac's, later sought, in their own way, to 'rectify' this omission. Certainly the tithes were valuable, for the Lacy demesne at Yarkhill was worth £20 per annum in 1160-70. Whatever the rights or wrongs of the case the Master, Hugh Cradock, and the brethren agreed to pay St Guthlac's a pension of £2 a year with their *Donebrugge* (Dunbridge) grange standing as security for prompt payment in lieu of 'all tithes due at St Guthlac's from the parishes of Weston and Yarkill'. Three copies of this agreement were made: the first, to be held by St Katherine's; the second, by St Guthlac's; and the third, by its mother house, St Peter's abbey, Gloucester. In Elizabeth's reign this pension of £2, 'late appertaining to the monastery or priory of Hereford, dissolved,' was being paid to Gregory Price Esq.[115]

Tithes

Tithes, greater and lesser, were the payment to the church of a tenth part of 'all things that yield a yearly increase by act of God', whether the product of land or beasts. They were justified by reference to Jacob's vow in Genesis 28:22: 'of all that thou shalt give me I will surely give the tenth unto thee' and to Leviticus 27:30-3. The greater tithes went to the rector, but the lesser came to be regarded as part of that 'sufficient proportion' of the parochial revenues that should go to the perpetual vicar. The hospital thus received a tenth part of all major crops—wheat, oats, barley, beans etc—whilst the vicar received merely a tenth of such produce as hay, flax, hemp, fruit, wood, calves, lambs and wool, piglets, chicken, goslings, doves, eggs, milk, garden produce and even bees with their honey and wax. Such minor tithes provided but a small income and many were extremely troublesome to collect. At Weston, however, where the emphasis on dairying was crucial, the master and brethren retained the tithes of hay. In addition to the lesser tithes 'altarage', all offerings at the altar, the collection in contemporary parlance, went to the vicar.

Table 6: Weston and Yarkhill. Greater and Lesser Tithes, 1535

		Weston			Yarkhill		
		£	s	d	£	s	d
Greater tithes	Grain	4	0	0		5	0
	Hay					10	0
Lesser tithes	Eggs		1	0		1	6
	Lambs & wool		10	0		13	4
	Flax			8		1	0
	Wax & honey		1	0			8
	Piglets & goslings		4	0		6	8
	Doves			4			
	Pasture					7	4
	Firewood & kindling					1	0
Total		4	17	0	2	6	6

Valor Ecclesiaticus III, 36, 44

Details of greater and lesser tithes at Weston and Yarkhill are available for 1535. These give interesting hints as to the domestic economy of the parishioners, for lambs and wool and pigs and goslings were the major elements in the vicar's lesser tithes, but doves, flax, and honey and wax are also included. The omission of any reference to calves and milk suggests that these were arbitrarily removed by the hospital from titheable produce, as was hay at Weston. It is also of interest that tithe payments on chickens, fruit and garden produce are not included (Table 6).

Collection of the greater tithes often met with stout resistance from the parishioners. Yet the task, if left to the hospital's bailiff, offered many temptations. The alternative was to lease out the tithes to a local person of sufficient standing to enforce payment. Such 'farming' has been described as 'the lesser of two evils: the substitution of waste by farmers for the peculation of bailiffs'. The benefit for St Katherine's, after a long period of very poor harvests due to bad weather, was a known and stable income.[116] By 1342 the greater tithes at Weston and Yarkhill were already farmed out for a fixed annual rent of 14 marks, £9 13s 4d. They were specifically excluded from John Hunt's lease of *Frere Courte*, Weston. By the 16th century such farming of the tithes had come to be described as the farming of the 'rectory' and their value was appreciating considerably. In 1503, when John Sherd was farmer of the Yarkhill 'rectory' and John Elyatt that of Weston, the respective sums they paid were £12 8s 8d and £4. By 1528 St Katherine's steward, Richard Seaborne of Sutton, was paying £14 13s 4d for Yarkhill and £4 for Weston. In the 1580 survey they were valued at £19 13s 4d and £6 respectively.[117]

At Kempley there is even less evidence for the tithes than for presentations to the vicarage. A rental of 1528 refers to William Ludbye, tenant of *Frerecourt*, paying one mark, 13s 4d, annually but only for the tithes of his own corn. In the 1580 survey the greater tithes are included as part of the valuation of Friars Court.[118]

Glebe lands

The glebe, like greater tithes, were for the most part in the hands of the rector. In a charter, described in the margin as 'Yarkhill rectory appropriated to the hospital', Master Moyses, priest at the time of St Katherine's foundation, granted 32s 6d rents to master and brethren for which he was to receive their prayers for 'the salvation', not only of his own soul but 'that of his wife and ancestors and successors'. There, and presumably at Weston and Kempley as well, the hospital, as rector, had formally undertaken from 'ancient days', presumably from Moyses' death, to furnish the perpetual vicar with an annual pension of £2 and a fixed allocation of grain, two loads of wheat and two of barley, as his 'sufficient provision'.[119]

The glebe was leased out. A part of Kempley's glebe is first referred to in the court rolls for 1362 when William le Brut, Master, granted a croft called *Parsonesfeld* to Hugh de Lynche and Walter, his son, for their lives at an annual rent of 16d. In 1364 Hugh Cradock, Master, granted the croft to Hugh, his wife, Margery, and their corporeal heirs for their lives, on the same terms but with an entry fine of six pullets. A century later, in December 1484, Margaret Velmyll showed by a copy of the manorial roll that Walter, her husband, had held *Parsonagesfeld*, an orchard or close called *Parsonesorchard*, a croft called *Wodwalparrock*, a field called *Bradfelde* and a meadow, *Maylagardesmedowe*, for which she paid an annual rent of 7s rent with suit of court etc.

By 1492 this parcel of lands had passed to Thomas Wilse who undertook to build a house of two bays, *spaciorum*, on 'the unbuilt messuage called Parsonage Close on which the rectory house was once built'. This was to be completed within four years and suitably maintained throughout the 90 years of the lease. However, when Wilse renewed his undertaking in 1515, a 'two-floored house' was specified. This was built, for numerous leases from 1581 to 1794 refer to 'a messuage some time ago rebuilt in which the rectory ... stood'. Bradfeld, now eighteen acres of pasture, and Maylars Meadow, now called Maddocks, continued to be associated with this messuage but the three other parcels, Parsonage Field and Orchard and Woodwall *parrock*, tended to come and go. The final episode in the story of Kempley church, parsonage and glebe land will be described in the second part of this *History*.

A marginal note, attached later to the deed of Moyses' grant of 32s 6d rents to the hospital, explains that this related to 'the appropriated rectory'. The subsequent history of the glebe can be reconstructed from the court rolls and terriers between 1321 and 1503 and then in deeds to 1718. The first evidence comes from a lease of 1321 which refers to a small parcel of land: a messuage, three acres of arable and one *peroc*, formerly in the tenure of Thomas *Partrich* of Little Hyde. *Parrock* and *peroc* are described in Chapter 5. This Robert *de Wytewykes*, his wife and son leased for their lives. The rent was 3s 6d, plus 6d in lieu of four hens, for all services but included suit of two courts annually at Weston. In 1325, however, Philip de Chaddesley, as Master, leased all the lands formerly held by Robert to Ralph *le Couherde* and in 1327 to William *Courant* and his wife, for 33s 4d, a sum very close to the 32s 6d annual rents granted by Moyses. The next year, described as 30 acres of arable with half an acre of meadow, this was leased for 50 years to John Hawkynes of Monks Hide and Alice, his wife, with Ralph *de la Brugges* of Weston, and their heirs. The rent, 30s, was to be paid quarterly at the feasts of St Andrew, the Purification, the Nativity of St John the Baptist, the saint to whom the parish church was dedicated, and Michaelmas. It is notable that in both the 1321 and 1327 leases the rent, at 1s per acre for arable, is double the 6d valuation of the 1316 inventory (Table 3).

The combined property is next referred to in a court roll of 1503 when James Tomkyns acknowledged that he held 30 acres of customary land with two messuages, now called *Mawdeleyns*, at a rent of 20s. In a lease of 1516 to James and his son John, it is described more fully as 'two messuages called *Magdleyn's* and *Partrych's*. The rent was now 22s, but the four fowls mentioned in 1321 were specified as a pair of capons at Michaelmas, 29 September, and of hens at the feast of the Purification, 2 February. Three highly detailed terriers follow: to John Tomkins in 1564, Richard in 1655 and finally, in 1718, to Francis Tomkins and his wife, when the property is described as 'the ancient parsonage or farm and glebeland thereunto belonging', assessed at 33 acres. Here, with the two pastures, Parsons Closes, and a meadow, Parsonage Meadow, leased separately, we have Yarkhill's ancient glebeland, entire.[120]

Fig 7.2 St Mary's, Kempley from the south

Fig 7.3 St Mary's, Kempley: Christ in Majesty

Maintenance of the Fabric

The parish was responsible for the maintenance of the nave of the church, the rector for the chancel. That St Katherine's was reluctant to spend any more than the absolute minimum on such works is evident even today at Kempley and Yarkhill. Kempley church is an early Norman building, *c*1120-30, to which the only additions were the west tower, built for purposes of defence *c*1276, and the south porch, built of timber in the fourteenth century (Fig 7.2). The Norman windows of the chancel show that no structural alterations were undertaken after master and brethren had been granted the advowson, but the undistinguished chancels of many neighbouring churches show that the hospital was not alone in this respect.

At Kempley the hospital's concern to minimise its maintenance charges for the chancel has been to our inestimable gain. It has ensured the preservation of the chancel paintings of *c*1130-40. These have been described by E.W.Tristram, the pre-eminent authority, as being 'as magnificent in conception as the Cluniac paintings of central France'. They enable us 'partially at least', he explains, 'to realise the splendour of our Norman cathedrals when their richness was enhanced by the intricate beauty of painted diapers and the play of bright colours'. The subject is the 'Glories of Heaven': Christ in Majesty, within a triple mandorla and seated on a rainbow, holds the Book in His left hand and with His right gives the blessing; above are the sun and moon, with human faces, and on either side the symbols of the four evangelists together with the seven golden candlesticks of the apocalyptic vision of St John, and pairs of cherubims and seraphims

Fig 7.4 St Mary's, Kempley: Peter and five other apostles look up at Apocalyptic scene

(Fig 7.3). The Virgin, crowned as Queen of Heaven, and St Peter with his keys complete the composition. From either side, apostles seated under an arcade look up in awe, as do their sculptured counterparts in the porch of Malmesbury abbey (Fig 7.4). Perhaps inaction on the part of master and brethren was due not so much to niggardliness as to the compelling power of this scene? Certainly its power prompted the parish into further schemes of wall painting in the nave, of which the Martyrdom of Becket and the St Christopher with the Child Jesus of 1370-80 and the 15th-century Wheel of Life are now the most impressive.[121]

Fig 7.5 Yarkhill: Nave, chancel and west tower

Fig 7.6 Weston Church: Nave, chancel and west tower, early 14th-century, from the south

In terms of structure, however, the parish followed its rector, with similar inaction in relation to the nave. This, dendrochronology has shown, has the earliest and most complete roof structure scientifically dated in Britain. The door between nave and tower is of the same period. Boring samples have produced an estimated felling range of 1120-50 for the nave roof and 1114-44 for the doors. Together with the 12th-century date for the chancel paintings, this points to the church being built by Gilbert de Lacy, who died after 1163, and the lay figures depicted on the north and south walls of the chancel as Gilbert and his grandfather, Walter I, the dynasty's founder.[122]

At Yarkhill the south doorway, tower arch and some capitals found at the vicarage 70 years ago, all suggest a church built about 1200. To this the west tower was added in the late 13th century, the upper stage probably in 1466. Although the nave was rebuilt and the chancel drastically restored by Thomas Blashill in 1863, there is no evidence in the chancel of work subsequent to 1200 (Fig 7.5).[123]

At Weston the situation is quite different. The chancel arch and south porch indicate that the church was originally built, as at Yarkhill, about 1200. In the early 14th century the chancel was rebuilt and lengthened, as shown by two windows of that date in its north wall. The east window and those on the south are part of Nicholson's 1881 restoration (Fig 7.6). In the north and south walls of the chancel are two contemporary tomb recesses, the latter described by Pevsner as 'uncommonly sumptuous'. Both belong to the type known as gabled canopy tombs of which the earliest are the free-standing tombs in Westminster abbey of Henry II's son, Edmund Crouchback, and his wife, Aveline, who died in 1296 and 1276 respectively. The fashion spread quickly to the provinces, where most tombs, as at Weston, were not free-standing but placed against a wall.

Similar tomb recesses can be seen at Hereford cathedral: one attributed to Thomas de Pembridge, treasurer died 1329, in the nave south aisle; the other to Bishop Thomas de Charlton, died 1344, in the north transept. Like the southern tomb at Weston, they have crocketed gables and arches decorated with cinquefoil cusping and a finial. At Weston the cusping is decorated with low relief foliage and four shields. At Hereford the tympana are decorated with trefoils, but at Weston with the low relief foliage and another shield at the head. On either side of the Weston tomb are pinnacled standards. With no trace of the original colouring, there is no clue to the heraldry on the five shields (Fig 7.7). The gabled canopy tomb on the north side of the chancel is simpler in design, but the gable is decorated with ballflower ornament (Fig 7.8). This made its first appearance in the county *c*1320. Locally, dated 'probably 1330 or later', ballflower is found in the north chapel of Ledbury parish church, covering both windows and doorway in profusion. Built into the tower are fragments of an early 14th-century coffin lid, with part of an inscription, which may well originally have been in the chancel.[124]

Neither rebuilt chancel nor tomb recesses were the work of St Katherine's. They were part of a chantry chapel dedicated to the Virgin. Notes collected by the 18th-century Hereford antiquary, James Hill, explain that 'under the chancel arch was painted the Blessed Virgin with the Infant Jesus; on each side kneels an angel with a trumpet. From the point of the Arch descends a Glory'. The chantry is first mentioned in the episcopal registers in 1362, when Bishop Lewis Charlton, by lapse of the patron, was obliged to present John Mason as chaplain, but the architectural evidence suggests it was founded some thirty years earlier. In 1369 however it was Roger *de Stepultone* (Stapledon?) who presented John Wele as chaplain. Three years later, when Wele became rector of the neighbouring church at Pixley, a Robert *de Stepultone* presented Richard Lene as chaplain. This is the last reference to the family which, as patrons, funded the building of the chantry and, in all probability, also the chancel and handsome west tower.[125]

Fig 7.7 Weston Church: Southern tomb recess in chancel

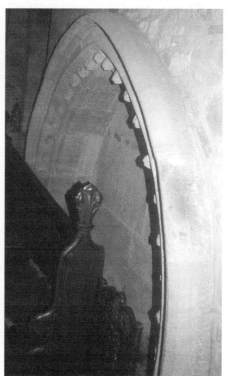

Fig 7.8 Weston Church: Ballflower decoration on northern tomb recess

71

The *Stepultones*, by assuming responsibility for the chancel at Weston, had converted it, effectively, into a family mortuary chapel, with the mail-clad knightly figures of two members of their family lying within the gabled canopies of the wall tombs. Hence the dramatic difference between the condition of the chancels at Weston and Yarkhill. Whether they were related to the Devon Stapledons is unknown. Certainly a close connection was built up between St Katherine's and Exeter, when John de Grandison was consecrated bishop on Walter de Stapledon's death in 1326.[126]

The chantry continued to be served. John Smyth was rector from 1433 to 1444 and then held the chaplaincy until his death thirteen years later when John Syrelle was presented by Thomas Walwyn as heir to the *Stepultones*. Whether Thomas was a member of the Hellens, Much Marcle, or Longworth, Lugwardine, branches of the Walwyns is not known. Indeed there was another branch just across the river from Weston, at Stoke Edith between 1308 and 1402. The physical condition of the chantry deteriorated. In 1512 when Bishop Booth was prevailed upon, by the Walwyns no doubt, to grant an indulgence to all assisting 'the inhabitants of Weston for the repair of their church and the chantry of the Blessed Virgin therein', no reference was made to the responsibilities of St Katherine's as rectors. Restoration must have met with some success for Thomas Walwyn presented in 1524 and John Walwyn presented the last chaplain, Thomas Ruckley, in 1536. Eleven years later the chantries were dissolved but in 1554 Ruckley, described as 'of honest fame and never married', was still receiving a pension of £4 7s 8d a year from the crown. Henry VIII's survey of all benefices, the *Valor Ecclesiasticus*, gives the value of the vicarage as £5 15s 3d. The chantry funded from the rent of 'Our Ladies Farm' was worth £3 6s 6d.[127]

Only in the 16th century do we learn how the hospital placed responsibility for the maintenance of Weston's chancel on other shoulders. Under the terms of a lease of *Freyrs courte* to Henry Wotton of Hereford city in 1565, Wotton was obliged to 'maintain the chancel of the parish church of Weston in (roof) tiling, walling and all kinds of repairs at his own cost and to pay out rents and charges, ordinary and extraordinary'. From the late 17th century such responsibility for Weston's chancel appears as a standard clause in all leases. Evidence of a similar arrangement at Kempley is found in a lease of *Fryars Court* in 1781.[128]

As well as maintenance of the chancels, St Katherine's had other financial responsibilities for its appropriated churches: the costs of the archdeacon's official parochial visitations, his annual procurations, and of the bishop's synodals, the parish's contribution to the expenses of holding diocesan synods. In 1315/16 such procurations and synodalia for Weston and Yarkhill cost 6s 8d and for Kempley, 7s 8d.

Episcopal Visitation

In the spring of 1397 Bishop John Trefnant conducted a visitation of the parishes of his diocese. Almost all references to such visitations in the Hereford bishops' registers are fragmentary. For this visitation, however, the clerk's rolls giving details of the issues raised at each parish were discovered and published, in 1929, by Canon Bannister, Master of St Katherine's 1909-36. The bishop's visit was usually preceded by the submission of searching questionnaires. These, which had to be completed in full, thus formed the basis for further enquiries on his arrival. In each parish his overall purpose was twofold: to establish the moral state of both clergy and laity and the physical condition of its church, churchyard and parsonage house. Such visitations could be fearful occasions, for the bishop came 'not only to admonish and exhort but also to punish and condemn'. For each of St Katherine's churches the visitation records provide us with remarkable evidence relating to the quality of parochial leadership exercised by the rector, William Pykesley, a man who had been master of St Katherine's for almost a decade and a half.[129]

The parishioners of Weston were called to Lugwardine on 1 May to make their formal presentments. From these it is evident that, although the physical condition of Weston church was sound, they had considerable fears for its spiritual life. They reported that John Pole, the chantry priest, would not obey the just and honest orders of the vicar and refused to conduct services with him. This they believed was highly detrimental to the spiritual well-being of the church, its oblations and emoluments. As to his own office, instead of celebrating his daily masses, Pole was often absent for three weeks or a month at a time. Further, he had removed two or three cartloads of church masonry from the graveyard without their licence and had refused to return it.

A much more serious charge was then brought against Pole by the parishioners, one which reflected some of their deepest fears. In 1236 Archbishop Edmund Rich had ordered that all fonts should be decently covered and locked. The reason was that the water, which was hallowed only at certain festivals, particularly Easter, had thus to remain in the font for considerable periods of time. This, many country people believed, made it highly vulnerable to theft and pollution—for use in the black arts. Pole had removed the lock from their font cover. His fate is not recorded but Trefnant took immediate action with John Stogursley, the vicar. In 1390, as vicar of Preston-on-Wye, Stogursley had exchanged benefices with Michael Inge, presented to Weston by Pykesley in 1388. A further exchange was now arranged, with the support of the abbot and convent of St Peter's, Gloucester, who, as proprietors of the Middle Court, Monksbury Court and Grove and Old House tenements, had an interest in the well-being of the parish. Stogursley was presented to St Peter's appropriated church at Mansell Gamage with John Harvey, its priest, taking his place at Weston in June 1397.[130]

The Kempley parishioners appeared before Trefnant at Dymock on 25 May. Explaining that their church house was 'ruinous and flat with the ground', they presented the rector, William Pykesley, still master, for failing to provide the vicar with a manse close to the church where they could have recourse to him in their 'times of necessity', that is for the rights of baptism and extreme unction. For the former water had to be kept ever ready in the font. Indeed such importance was attached to the baptism of the newborn that, if the life of such a child was in any danger then the midwife, or failing her any person present, had to pour water over its head, saying 'In the name of the Father, in the name of the Son and in the name of the Holy Ghost', to ensure removal of the stain of original sin which would otherwise bar the newborn from Heaven. Such a ceremony was acceptable even if the *In nomine* was uttered in English. The midwife was instructed that, in the case of a difficult birth, to ensure baptism even the mother's life should be risked. Similarly, parochial clergy had always to be ready to administer extreme unction, the *viaticum*, to strengthen the dying with grace on their way to the afterlife. Pykesley had to face another charge. The jurors further presented that for the last ten years as rector he had withheld the 2lbs of wax due to them annually for St Leonard's light.

The Yarkhill parishioners made their presentments at Much Cowarne on 30 May. Their chancel roof, they reported, was so defective, through the neglect of the rector, that the chaplain could not celebrate mass there when it was raining, and that the windows were broken. Presumably on wet days mass was celebrated in the nave, which was maintained in a reasonable state by the parish. The jury further pointed out that, since his appointment, the rector had withheld the vicar's annual pension of £2, two loads of wheat and two of oats, which pension, they stressed, had been 'ordained in ancient days', that is at the time of appropriation, c1231. Pykesley had also failed to supply the straw that should have been strewn, thrice a year, on the floor of the church. That was not all. As at Kempley, the vicar's house was ruinous and almost flat with the ground. This, the parishioners admitted, should have been a joint responsibility of rector and vicar but the latter could hardly be expected to contribute when Pykesley had withheld his pension for so long. Not surprisingly, the vicar, Roger Woodwall, who had served the parish faithfully for fourteen years, had made off with the timber from his manse and retained 5 marks, £3 6s 8d, 'owing to the service of the holy Virgin'.[131]

Further evidence as to Pykesley's shortcomings as master will be considered in a later chapter, but his failings as rector should be placed in context. Of the four parishes examined on the first day of Trefnant's visitation, the chancels of two, Brinsop and Burghill, had been found defective. Both churches had been appropriated by the Augustinian canons of Llanthony Prima. Eight parishes made presentments at Much Cowarne on 30 May. At Stoke Lacy, an appropriated church of St Peter's, Gloucester, the chancel and rectory were defective. At Ullingswick St Peter's, which held two-thirds of the rectory, had made off with a service book, the great portiforium. For the most part, however, presentments were dominated by reports of moral lapses of clergy and laity. At Kempley the jury referred to the lapses of Giles Absolon who, for his mortal sin, had for twenty-six years had an 'abundantly' incestuous relationship with Margaret Onlyth, *in amplexibus incestuosis*. At neighbouring Bromsberrow, beyond Donnington, there was the further report that 'Geyles Absolon, unattached, and Maiota Onlyth have committed incest'.

8 The Early 14th Century: Relics, Patronage and Maladministration

The Relic List

Most treasured of the possessions of the greater religious houses were the relics, cherished for their miraculous powers. Some hospitals also acquired relics which became the 'means of bringing resort and thereby enriching the hospital'. The hospital of the Holy Cross, Colchester, claimed a fragment of the True Cross. This was enclosed in 21oz of gold. Hospitals on major pilgrim routes fared well and those on the Pilgrims' Way to Canterbury best of all. As late as 1519 one of the brethren of the leper house at Harbledown, founded c1100, ran into the road and sprinkled the passing Erasmus and Dean Colet with holy water, offering them their relic of Thomas, the glorious martyr, to kiss, the mangled upper part of a shoe, set with a piece of glass like a jewel. On this the community was believed to depend for its maintenance. The hospital of St Katherine-by-the-Tower in London, founded in 1148 by Stephen's queen, Matilda, was granted part of their saint's tomb by the pope, at the special request of Catherine of Aragon.[132]

St Bartholomew's, Oxford, had one of the most important collections. It claimed a piece of the skin of its patron, Bartholomew the apostle, who was flayed alive and whose symbol was the butcher's knife, as well as bones of Stephen the protomartyr and a rib of St Andrew. Laid up in several repositories in its chapel, the relics were exposed to view 'at high and select times, especially at a general concourse of people. Unhappy did he account himself that could not come neare either to touch or kiss them.' Treasured above all was the comb of their local saint, Edmund Rich of Abingdon, archbishop of Canterbury 1233-40. He was famed for restoring to health those 'troubled with continuall headaches, frenzies or lightheaded'. Not infrequently relics were stolen. The Augustinians of St Osyth's removed a fragment of the True Cross from Holy Trinity, Dunwich, 'whither many resorted who bestowed much alms'. The king himself obliged the abbot to return it. St Bartholomew's, Oxford, was not so fortunate, for all its relics were appropriated by Oriel College when it became the hospital's 'protector' in 1327. But at Colchester thieves coming by night were, no doubt, more interested in the 21-oz gold reliquary than in the relic itself.[133]

St Katherine's 1316 inventory contains a list of relics of astonishing range and quality. In terms of recorded relics they must have rivalled, possibly outshone, even those of St Bartholomew's (Appendix 1). Of the special virtues or healing properties of Ledbury's relics we have no hint. All we have are the details listed in the inventory. Most of the relics were kept in six purses, two phylacteries and a pyx. In origin the phylactery was a small leather case containing vellum strips with religious texts, but by the 13th century the term was used for any small vessel or case containing relics or other precious objects.

Always held in the highest regard were relics of the Holy Family. Pride of place would therefore have gone to the first two items listed, a 'small part of the vestment' of the Virgin in one phylactery and another 'part' in the other. This also held part of 'the vestment of St Thomas'. Third on the list was a fragment of the 'Cross of (Our) Lord', with another from St Andrew's cross. As to how these two were protected there is no indication. Next was the silver pyx, a glass receptacle or box, normally used to protect the consecrated host but quite often mounted in precious metal to display relics. This contained the 'oils of St Thomas'. Then follow the contents of the six purses, made from rectangles of cloth with two lateral seams and drawstrings at the top and, usually, lined. The first, of silk, contained relics of St Stephen, the Pope. In another were 'the bones of Saints Simon and Stephen'. The white purse contained 'items of the blood, hair and vestment of the blessed Thomas, the martyr'. In the purse of red muslin was 'a small piece of the chasuble of "the blessed Denis"', whilst the black purse contained 'a small bone of the blessed Andrew', a second piece of wood from his cross and a piece of the tunic of St Thomas. The sixth purse contained 'tiny stones'.

This apparently miscellaneous collection can be reduced to some order. After the three relics of the Holy Family, most of the identifiable items are of Roman provenance. Pope Stephen I died *c*257, naturally according to the earliest tradition, but later it was believed he died a martyr during the persecutions of the Emperor Valerian. Stephen was the only Roman; the other saints had been translated, by fair means or foul, from their resting places in the eastern Mediterranean. Simon the apostle, with his companion, Jude, had been hacked to death by 'the heathen priests of Persia'. He can be seen with the instrument of his martyrdom, the falchion or curved sword, amongst the other apostles in the lower tracery lights of the great east window of Great Malvern priory. Claim was laid to three relics of St Andrew: the small bone and two pieces of his diagonal cross. His body was believed to have been translated from Patras, the city of his martyrdom, to Constantinople whence crusaders, after they had stormed the city in 1204, took his body to Amalfi and his head to Rome. The bones of St Stephen are carefully distinguished from those of Stephen the pope, thus representing a claim to a relic of the church's protomartyr and first deacon, stoned to death for blasphemy, his assailants' clothes having been laid at the feet of Saul, later Paul. Stephen's relics were also taken to Constantinople and thence to Rome.

One relic was French in origin. The small piece of the chasuble of the blessed Denis, Bishop of Paris, beheaded *c*250, must have come from his native city. The others were English. The blood, hair and vestments of the blessed Thomas, martyr, in the white purse, are those of Thomas Becket but the St Thomas, part of whose vestment, tunic and oils are claimed, is a quite different saint, considered below. The part of 'a wax candle kindled with celestial fire on the vigil of Easter' is in a category of its own. Was it 'the treasured remembrance of an Easter spent by a pilgrim' at the church of the Holy Sepulchre in Jerusalem?

Three crosses were included under the heading 'relics' rather than the preceding category of 'ornaments'. They were a small cross of silver, a larger silver cross with unidentified small silver images and another, of latten, that is covered with sheets of brass. This is merely described as 'old'. About other items the brethren were wholly ignorant. In the first phylactery, with part of the Virgin's vestment, were 'other unknown relics'. In the second, with a further relic of the Virgin, were 'certain other relics'. The pyx contained not only the oils of St Thomas but also 'other minute items'. The silk purse contained 'certain other minute items', another merely 'tiny stones, *lapides minuti*', possibly chippings from holy sites. It would seem that at least a major part of the collection had passed through a number of hands. However minor, each item would have been of vital significance to its original owner, but lost its identity as it passed on the various stages of its journey to St Katherine's.

St Thomas Cantilupe

The clerk who drew up the list took great care to distinguish between the relics of St Thomas the Martyr, that is Thomas Becket of Canterbury, murdered in his cathedral in 1170, and those of another St Thomas, of whom there were three relics: part of his vestment being with that of the

Virgin in the second phylactery, the oils in the silver pyx, and part of his tunic in the black purse. These were relics of either Thomas the apostle or Thomas Cantilupe. The apostle's relics were claimed by Mylapore, near Madras in India, the site of his martyrdom. On the other hand, according to the *Roman Martyrology*, they were translated first to Edessa in Syria, *c*230, thence to the island of Chios and eventually to Ortona in the Abruzzi mountains where they are still venerated.[134] If St Katherine's had claimed the apostle's relics, they would have been so identified. The reference to oils is, however, conclusive. As Thomas the apostle's martyrdom had been early in the first century, it would be strange indeed to make such a claim to his 'oils'.

Thomas Cantilupe died near Orvieto in August 1282. To fulfil his wish to be buried in his cathedral at Hereford, his body was boiled to separate flesh from bones. The 'oils' could well be the resultant fluids. Heart and bones could then be brought to England. On the other hand, when the relics of St William of York and St Hugh of Lincoln were translated, a clear oil was found. From this may have arisen the 'odour of sanctity', often referred to on such occasions. Both Westminster abbey and Salisbury cathedral claimed phials containing St Katherine's oils. In the early eastern church the tradition was that oil would be poured into the top of reliquaries kept in a special mortuary chapel. After contact with the saint's bones they poured out from below and were kept in phials to be used to anoint, and on occasions to be drunk by, the sick, in the firm belief in their miracle-giving powers.[135] When the seven-year-old Henry VI was crowned King of France, anointment was with the sacred oils of St Thomas Becket.

Fig 8.1 Credenhill Church: Thomas Becket and Thomas Cantilupe window c1310 'to stimulate rather than celebrate a canonisation process'

Any attribution to St Thomas Cantilupe has, however, to meet the apparent difficulty that formal canonisation, by Pope John XXII, took place in 1320, four years after the inventory of St Katherine's relics was drawn up. This is not such a problem as at first sight it might appear. Papal control of the canonisation process had only been established by Innocent III (1199-1216).[136] Historically canonisation had always been a popular process, its outward manifestation being the miracles wrought.

This remained the fundamental criterion, but canonisation was now subject to formal investigation by papal commissioners. Evidence of miracles was given to such judges-delegate at Hereford between August and November 1307, but the popular cult of Thomas Cantilupe, with its abundant miracles, had been initiated at Easter 1287. This was achieved through the unswerving devotion of his immediate successor, Bishop Gilbert Swinfield (1283-1317) who for eighteen years had been his personal clerk and confidant. In April 1287 Swinfield organised the formal translation of Thomas's relics from their first resting place under a flat stone in the lady chapel to a new tomb, still to be seen in the north transept. The translation was timed to coincide with the diocesan Holy Week celebrations, characterised, as always, by great anticipation.

'Thomas's miraculous powers were fully released on Maundy Thursday, 3 April, the day of his translation' to the tomb in the north transept (Fig 8.2). Locals had no doubt as to Cantilupe's sanctity, and the impact on Ledbury must have been even more electric than on the other estates of the church of Hereford, for the beneficiary of the first miracle that day was a John *de Masintone*, almost certainly the man who, the *Red Book* tells us, held 120 acres at Massington of the bishop by military tenure and who, with other major tenants, witnessed a number of St Katherine's late 12th-century charters. Many of the other early pilgrims also came from the manors of the bishop and dean and chapter. By the end of April 71 miracles were recorded. By 1300 there were 250 more and in 1312 the number had reached almost 500.[137]

This was part of a carefully orchestrated campaign. The year prior to the translation Swinfield canvassed his fellow bishops to grant indulgences to all praying for the repose of Cantilupe's soul. On his perambulation of his own estates and the diocese generally he preached forcefully on Thomas's sanctity. Other means were used to promote the cult. St Mary's, Credenhill was a church in which the dean and chapter had a considerable interest. Half the manor belonged to them in 1086 and as late as 1385 the rector had to pay the dean and chapter an annual rent for a licence to inter the dead in his own churchyard instead of the cathedral close.[138] Here the famous stained glass windows, with the twin figures of Becket and Cantilupe, are further evidence of Swinfield's campaign. These are dated *c*1310, not only on the character of the glass but also 'the ambivalence

Fig 8.2 Cantilupe tomb

suggested by the absence of haloes and *sanctus* inscriptions presupposes an image designed to stimulate a cult rather than to celebrate a canonisation process' (Fig 8.1).[139] As early as 1289 Swinfield even refers in his formal register to the offerings of wax at the tomb of *Saint* Thomas. Two years prior to canonisation Edward III himself, writing to the pope and a cardinal, refers to Cantilupe as *beati Thome de Cantilupo.*[140]

Where were such precious relics kept in safety? The chapel's two chalices of silver gilt, with patens used at the altar service, would have been kept in the aumbry. In the chapel are the remains of two such aumbries, that near the altar being replaced by another in the north wall when the new, larger central east window was built *c*1330-40 (Figs 8.3a&b). Both aumbries were larger than required for the chalices and patens and both were quite elaborate in design. Sides and sills were of well-cut stone and well rebated to accommodate a pair of wooden doors. The aumbry beside the altar has an arched head. Its size and design suggest its construction was not coeval with the original building, for it was usual to have a plain, square or oblong, shape which 'simplified the construction of the timber doors' and, more important, 'in no way competed with the richness of other fittings'. The implication is that the first aumbry was purpose-built *c*1300 for the safe custody of the newly-acquired relics in their two phylacteries, silver pyx and six purses, to be replaced by the second *c*1340.[141]

About the overall form of the replacement aumbry we can only conjecture. The sides, as they remain, are vertical but the upper part with the head has gone. Given the final canonisation of Cantilupe in 1320, one would anticipate that this second aumbry, of *c*1330-40, would have been somewhat grander than its predecessor. Removal of the head is quite unusual. As there is no evidence of structural faults, its subsequent truncation can only be satisfactorily explained if it was being used as a reliquary. In 1538 Edward VI's government launched a violent attack on images and relics as 'idolatrous and superstitious'. As all relics had to be disposed of, this would have left the chapel with an aumbry too large for its normal requirements, chalice and paten, but this would certainly not justify the expense of modification. In all probability this was undertaken by the master as a visible expression of his adherence to the new theology. Recent archaeological investigation illustrates his anxiety to minimise the costs of conformity to the new political correctness.

Fig 8.3a St Katherine's: 1st Aumbry in chapel, east wall left of altar

Fig 8.3b St Katherine's: 2nd Aumbry in chapel, north wall

Well-cut stone, to match the existing sill and sides, was not used. Instead, two timber lintels carry the weight of the rough masonry infilling above. One of these had collapsed. It is, at the least, unfortunate that, in replacing the rubble after this investigation, those involved used a mortar the pinkish colour of which clashes so sharply with that of the rest of the chapel, that the visitor's eye is distracted from its many other objects of interest.[142]

How did such a remarkable relic collection come into the possession of a small hospital, tucked away in the Welsh marches? The donor, or donors, must have been figures of national stature. The inclusion of relics of Thomas Cantilupe, who died more than half a century after its foundation, excludes Hugh Foliot as donor of at least part of the collection. Moreover, if Foliot had had a personal relic collection, it would not have been granted to St Katherine's, Ledbury, for a year or so after the hospital was established he founded another chantry in the episcopal chapel at Hereford. If Foliot did indeed have any relics his chapel by the cathedral would have been their resting place, for here they would have attracted much larger crowds and thus offerings.

The de Grandison Family

There are, however, significant clues as to the donors. The Annals of Dore Abbey for 1321 record that on '6th October, a Tuesday, the lord W(illiam) de Grauntson (of Ashperton) came to Dore bringing with him a fragment of the wood of the Holy Cross adorned, very beautifully, with gold and precious stones. In return for the grace and favour of the lord Straddel, abbot, ... he handed it over to the monastery.' The favour, it seems, was the right for William and Sybil to be buried close to the high altar of this Cistercian abbey, founded by one of her forebears in 1147. Almost a century

Fig 8.4a Caernarfon Castle, Eagle Tower: Imperial Imagery

Fig 8.4b Harlech Castle

ago, during his restoration of Dore, Roland Paul found delicately carved architectural fragments, gilded and coloured, by the site of the rood screen. These were possibly part of a suitably elaborate setting for William's gift. A similar gift was made by William's second son, John, bishop of Exeter 1327-69, to his cathedral church: a part of the True Cross in a reliquary decorated with images of St Peter and Paul, nine pearls and 78 precious stones.[143]

These fragments of the True Cross presented to Dore Abbey and Exeter cathedral by William and John, his second son, had in all probability belonged, together with many other relics, to William's elder brother, Otto, a Savoyard from near Lausanne, one of Edward I's closest personal friends and one of the great soldiers and diplomats of his age. It was Otto who brought William to England. The brothers played a major role in the Edwardian conquest of Wales. In 1284 Otto was justiciar of north Wales with his headquarters at Caernarfon. In 1287 William was constable of the newly-completed castle at Harlech, but in the following year took Otto's place at Caernarfon as acting justiciar (Figs 8.4a and b). He was responsible for building works not only there but also at Conway, Harlech, Bere and Dolwyddelan. Enormous sums were involved. A single account which he rendered to the chancellor totalled almost £1,000.[144]

Dominating Caernarfon castle from its western end is the great Eagle Tower, named from the three eagles that crowned its three turrets and intended as the residence of Edward I's Justiciar. The unusual use of polygonal rather than round towers and, for Britain, the unique patterning of the walls by different coloured bands of stone, recall buildings of the imperial city of Constantinople. Such imperial references, combined with the use of eagles, probably represent an important element in Edward I's policy. It seems more than a coincidence that William de Grandison's coat of arms carried a bend with three eaglets displayed, which he may well have adopted as his mark of difference after leaving Caernarfon.

Two of those with whom Otto and William were most closely associated in their work on the north Welsh castles were Hugh of Leominster, 'clerk responsible for the (accounts of) operations

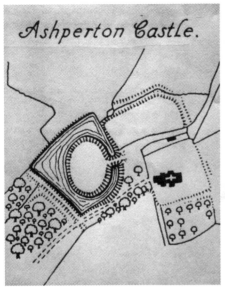

Fig 8.5 Ashperton: Plan of castle site

at Caernarfon and Harlech', and Master Walter of Hereford, 'keeper of the royal works' at Caernarfon. It was with Herefordshire manors, at Ashperton and Stretton (Grandison), that Edward I rewarded William for his services. In 1292 he granted William a licence to crenellate his Ashperton mansion with walls of stone and lime.[145] Of this fortified manor house nothing can now be seen but both the circular island of more than half an acre on which it stood and the extensive moat by which it was defended are still there, hidden in the dense trees immediately west of St Bartholomew's church (Fig 8.5). The church stands in what was apparently a rectangular bailey, still marked to the north and east by a dry ditch. William and Sybil had a number of children. Peter, their eldest son, succeeded on William's death in 1335 (Fig. 8.6); their second son, John, became Bishop of Exeter in 1327; and a third was christened Otto. As Otto senior had no family, William's sons were his beneficiaries.

Otto was the last of our crusading leaders. He accompanied Edward I on crusade in 1270 when he is credited with saving his sovereign's life after an assassination attempt. In 1290 he led the advance guard of what was intended to be Edward's second crusade but in the following May the Mamluks launched their final assault on Acre, capital of the second crusader kingdom and headquarters of both the Templars and Hospitallers. Now it was the last major toehold in the Holy Land. Otto was joint

Fig 8.6 Hereford Cathedral lady Chapel: Effigy of Peter de Grandison

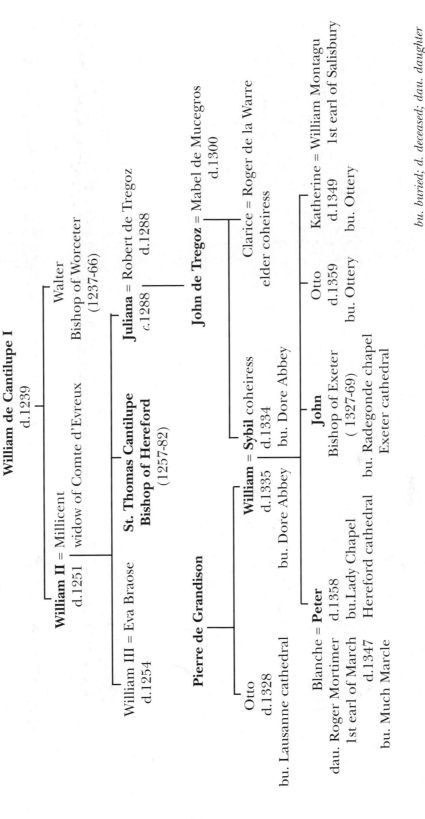

Fig 8.7 *Cantilupe, Tregoz and Grandison Families*

bu. buried; d. deceased; dau. daughter

William de Cantilupe I
d.1239

Walter
Bishop of Worceter
(1237-66)

William II = Millicent
d.1251   widow of Comte d'Evreux

Juliana = Robert de Tregoz
*c.*1288   d.1288

St. Thomas Cantilupe
Bishop of Hereford
(1257-82)

William III = Eva Braose
d.1254

John de Tregoz = Mabel de Mucegros
d.1300

Clarice = Roger de la Warre
elder coheiress

Pierre de Grandison

William = **Sybil** coheiress
d.1335   d.1334
bu. Dore Abbey   bu. Dore Abbey

Otto
d.1328
bu. Lausanne cathedral

John
Bishop of Exeter
(1327-69)
bu. Radegonde chapel
Exeter cathedral

Otto
d.1359
bu. Ottery

Katherine = William Montagu
d.1349   1st earl of Salisbury
bu. Ottery

Blanche = **Peter**
dau. Roger Mortimer   d.1358
1st earl of March   bu.Lady Chapel
d.1347   Hereford cathedral
bu. Much Marcle

83

commander of the combined Christian force defending the city. He was one of the last to leave and the removal of the cathedral's relics, to prevent them falling into the hands of the infidel, would have been an imperative. Acre cathedral was dedicated to the True Cross. The cross itself had been lost to Saladin at the battle of Hattin, 1187. Despite Saladin's various promises, it was never recovered. However, following its discovery by the empress Helen in the early 4th century, fragments were distributed to many churches. Further fragmentation took place after its recovery from the Persians by the Emperor Heraclius in 630 and on the conquest of Jerusalem by the crusaders in 1099. Like many medieval relics, the True Cross apparently had the capacity for almost infinite fragmentation. Given Acre cathedral's dedication, it may well have received its relic as early as the 4th century. It will certainly have acquired many other relics as the crusader lands contracted in the later13th century. Indeed, after the fall of the Holy City in 1187, the patriarch of Jerusalem had had to establish himself at Acre.[146]

Subsequently Otto conducted at least four series of negotiations on Edward I's behalf at the papal court: at Rome in 1289 with Nicholas IV, with Boniface VIII in 1298 and in the Great Jubilee year of 1300 and finally, in France, with Clement I, the first of the Avignon popes, in 1305. All were concerned with a possible re-opening of the crusade. On such occasions gifts of relics would not have been out of order. Indeed Boniface VIII, although 'one of the greatest authorities on canon law', not only treasured relics but was superstitious enough to believe in magic and the protection of amulets. Otto was not slow in pressing both his own and his family's interests. From the pope he received 3,000 marks (£2,000) for his 'heavy expenses and losses in the sack of Acre' as well as lucrative ecclesiastical offices for three of William's sons, at a very early age. Thus it may well be that the considerable Roman component of the St Katherine's collection was built up by Otto.[147]

The evidence suggests that the Cantilupe relics in the St Katherine's collection came from a different source. William de Grandison of Ashperton married Sybil, the younger daughter and joint heiress of Sir John de Tregoz, lord of Ewias Harold, c1285. Sybil's grandmother, Juliana, was Thomas Cantilupe's favourite sister and his only relative living close at hand. She figures in a number of episodes in his *Life* and it was to her that he left his interest in the manor of Earley, near Reading, where he often broke his journeys between Hereford and London.[148] Juliana Cantilupe married Robert de Tregoz of Ewyas Harold, patron of Dore Abbey. Their one son, John, who died in 1300 had only two daughters, Clarice and Sybil. Clarice, the elder, predeceased her father and the family relics, which John had inherited from his mother, Juliana, thus passed to Sybil de Grandison (Fig 8.7). The Cantilupe relics in St Katherine's collection are, with little doubt, those of his sister, Juliana. When Cantilupe's remains arrived in England in 1283, the family removed many small relics. These included his knife, parts of his shirt and other shreds of his clothing and his iron-link belt. Minor shrines were founded with such relics at the family manor of Hambledon, Bucks, and at Winchester and Leominster. His heart was buried in Ashridge but his bones, the Worcester annals tells us, were interred in front of the altar in the lady chapel of Hereford cathedral, under a flat stone. Swinfield's translation of Cantilupe's remains from the lady chapel to the north transept in 1287 provided the family with a further opportunity for relic acquisition. The small piece of St Denis's chasuble may well have been acquired by Cantilupe who spent many years in Paris, first as a student and later as a lecturer at the university.[149]

Maladministration

There is firm evidence of the Grandison family's patronage. At St Katherine's the combination of institutional wealth and virtual corporate independence was not a happy one and supervision by dean and chapter appears, at best, to have been ineffective. The first evidence of maladministration comes in 1322 during Philip de Chaddesley's mastership. Accusations of culpable mismanagement, in particular the granting of long leases at low rents, were brought against master and brethren.

Fig 8.8 Exeter Cathedral, west front: Image screen begun by John de Grandison

The motives were either a concern to secure large reliefs, that is entry fines, thus sacrificing the hospital's future for short-term benefit, or a culpable wish to grant favours to friends or relatives. As the leases, pointedly, indicate the brothers' and sisters' 'unanimous consent', they were probably under considerable pressure from Chaddesley. In 1323, these charges being brought to the attention of Pope John XXII (1316-34), he commanded the abbot of Wigmore to carry out an inquiry.[150]

How did details of the shortcomings of this small, remote English hospital reach the ears of the pontiff at Avignon, and why did he intervene so decisively? The answer is not difficult to find. William de Grandison's second son, John, born at Ashperton in 1292, advanced rapidly through the ecclesiastical hierarchy under the patronage of his uncle, Otto. Indeed, on hearing of his uncle's death in 1328, he wrote 'the news has stricken me to my inmost heart, with him the crown of my head has fallen'. John held a prebend at York minster when only seventeen and the archdeaconry of Nottingham at eighteen. He attended the university of Paris where his tutor was Jacques Fournier who was to succeed John XXII as pope Benedict XII in 1334. By 1322, the year of the abbot of Wigmore's inquiry into the irregularities at St Katherine's, John was a papal chaplain. In 1326 he was a papal nuncio and, following in his uncle's footsteps, was negotiating between the English and French monarchs. In 1327 John XXII provided John de Grandison, at 36 years of age, to the bishopric of Exeter, which office he held with great distinction for forty-one years (Fig 8.8).[151]

John XXII's appointment of the abbot of Wigmore was an outright condemnation of the dean and chapter's failure to exercise their trust, but the years 1262 to 1320 had been a period of great difficulty for the cathedral. About 1262 the notorious Savoyard bishop, Peter de Aquablanca, 1240-68, had deprived Dean Avenbury of his office and appointed his nephew, John, in his place. For a time there were rival deans and the conflict was taken to the papal court which—in 1282—found in favour of John de Aquablanca, who then held office until 1320. Both Philip de Chaddesley and John de Marcle, his predecessor, would thus, as masters, have been Aquablanca appointees.[152] What

85

influence the abbot's findings had on the management of St Katherine's is not known but Brother Philip was still master in 1328. Two years later John XXII intervened once more. He was prompted no doubt by John, now bishop of Exeter, acting on his parents' behalf. On this occasion the papal penitentiary granted a forty-day indulgence to all making donations to the hospital or attending masses or canonical hours celebrated on certain days by Brother Peter de Esebache.[153]

9   Stained Glass and the Reconstruction Programme *c*1335-40

A major campaign of reconstruction was undertaken in both chapel and hall about the years 1335-40. There were two principal elements. The first was the building of a new roof. This has trusses with two double collar-beams, the lower strengthened by a pair of curved braces. They are spanned by two purlins, strengthened, in the four eastern bays, by attractive curved and double cusped wind braces which catch the eye of all visitors. (Figs 9.1, 9.2) It is interesting to compare this roof with that of north aisle of the parish church, which also dates from the prosperous era prior to the outbreak of the Black Death in 1349. The trusses of its 15 bays have curved braces to a single collar and curved but uncusped wind braces. At St Katherine's the western truss is much simpler and probably of 17th-century date. With the position of a doorway close to the west end, this suggests that there may have been at least some services at this end of the building.

The second element was the provision of new doorways and the replacement of a number of the 13th-century lancets with larger windows, in the Decorated style, providing much more light for the chapel and hall. Two of the new doorways, with chamfered jambs and segmental heads, are still in use on the south side of the hall. A third has been blocked up and a window inserted above. (Figs 9.3a&b) There are remains of two of these windows in the south wall, that in the chapel being well preserved. In the north wall are two more, but here the stone tracery has been replaced in wood,

St Katherine's, early 14th-century roof
Fig 9.1 Above: Trusses with double collar beams
Fig 9.2 Right: Purlins to each bay strengthened by two pairs of curved and moulded windbraces

St Katherine's
Fig 9.3a Above: Door on south with chamfered jambs
and segmental head
Fig 9.3b Right: Blocked-up door on south

St Katherine's
Left: Fig 9.4a Two-light window in chapel; Centre: Fig 9.4b Two-light Decorated window in hall with timber
tracery; Right: Fig 9.4c East front, Decorated window with three ogee trefoiled lights, reticulated tracery in
head and pair of quatrefoils

probably in the 18th century. (Figs 9.4a&b) The archway still to be seen in the north wall of the hall may well be a replacement of this period, for the head has chamfering similar to that of the two doors, but it lacks the projecting hood held on corbels which is a marked characteristic of early-14th-century fireplaces. Most important of all, however, was the replacement of the central lancet of the triplet in the east wall of the chapel with a Decorated window of three ogee trefoiled lights and netlike curvilinear tracery with a pair of quatrefoils in the head. Such window tracery confirms the proposed date, c1330-40, given by the Royal Commission for the roof structure (Fig 9.5).

Although little now remains of the glazing programme of the large new east window and its companions, the lancets to north and south, it is a subject of great interest. Fortunately, the vestiges of its 14th-century glass have been brought together with considerable ability. Most significant are the composite figure of a female saint and the Grandison coat of arms. Despite the loss of almost all St Katherine's glass after the Reformation, the east window still carries this striking reminder of Grandison patronage. On the left-hand side of the central light is a coat of arms: *paly of six argent and azure a bend gules bearing three eaglets displayed*, that is six vertical bands alternately blue and silver across which there is a diagonal red band with three gold eaglets, their wings outspread (Fig 9.5a). The replaced upper parts of the three blue bands do not have the intensity of medieval glass but this heightens one's appreciation of the glass below, which retains its original appearance. Here the depth of the colour is intensified by the use of diapering, a delicate repeating pattern of foliage on gracefully curling stems, the same pattern being applied to both the blue and silver glass. During restoration the heraldic glass was inadvertently reversed and the bend is now incorrectly placed. It should cross the field from top left to bottom right instead of which it crosses from top right to bottom left in the form of a bend, or more frequently bendlet sinister, a mark of illegitimacy.

The arms of Otto de Grandison, the senior member of the family, were merely *paly of six argent and azure a bend gules*. To this William de Grandison of Ashperton, Otto's younger brother, added the *three eaglets displayed* to the bend, as a mark of difference. This coat was carried only by William and, after his death, Peter, his eldest son, who died without a direct heir. William's second son, John, bishop of Exeter, substituted a golden mitre for the second eaglet as a mark of difference (Fig 9.5b) and third son, Otto, replaced the eaglets with three escallops.[154] William died in 1335 and Peter 23

Above: Fig 9.5a Arms of William and Peter de Grandison, reversed
Right: Fig 9.5b Ottery St Mary: Misericord with Bishop Grandison's arms

Above left: Fig. 9.6 St Katherine's composite female
saint
Above: Fig 9.7 Christ Church, Oxford:
The Virgin Mary
Left: Fig 9.8 Christ Church, Oxford:
St Margaret holding staff with cross head

years later, in 1358. Which do the arms commemorate, father or son? Given Peter's magnificent tomb in Hereford cathedral, he must surely be excluded as a candidate?

The figure of the St Katherine's composite female saint is a skilful reworking of assorted fragments into a credible overall composition (Fig 9.6). On either side are vestiges of the characteristic border of the period: four white vine leaves project from a vertical golden stem decorated with a wavy line, all against a ruby background. The figure looks to the left. The strong character of the face is created by the utmost economy of line combined with a restricted but highly effective use of 'smear' shading under the eye. This, a wash laid on with a brush to varying depths according to the degree of opacity required, was also used on the folds of garments. Golden hair descends in deep waves down either side of the face. This is highly characteristic of the period, for the early decades of the 14th century witnessed a revolution in the glazier's art—the use of silver stain. No longer was it necessary to cut to size individual sheets of yellow pot metal glass, that is glass coloured during its manufacture in a pot or crucible. Silver oxide solution was painted on the exterior of the glass and then fired in a kiln to produce a range of colours from light yellow through gold to deep bronze. Hair, crowns, crosses, elaborate canopy work etc could be applied on white glass at will 'freeing the glazier from the constraints of leading'. The glass-painter now enjoyed extraordinary flexibility and delicacy of touch, from which a new aesthetic developed.

About 1330 figures similar to that at Ledbury became the dominant feature in the display of stained glass. They were characterised by increasing naturalism, many assuming an attractive S shape, as with the Christ Church Virgin. (Fig 9.7) Such figures were placed under canopies. Based on architectural models, they were adopted universally by stained glass artists to house their saints. Forming an integral part of the overall design, they were to grow rapidly both in height and elaboration. Although no vestiges now remain, we can be confident that the saints which filled the eastern windows at St Katherine's would have stood under such canopies. Just as at night-time the candlelight falling on the statues of the Virgin Mary and St Katherine must have given succour to the sick and dying, so during daylight hours the saints, under their golden canopies and against their richly painted backgrounds, must have fulfilled the same purpose. No trace of the canopies remains, but there is considerable evidence of the border design, of trailing vine tendrils, which was used to enclose the whole composition within the individual window frames. Here the foliage, like the figures, is naturalistic.

The most distinctive feature of the composite figure is the tall cross-staff which she holds firmly in her right hand. This is an attribute of St Margaret of Antioch who, professing herself a devout Christian, rebuffed the advances of the local governor. Her tortures included being swallowed by Satan in the guise of a dragon; but when she made the sign of the cross it burst asunder and she emerged unscathed. Although the Legend was denounced by the pope as early as 494, she was one of the most popular medieval saints, probably due to her association with childbirth.[155] At Christ Church cathedral, Oxford, and Kempsey (Worcs) she can be seen grasping her cross-headed staff, with which she is piercing the dragon. (Fig 9.8) At Ledbury the lower part of her staff, and presumably the dragon, have been lost. The head is unlikely to be that of Margaret, for she is usually depicted wearing a crown. Whether or not it is the head of St Katherine is difficult to decide. The figure lacks any of her usual attributes, the toothed wheel which failed to bring about her death, or the sword with which she was finally executed, but the critical question is whether she also should be wearing a crown. She is shown crowned in panels of the first half of the 14th century at Kempsey (Worcs), Deerhurst (Glos) and at Oxford cathedral and, of the late 14th century, in the east window of Exeter cathedral; but without a crown in the restored wall painting of c1300 at Hailes church (Glos). The attributes of saints only came to be standardised early in the 14th century.

A detailed examination of the glass, especially the composite saint, the fragments below the coat of arms, and the remnants of the borders, shows that it can be attributed to a workshop active

Fig 9.9 Christ Church, Oxford: Gabriel's nimbus

in the West Midlands 1330-50. Some of the most notable products of this workshop are to be found in three windows of the Latin, that is the north-eastern, chapel of Christ Church cathedral, Oxford, until the dissolution the Augustinian priory of St Frideswide. These windows, it has been said, represent 'some of the most important glass of the second quarter of the 14th century'. Following the work of contemporary manuscript painters the glaziers who created the figures were, as the Oxford canopies show, deeply concerned with 'the creation of an illusion of three-dimensional space.'[156] The glass is in three of the five northern windows of the chapel. In two of these sets of triple windows are five female saints: SS Katherine, Frideswide and Margaret in the first; SS Hilda and Katherine, together with the Virgin and Child in the third. Each figure is set against a dark blue or dark red background, under an elaborate, crocketed, towered and spired canopy. A third set of windows portrays the Annunciation, with Gabriel on the left and Mary on the right, each against a dark green background. Between them the much larger figure of an archbishop is obviously an intruder. It is the figures of Gabriel and Mary that provide striking parallels to that at Ledbury but also Margaret with her staff has marked similarities.

A face composed of white glass and painted with golden hair falling in waves on either side was a common feature of the glazier's art of this period but within the convention, as one would expect, there was considerable individuality. Thus in the case of the prophet Ezekiel at Madley and of Joel at Tewkesbury, the hair is much wilder, for Katherine at Deerhurst more restrained, whilst the archangel Michael at Eaton Bishop has been given a double set of such waves. However both the facial expressions and the portrayal of the hair of the Oxford Virgin of the Annunciation and of the Ledbury female saint are very similar, if not from the same cartoon. Both look to the left but, as appropriate in the case of the Virgin, Her head is bowed. However the hair on either side of the face is deeply waved, descending on one side in four waves as far as the shoulder. (Fig 9.7) These features are replicated at Ledbury, especially about the long neckline. Both figures drape their outer garment over the crook of their left arm, permitting it to fall in similar graceful folds from the elbow. In each case the artist has had considerable difficulty depicting the left eye.

The most compelling evidence, however, is in the similarity of the minor details found at Ledbury and the Latin chapel but not elsewhere. In the Oxford Annunciation scene the nimbus of both Virgin and Archangel Gabriel (Figs 9.6, 9.7, 9.9) is decorated with an unusual pattern of semi-circles, found also on the halo of the Ledbury figure. At both Oxford and Ledbury St Margaret's staff has a floret of five petals at the ends of the arms of the cross and the way in which the hand grasps that staff is almost identical. There is only a limited amount of original vine trail in the borders at Oxford, yet even the stems of the vines in the 14th-century glass and the 19th-century copies are decorated with a wavy line similar to that on the vine stems at Ledbury. Finally, the borders of the green diapered background of both Virgin and Gabriel have a delicate white design of quatrefoils within lozenges on a black background. Beneath the coat of arms in the central window at St Katherine's are the remnants of another inner black border. It is decorated on either side with a pair of thin gold lines. These enclose a pattern of quatrefoils within lozenges, similar to those at Christ Church, but here the white pattern is picked out more delicately. (Fig 9.10b-e) What appears to be an early precursor of this design can be seen at the head of the columns and in the fenestration of the Decorated windows which form the borders of the figure of St Katherine at Deerhurst, an earlier and frequently illustrated example of the work of the West Midland school.

Peter was amongst the saints who looked down from the east window at the poor and infirm at Ledbury. At the centre of the St Katherine's lozenge pattern is part of a key, the symbol of Peter and his successors. 'Thou art Peter and upon this rock I will build my church ... And I will give unto thee the keys of the Kingdom of Heaven.'[157] The Ledbury key fragment looks large indeed in relation to the head of the female saint, but this is quite usual for glass of the era. As at St Peter's, Stanford-on-Avon, Northamptonshire (Fig 9.10a & b) and Merton College, Oxford, St Peter is often depicted holding keys of a size similar to his head.

From the left: Fig 9.10a St Peter's, Stanford on Avon, Northants: Peter holding keys;
Fig 9.10b St Katherine's: Key and Lozenge with quatrefoils within; Fig 9.10c Christ Church, Oxford:
Lozenge; Fig 9.10d St Katherine's: Vine trail; Right: Fig 9.10e Christ Church, Oxford: Vine trail

The remodelling of the Latin chapel has been dated by Richard K. Morris. 'The work ... most probably belongs to the decade c1330-40.'[158] The close similarities in the glazing of the windows at Oxford and Ledbury suggest that the arms on the St Katherine's east window are those of William de Grandison rather than those of his son, Peter. The circumstances of their respective burials confirm this. On his death in 1356 Peter was provided with a splendid memorial, a magnificent tomb directly facing the shrine of St Thomas Cantilupe, the brother of his great-grandmother, Juliana. William was buried in much humbler circumstances. When his wife, Sybil, died in 1334 it had already been arranged that she was to rest in the choir of the Cistercian monastery which her family had founded at Dore. Only nine months later her husband, William, was buried, in accordance with his wishes, by her side.

Is one coat of arms sufficient evidence to suggest that this east window was a memorial to William, who died in 1335? Certainly the Grandisons were by far the wealthiest family in the district. The local tenants of the bishop, who formed the dominant group amongst those seeking to promote the hospital in its early years, were minor figures, holding at the most 200 acres of land. This project was far beyond their means. The only other possible candidate could be one of the Pauncefots, but they already had their own chapel at the Hazle, and it is highly unlikely that they could have conceived let alone funded such an extensive programme.

The Grandisons, on the other hand, were outstanding in terms of both wealth and status. In administering Edward I's castle building programme in north Wales, William on occasions handled £1,000 at a time. His sons were to inherit their uncle Otto's wealth in 1328. Bishop John's extensive patronage of the arts shows that, after this time, he had very considerable financial resources at his disposal. The richness of the tombs of both Peter, in the Lady Chapel of Hereford cathedral, and of his wife, Blanche, at Much Marcle, confirms that he too was a man of great wealth. (Figs 9.11-12)

From Bishop John's personal correspondence it is known that he was particularly close to his parents. After his consecration as bishop by Pope John XXII at Avignon in 1327, he seized the opportunity to spend two months with them locally prior to travelling to Exeter for his enthronement on 18 October 1327. It was now that John obtained, on behalf of his parents, a papal indult, allowing a specific deviation from the church's law, by which their confessor was permitted to give, at the hour of death, a plenary remission of sins. Between 1337 and 1342 much of Bishop John's energy was devoted to

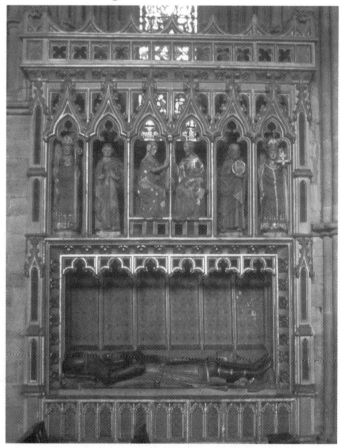

Fig 9.11 Hereford Cathedral, Lady Chapel:
Peter de Grandison's Tomb

94

the conversion of the church of Ottery St Mary, which he had bought from Rouen cathedral, into a college of chantry priests. Here eight canons, eight priests, 12 clerks and eight choristers were to offer up prayers to 'insure the never-ending remembrance of the deeds of valour and charity wrought by his family, whether in England, France, Scotland, Wales or the Holy Land'. In the list of the 16 family members to be remembered, his father and mother came first, followed by himself and his four brothers and four sisters. It was at Ottery that his sister, Katherine, and younger brother, Otto, with his wife, Beatrix, were buried (Fig 9.13). Their tomb has been described as 'amongst the best works of its date in the south-west'. As neither John nor his elder brother, Peter, could exercise any real influence over their parents' tombs at Dore in the remote and unstable southern march of Wales, there can be little doubt that the refurbishment of St Katherine's chapel was intended by them to serve not only as a chantry but as a local memorial chapel for their father and mother. Bishop John himself was to be buried in a small chantry chapel to the right of the central doorway through the great image screen which he caused to be erected at the west front of his cathedral. (Fig 9.14)

Fig 9.12 Blanche de Grandison, tomb in Much Marcle church

The quality of the stained glass strongly suggests that it was masterminded by John who, having spent a number of years at the university of Paris and then at the papal court in its exile at Avignon, revelled in their rich intellectual and artistic life. The same decorative treatment of the nimbus at Oxford and Ledbury is to be found in two panels depicting the Annunciation to the Virgin of *c*1325 in the choir of St Ouen in Rouen, suggesting that these inspired the scene at Oxford. Furthermore, the Rouen glass, we are told, 'exemplifies the refinement of Parisian styles of the first quarter of the century', although little survives in the capital. If this is accepted, the lineage of the Ledbury glass can be traced by way of Oxford and Rouen to Paris.[159]

Fig 9.13 Ottery St Mary: Effigy of Otto II de Grandison

Fig 9.14 Exeter Cathedral: Bishop John's chantry

All the evidence underlines Bishop John's very keen sense of his family's honour and his responsibilities. At his college at Ottery the Grandison heraldry embellishes both bosses and reredos, all the surviving liturgical fittings and even the orb which bears the golden eagle on the lectern. Of the many precious items John left to his cathedral, fifty-six bore his arms; in the case of one, sixteen times. Even his personal ivory triptychs, now in the British Museum and the Louvre, uniquely, carry his arms. At St Katherine's the single remaining Grandison arms forms a fitting tribute to both father and son.

10 The Black Death
and the Age of Crisis, 1349-97

The full force of the Black Death was felt in Herefordshire early in 1349. It has been estimated that, as a result of this and subsequent outbreaks, the population fell nationally by some 30 to 45 per cent but regional and local variations were considerable. A decline of some 42 per cent in tenant numbers has been proposed for the Worcester episcopal manors, but this takes into account some recovery in the plague's aftermath.

The local impact is graphically illustrated by clergy institution lists in Bishop Trillek's register. They provide the most reliable and complete data for monthly mortality rates in the diocese. Until late in July the bishop's clerk gives death as the cause of vacancies. Only later is it assumed. Institutions averaged six a year between 1345 and 1347, but in 1349 there were 159.[160] The first death, in March, was of John Prato, chaplain of the chantry of the Blessed Virgin in Ledbury parish church. On 20 April Brother Gilbert de Middleton, Master of St Katherine's, inducted John's successor. At Weston on 26 May, after the death of 'Sir Roger', 'the warden and brothers' presented Richard de Weston as the hospital's vicar. Shortly afterwards Gilbert himself died.

Other local clergy followed in rapid succession: three priests died at Bosbury and two at Evesbatch within the next six months. Death led to presentations at Bishops Frome on 30 May and at Bosbury on 6th and Evesbatch on 29 June; in July there were six: at Bromesberrow on 2nd, Munsley on 12th, Ledbury on 19th, after the vicar's death, Bosbury on 21st, Castle Frome on 28th and at Donnington on 31st. The mortality rate now began to subside. There was only one presentation in August, at Canon Frome, two in September, at Much Marcle and Bosbury, one in October at Evesbatch. The final death that year was of John Golafre, vicar of Little Marcle, in December. The full force appears to have been spent for there were but two clerical mortalities in 1350, at Coddington in March and of Stephen de Estenore, at Eastnor, in July. According to the register, only at Colwall and the chapels at Pixley and Aylton did local clergy escape the plague. Of fatalities among the chaplains, brethren and poor at St Katherine's there is no record. A conservative estimate puts the death toll of the beneficed clergy in the diocese at some 40%. There was a second major outbreak, the Grey Death, in 1361 and lesser outbreaks in 1368-9 and 1375, with another major outbreak in 1391, and it has been suggested that high mortality rates were almost as much a phenomenon of the 15th as of the 14th century.[161]

The profound economic and social consequences of such dire demographic decline were felt first as a chronic shortage of manpower with a consequent decline in production and therefore revenue. Landowners were squeezed by increased costs due to the acute shortage of labour. In many places the wages of agricultural workers doubled. At the cathedral, where at least eight of the canons had died, the dean and chapter's income was halved. Rarely after 1349 were more than eight of the twenty-eight canons resident, as compared to fifteen or so immediately prior to the outbreak and more than twenty c1300. So straightened were the finances of the see, that in 1356 five of the bishop's palaces, at Ledbury, Colwall, Bishops Frome, Bromyard and Ross, more than half of those in the county, were abandoned.[162]

The precise impact of the great plague on St Katherine's estates is difficult to assess due to the random nature of extant records but the full text of the last court rolls of the Hyde, Cradley in July 1349 provides a graphic illustration:

> Henry *de la Barwe* held 1 messuage and $^1/_2$ virgate (30 acres) of land. It lies uncultivated so it is in the hand of the lord. John son of William de la Hyde held a virgate (60 acres) and 1 noke (15 acres) of land. It is not occupied so it is in the hands of the lord. Hugh Schyppathe holds 1 messuage and 8 acres of land which Richard le Colyar held.

The court rolls show that between 1314 and 1318 the annual rents from the Hyde were some £1 18s, but in 1349 St Katherine's received only Hugh *Schyppathe*'s rent of 2s 6d. At Berrow such was the shortage of people in 1369 to take up tenancies still vacant through plague mortality that Richard *Maundevyle* senior, holding a messuage and curtilage, felt free to come to the manor court, acknowledging that 'for a great time he had occupied it unjustly' that is without any action being taken.

Although, with the ultimate threat of flight to greener fields or neighbouring towns, peasants were able to bargain hard to reduce their customary dues and entry fines, not all the hospital's villeins realised the strength of their bargaining position. In fact on the predominantly arable lands at Kempley changes in the labour market came slowly. There labour services were already being commuted to cash payments well before the outbreak, and the lord's control of wardship and marriage had, in the case of that 'awkward character', John Geffrey, been challenged in 1316. However it was some time before other personal services were challenged.

In 1361, more than a decade after the Black Death, Robert and Alice Nicholes took up the 23 acres of villein land formerly held by Alice *Wodeward*. They paid the same rent, 6s 2d, and accepted

Fig 10.1 St Katherine's: Development in the Market Place

the full range of services: autumn work, meadow mowing, lifting the hay, *hundredsilver, yeldsilver* and pannage, but this is the last reference to villein services at Kempley. In the next extant roll, for 1364, all were reduced to money payments. In 1370 three Kempley men did fealty for their existing hold-

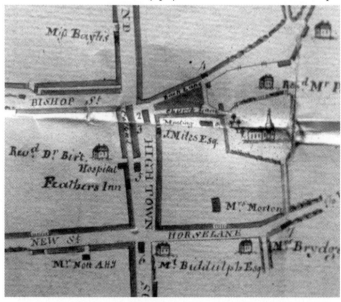

Fig 10.2 Plan of Ledbury by J. Lydiard, showing Katherine Row, 15th-century Hospitalys Rowe, *Butchers Row and Cathol between*

Fig 10.3 Ledbury: Early 19th-century view of the Market Place and Butchers Row and showing the confined character of the Cathol and thus Hospital Row

ings but two couples were granted the lands of former tenants without spec-ification of terms. Interestingly, however, Kempley rent levels were maintained, 6s being paid for 30 acres in 1370 and 1380. By the time of the next extant court rolls, at the end of the 15th century, rents had dropped by 33%.

For the cultivation of its demesne St Katherine's had been dependent on the labour services of its customary tenants, the villeins. Now the commutation of such services combined with rising labour costs led to a dramatic change in the way the demesne was exploited. As early as 1370 Robert Edwyn at Kempley had negotiated the lease of 2 acres of the hospital's demesne lands. This process accelerated rapidly. By 1397 the hospital's demesne economy had collapsed. The master was leasing all its lands to laymen. He was but following the example set locally by great landlords such as the bishops of Worcester and abbots of Westminster.[163] The master now had at his personal disposal, not agricul-tural produce for home consump-tion, but an annual income from the demesne rents, with all its blandish-ments.

Such leasing of hospital lands was not restricted to the countryside. On the market frontage of *Middletown*, now High Street, the land either side of the Great Gate was developed (Fig 10.1). Given the popu-lation collapse, there was plenty of vacant and abandoned property in Ledbury but sites in and close to the market were always at a premium. Even in the depressed economy of the post-plague years they will have been eminently saleable. The first evidence of such development is in a deed of 1363 by which master and brethren granted land lying between the hospital building and the Booth Hall or Hundred House, now the Feathers (Figs 10.1 & 2.10a).[164]

The first reference to buildings on the opposite, that is the northern, side of the gatehouse comes in 1403. Described here as *Hospitalys Rowe*, in later records it is the Catherine Row. The records suggest that some almsfolk were transferred from communal life in the hall to individual accommodation here, either late in the 15th or early in the 16th century. It was situated beyond 'the little land called *Cathole*', the alley between Butchers Row and the hospital. Both John Devereux's plan in his *Ledbury Guide* of 1824 and an early 19th-century view of the Market Place and Butchers Row show just how dark and confined both the *Cathol* and Hospital Row must have been (Figs 10.2 & 10.3). Although later in date, Abbey Cottages in Church Street, Tewkesbury are a similar type of peripheral development. Only three years earlier Bishop Trefnant had been raising capital in the town by granting a 40-year lease of the old Booth Hall at an annual rent of 6s 8d, to Richard Glover, who contracted to build a house of three bays. The bishop gave the oak, but without carriage. Against this new house he built a solar to serve as his court and gaol. The same year Trefnant, Dean Prophet and the chapter were engaging in similar property development in London where they granted a 60-year lease for a house to be built on a plot in the garden of their Inn, close to Old Fish Street. The hospital also developed land along Bishop, now Bye, Street where, as late as 1933 there was the four-bay hall of a 14th-century house, of which a bay still stands to the right of the entrance to the car park. Although then a working men's lodging house, it was known as the 'Bishop's Palace', like 'Bishop Street' probably a reference to the pre-1230 use of the site.[165]

With the arrival of winter the pestilence abated and bishop Trillek embarked upon a major ordination programme in an attempt to fill the depleted ranks of the parochial clergy of his diocese (Fig 10.4). Using his Ledbury palace as a base, he undertook almost 750 ordinations in ceremonies at the parish church on 19 December 1349 and 20 February and 13 March 1350. Candidates passing through orders to the priesthood included large numbers from Wales. Archdeacon Gruffudd ap Rhys of Brecon herded, in all, 108 candidates from St David's in 1349, and a further 50 the next year. The death of bishop Bransford from the plague on 6 August meant that Trillek had to ordain many others from Worcester diocese which then extended to the Avon at Bristol. On this, as on a further occasion a century and a half later, Ledbury church was well situated to serve both dioceses.[166]

Despite the best efforts of Trillek and other bishops, the great gaps caused by death in the clerical ranks became increasingly difficult to fill. According to Henry Knighton, the Leicester abbey chronicler, 'so great was the scarcity of priests that many churches were desolate, without divine office'. Before the plague chaplains were so numerous that 'one could be got for 4 marks, or 2 marks with board. Now scarce any would minister in a church for under £10 or 10 marks and none would accept a vicarage for under £20 or 20 marks'. The consequence was that 'shortly a multitude (of laymen) whose wives had died, most of whom were illiterate, came crowding into orders'. Even though Knighton was no doubt exaggerating, the increased salaries demanded by chaplains came at a time when the hospital's financial resources were sorely reduced. Even more important, however, was the crisis in leadership. St Katherine's was now entering a period of profound danger, which was only to be overcome by the intervention and reforms of Dean Prophet in 1398.[167]

Dean and chapter had great difficulty in finding not only chaplains and brethren but also a suitable master as successor to Gilbert de Middleton who had died of the plague. A Brother Richard was acting with 'the unanimous consent of the community' on 12 March 1350 but was replaced by Thomas de Ledbury, a brother of St Oswald's hospital, Worcester, presumably strongly recommended. Thomas was ordained acolyte, subdeacon and then deacon by Trillek in Ledbury church between 19 December 1349 and 13 March 1350 but in 1351, at the annual visitation, traditionally held at Michaelmas, the dean and chapter uncovered 'errors and excesses' of the brothers and almsfolk. Thomas was warned against such negligence and ordered to correct these matters. Dean and chapter did not wait long for improvement. On 18 November he was commanded to appear before them, for failing to correct these abuses and to answer fresh charges, 'of wrongdoing'. On 2 December he was replaced by Thomas de Bradewardyn.[168]

The new master fared little better. In June 1353, when institutions of priests were beginning to approach their pre-1349 figures, Trillek embarked on a formal visitation of his diocese to discover for himself how far it had recovered from the impact of the plague. His concern lay with

Fig 10.4 Trilleck brass on north side of cathedral presbytery. He wears mass vestments, a mitre and holds a crozier in his left hand, whilst giving a blessing with his right

the spiritual and moral life not only of the parishes but also of the religious houses, the monasteries and hospitals. Given the methods employed, of preliminary questionnaires and subsequent statements made on oath before the bishop or his deputy, this was a far more searching enquiry than the dean and chapter's annual inspection. The evidence suggests that the latter often degenerated into a social occasion, with little more than indulgence in the warm hospitality of the master and brethren, a handsome and convivial meal at the hospital's expense. The Ledbury parishioners, on the other hand, in making their presentments to Trillek, will have identified with St Katherine's poor and infirm.

Bishop Trillek, alarmed by the 'excesses' of the brethren at St Katherine's and their failure to live up to standards appropriate to their high calling, intervened in September 1353. Impatient for action, he commanded Thomas Bellamy, his commissary, to correct and reform these errors and excesses and to warn de Bradewardyn against future negligence. The chapter's failure to monitor adequately events at St Katherine's may be explained by the long interregnum after the death of Stephen de Ledbury, dean for 30 years, early in the spring of 1353. His successor, Bishop Trillek's brother, Thomas, took up the office only in the autumn of 1354. In December 1353 the chapter, finding their commands to reform the unsatisfactory state of the hospital and the faults of the brothers and other members of the community had been ignored, appointed three of their members to act as a commission of enquiry. They were given powers to remove the master if necessary and appoint in his place a suitable person from amongst the brethren. The trio included Canon Adam de Esegar, a man who, in the near future, was to play a critical role in endeavouring to revive spiritual life at St Katherine's.[169]

Bradewardyn was dismissed and early in 1354 William le Brut was appointed master in his place. His career, like that of Thomas de Ledbury, was typical of many priests of his day. He passed through the three stages of preparation for the priesthood in exactly three months: ordained to acolyte's orders at Ledbury parish church on 7 March

1349, to subdeacon's orders at the next ordination service, in the bishop's palace at Stretton Sugwas on 28th, and to deacon's orders at Bosbury on 11 April. Ordained priest by Trillek at his Prestbury palace on 31 May, William could now celebrate the divine office and thus be appointed a chaplain. Within five years he was Master. Given his mandate to remedy their 'faults', relations between le Brut and the brethren must have been far from cordial. In March 1356 Trillek had to investigate accusations by the brethren that le Brut was responsible for 'delapidation of the goods of their appropriated churches at Weston, Yarkhill and Kempley'. There is no record of the findings, but le Brut successfully weathered this storm, for in 1362, in the Kempley court rolls, he is referred to as master; but by April 1363 he had been succeeded by Hugh Cradock.[170]

The decades following the Black Death were a time of crisis, not only for St Katherine's but for all such institutions. For many it was terminal. It is estimated that one in five of England's hospitals failed in the second half of the 14th century. St Katherine's was particularly vulnerable as it had become, virtually, a college for chantry priests. Initially with but two chaplaincies, founded by Bishop Foliot and William of Ockeridge, by 1361 there were at least five.[171] The others were funded by rents, such as those granted by the Grandisons. Due to the support and patronage of the Esegar family St Katherine's escaped the fate of so many other hospitals. Their injection of further resources in the early 1360s was critical but, like the Grandisons, the Esegars' interest was in the development of chantry services rather than support for the welfare of the poor.

The family was of humble origins. Its fortune was built by William I Esegar, a wealthy merchant and one of Ledbury's two members of Edward I's 1305 parliament, the second and last in which the borough was represented. The family was both wealthy and well connected, as shown by a deed of 1327 in which William Esegar bound himself to repay a loan of £200 made by Robert Goldhill of Gloucester. Goldhill had been one of the Gloucester bailiffs in 1314-15 and, as one of the community's leaders who had supported the rebels against Edward II in 1322, he was fined £100. His property included a tenement, stretching from the street between the bridges against the West Gate to the river Severn where he owned a fishery. In his will of 1334 he left money to Llanthony priory, three friaries, two hospitals and the bridge. The use to which Esegar intended to put such a large sum of money is, sadly, not apparent from the sources.[172]

In 1312 William I and Beatrice, his wife, began to acquire land in Ledbury foreign. In exchange for all their property in Northleach, Gloucs, John, son of John of the Hazle, granted them a farmhouse with one carucate, 240 acres of arable, meadow, pasture and ways, together with all goods, chattels, moveables and immoveables at *la Hulle*, halfway between Ledbury and Preston Cross, north of the main road, now Hill House Farm. To this holding their son, William II, and his wife, Sybil, added a further 47 selions and six butts close by: 22 selions at *Hullecroft*, 13 at *Horsehull* and 12 in *Baystefeld*. A number of these selions are described in detail. In *Horsehull* four extended 'from *Wallefeld* to the way leading to the vineyard'. In *Baystefeld* five extended 'on one head to the vineyard of the lord bishop and on the other from the vineyard gate to the way to *Pychehull*' (Pixley?). William II and Sybil then purchased a further 240 acres, for 100 marks (£66 13s 4d), from Roger de Borhnhulle (Burchull), knight, at *Erlingham* (Orlham), to the south of the same road and less than a mile from la Hulle (Fig 10.5).[173]

With land as well as money, the Esegars moved up the social scale and had links with two major local landed families, the Grandisons and Pauncefots, the latter possibly by marriage. A certain John de Aysshe had held land of Peter de Grandison by military tenure. On Aysshe's death custody of his heir, John, passed to Peter as feudal lord. These rights of wardship and marriage, with custody of John's lands, Peter then transferred in 1341 to William II Esegar with the proviso that his marriage should be 'without disparagement'. In due course John married William II's daughter, Beatrice, evidently named after her grandmother. With the Pauncefots the Esegars were involved in a number of property deals. The 240 acres at *la Hulle* had once belonged to Sybil, widow of Sir

Fig 10.5 Erlingham, *Orlham Farm today*

Grimbald Pauncefot. William II's grandson, Canon Esegar, later purchased *Tyrellsfrith* in Little Marcle from another Sir Grimbald.[174]

A clause attached to an Orlham deed declared that if William (III), eldest son of William and Sybil, had no heirs the property should descend to his brother, Thomas. For reasons which are not apparent Thomas came into the family property whilst William was still alive and furthermore had a son, Nicholas. By December 1361 Thomas was dead, possibly of the plague which returned that year. By the terms of his will all his lands at *la Hulle* and *Erlingham*, 480 acres of arable, 12 of meadow and three of more, were to be granted to the Master and brethren of St Katherine's to endow a further chaplaincy. First, however, Thomas's smaller debts and a number of legacies had to be paid, including 10 marks, £6 13s 4d, for the maintenance of Ledbury parish church, and £5 for that at Bridstow.[175]

William and his family were nevertheless provided for. By a proviso attached to the grant of the family's lands to the hospital, they were to be granted a corrody. This could take the form of either a pension, being used by the Crown and monasteries themselves to reward long service, or more frequently a type of annuity, food, clothing, fuel and lodging for life, purchased by members of the laity in exchange for a grant of land or even cash. In the case of William and his family it was the latter: a tenement in the Southend with a bushel of corn and 1d weekly, 13s 4d for a robe on the feast of St Andrew and 12 horseloads of wood annually, delivered at the master's expense. On William's death his widow, Juliana, was to receive a trug (two-thirds of a bushel) of corn and 1d each week; and on her death their son, Nicholas, was to be similarly treated. Presumably they would also retain the house.[176]

Normally the corrodian was granted private quarters within the precinct, but William was to receive out-relief. The Southend was evidently specified as suitably removed from the industrial and commercial hurly-burly of the principal streets of the borough. The inclusion of the wife as widow in such an agreement is not unusual but that of the son certainly was, for in normal circumstances this would mean the extension of the financial burden for many more years. For William and

Juliana the corrody guaranteed not only their well-being in old age but freedom from the concerns of managing an estate. In the case of their son, Nicholas, it was possibly a means of ensuring long-term provision for one ill able to fend for himself.

Although Thomas appointed two chaplains as executors, the dominant role in the execution of his will was played by Thomas's son, Canon Adam. Trillek's predecessor, Bishop Thomas Charlton had presented Adam to the Gorwell prebend in 1341. On Trillek's death in 1361 he was one of two canons appointed custodians of the temporalities of the see and served his successors, bishops Lewis Charlton (1361-70) and Courtenay (1370-5), as vicar general. To Thomas's grant of Orlham and *la Hulle* Adam himself added the gift of a wood lying in Little Marcle, commonly called *Tyrellsfrith*, formerly *Roselynesfrith*, acquired from Grimbald Pauncefot of the Hazle. This was part of

Fig 10.6 Hereford cathedral, North Porch: Esegar Chantry Chapel

Falcon Lane Wood and a house on the south side of the lane is still called Tyrellsfrith Farm. In addition nine bushels of wheat from Orlham were to be distributed to the poor annually, a dole which was still being provided in 1937.[177]

The principal beneficiary under the terms of this grant, however, was Adam. A chaplain was to say masses in St Katherine's chapel 'for the good estate of Adam while he lived and for his soul after he departed this life'; only then were the souls of his father and mother and other members of the Esegar family specified.[178]

After his part in the examination of the excesses of the brothers and dismissal of Thomas de Bradewardyn in 1353, Adam must have watched with great care, and anxiety, developments at St Katherine's under the mastership of William le Brut. The process by which Thomas Esegar's lands were transferred reflects the character of Adam's doubts. Firstly, in December 1361, the lands were conveyed, not to the Master but to six chaplains: William Knyt, Robert *atte Brugge*, Thomas Berde, William *atte Hulle* of Putley, John Balle and John Wynd. All were named in the deeds, apart from Robert *atte Brugge* who died in 1362, and all took a prominent part in the proceedings. Wynd was to become Master of the hospital. Secondly Adam ensured that all the proceedings were underwritten in a formal ratification by Bishop Lewis Charlton. Masses, it specified, were to be celebrated not only 'in perpetuity' but also 'each day'; and, in an attempt to ensure full compliance, a penalty clause was added. In case of default Master and brethren bound themselves to pay the dean and chapter £2. In the case of serious default the bishop and his successors were to take appropriate action.[179]

Despite these safeguards, Adam still lacked confidence in his chantry foundation. In 1367, following Bishop Hugh Foliot's example, he founded a chantry chapel at Hereford, dedicated to the Virgin Mary. It was established in a chamber above the cathedral's early14th-century inner north porch. Access is still by a turret staircase which projects into the eastern angle between porch and north aisle (Fig 10.6). This he endowed with a house and land in Much Cowarne and rents in Weston-under-Penyard to provide a chaplain to say further masses for the repose of his soul and those of members of his family. Adam's fears proved well founded. By 1397 there were but two chaplains at St Katherine's, and both neglected their duties.[180]

The Esegar grant of 480 acres represented a massive injection of additional resources, an increase of 42% on the 1,137 acres which the hospital had owned in 1316. Orlham and la Hulle had replaced John de Stanford's grant of the Hyde, Cradley as the most valuable of St Katherine's holdings, being more than two and a half times greater, both in area and value. In the bishop of Worcester's 1580 survey, the 180 acres at the Hyde were valued at only £2 13s 4d as compared to £7 for the 480 acres of arable plus 12 of pasture and three of more at Orlham and la Hulle. Orlham Farm remained in the hospital's possession almost to our own time.[181]

Between 1366 and 1368 Hugh Cradock was replaced by John Wynd but, with the appointment of William Pykesley in the early 1380s, renewed evidence of serious maladministration led to further papal intervention. Pope Urban VI required dean and chapter to ensure that all properties 'wrongfully alienated by the brethren and their predecessors' were restored. It is characteristic of Pykesley that, in unilaterally presenting Michael Inge to Weston church in 1388, he was the first Master to disregard the traditional role of the brethren in this process. In 1389 the chapter placed St Katherine's temporalities and spiritualities in the hands of Richard Knight, rector of Eastnor, and their fellow canon, Roger Hore.[182]

Pykesley however had regained control of the hospital from its two custodians by the time Bishop Trefnant opened his formal visitation of Ledbury parish in 1397. Information supplied by the parishioners at Weston, Kempley and Yarkhill had already drawn his attention to some of the master's failings. The evidence provided by the Ledbury jurors banished any hesitations the bishop may have had about removing Pykesley, whose shortcomings had reached crisis point. St Katherine's was utterly failing in both its roles, in providing alms and as a college of chantry priests. The master had wholly withdrawn in-relief for the thirteen 'poor and weak lying therein' and out-relief, the customary twice-weekly dole distribution to the poor of the town. To the scandal of the hospital, both brethren and those they tended had to beg their bread on the streets. The parishioners then gave evidence as to the condition of the chaplains whose duty, they explained, was to serve God, continually, within the hospital through the daily offices and recitation of intercessory prayers. Instead of the establishment of five chaplains which they knew of old, Pykesley now provided 'no more than two'. So bad were their conditions, in terms of food and submission to the master who had assumed arbitrary rights of dismissal, that wherever possible they had sought service elsewhere. As early as 1332 Emeric Pauncefot had granted the hospital 40s rent in Cowarne to enable one of its chaplains to celebrate divine service every Sunday, Wednesday and Friday and all feast days in his chapel at the Hazle, but this, it was ordered, should not be to the neglect of the chaplain's services at St Katherine's. The jurors concluded that the ills they described were a consequence of the leasing of St Katherine's lands and tenements to laymen, putting ready cash rather than demesne produce at the master's disposal.[183] St Katherine's was not, however, the exception. At St Bartholomew's, Gloucester, not only were jewels and pensions sold but also beds: 6s 8d was even extracted from a man who had lost both legs. Parts of the hospital were roofless, pigs wandered about freely and the inmates were deprived of both food and clothes. Such serious failings, often worse, were widespread.[184]

11 Prophet's Reforms, 1398 and the Building of the Master's House

John Prophet

During the nearly eight centuries of St Katherine's history there have been four major schemes of reform: the Ordinances of 1398; the decree of the Exchequer Court, in 1580; the order of the same Court, in 1819; and last, by the Charity Commissioners, in 1962. The 1398 Ordinances were the work of Dean Prophet (1393-1404). Most eminent of Hereford's medieval deans, he was an outstanding administrator who served three kings. A registrar at the court of the archbishop of Canterbury in 1382, he was then appointed a royal clerk. Prophet rose rapidly in the service of Richard II. By 1389 he was clerk of the royal household and by 1392 secretary to the royal council where he proved himself a man of quite exceptional energy and ability. He not only made the usual notes on the Council's work but introduced a Register, what we would call minutes, a daily summary of its proceedings. It was 30 years before the Council adopted this as a standard procedure. Prophet's Register began in 1392 and ended the next year, in the November of which he was elected dean of Hereford. He must have been well known to Bishop Trefnant who served with him on the royal council. In 1400, during the first year of his reign, Henry IV decided that Prophet should be recalled to attend council meetings. Without any other state office, he was retained at an annual salary of £100 'so long as he should remain in the King's Council'. In 1403 he was appointed Henry IV's secretary, receiving papal licence in November to withdraw from his Hereford deanery. When in 1406 he was appointed Keeper of the Privy Seal his reward was the York deanery. This he retained until his death in 1416, resigning the keepership only the previous year (See Fig 12.2).[185]

Prophet received many other ecclesiastical perquisites through the good offices of Richard II, Henry IV and Henry V. By 1404 he held prebends at Lincoln, Salisbury, York and St Asaph's cathedrals, Abergwili, Tamworth and Crediton, as well as the rectory of Ringwood, Hants. Within the Hereford diocese he had been presented to a prebend in the cathedral in 1384 which he held until 1407 and in 1390 to the Upper Hall portion of Ledbury parish church. A year after he became dean he was granted the free chapelry of 'St Tyrioc', the ruins of which are visible at low tide on the tiny island of Chapel Rock just south of Beachley Point in the Severn estuary. His career was in no way exceptional, for the granting of such sinecure livings to clerics holding major administrative offices under the Crown was by this time standard practice.[186]

The 1398 Ordinances

The evidence given to Bishop Trefnant at his visitation of Ledbury parish in 1397 starkly underlined the collapse of the system of annual inspections entrusted by Foliot to the dean and chapter. Conditions at St Katherine's shocked Prophet deeply. He acted swiftly and decisively, as dean, to remedy this failure. William Pykesley was dismissed and John Malvern, a man of very different character and background, appointed as master. Prophet's report and recommendations to the chapter in 1398 confirmed the jurors' evidence to Trefnant. By a series of ordinances, sealed in the chapterhouse on 2 November and taken to the bishop at his Whitbourne palace for confirmation on 16 December 1398, Prophet sought to secure full observance of the founder's wishes. Prophet accepted that, for masters of adequate calibre, full residence could not be required. Should however their periods of residence be deemed inadequate by dean and chapter, they would be removed. He sought to provide adequately for both the care of the poor and infirm and the cure of souls. To ensure the poor and weak were sufficiently served and suitably maintained, his Ordinance laid down that they were to receive at least seven small loaves weekly, baked from good grain, each to weigh 1lb 3oz. Similar provisions applied to their ale allowance. This is the first, brief, glimpse in the mass of St Katherine's records of the life of the 'poor and infirm' for whose wellbeing the hospital had been founded. In order that masses were performed according to the benefactors' wishes and that 'all in the said house' should be at their disposal, discipline over the chaplains was restored to the dean and chapter and only by their authority could chaplains be granted a licence to serve elsewhere, or be dismissed. How long, one wonders, did they continue to exercise this prerogative? In addition to their board the chaplains were to receive a fixed annual stipend from the master of £1 10s for 'life's necessities' and 6s 8d for their vestments. These were to conform in colour to those 'as used of old', and bear the traditional white cross on the chest.[187]

Although not referred to in the ordinances, some 70 acres of arable at Dunbridge and Little Marcle, 27 acres of coppice at Dunbridge, now Hospital Wood, together with the tithes of the Hazle, came in the 15th century to be designated as 'Master's Demesne', with the rents allocated for his personal use. For the canons of Hereford cathedral, who each enjoyed the separate estate attached to his prebend, this would appear the natural solution to the problem of raising the master's standing. In the bishop of Worcester's 1580 survey this demesne was valued at £12 14s 6d per annum, as compared to the £90 clear of all other outgoings which was reserved for the maintenance of St Katherine's dual functions as hospital and college of chantry priests.[188]

Such independent provision was essential if Prophet was to secure adherence to the founder's wishes. Above all, St Katherine's needed firm leadership. What evidence there is indicates that previous appointments to the mastership had, for the most part, been internal. In 1353 the chapter had instructed its three-man commission to replace Bradewardyn 'from amongst the brethren' and both William le Brut and John Wynd had been chaplains. Thomas de Ledbury's toponym shows that, although an outsider, a brother of the Worcester hospital of St Oswald, he was of a local family. After 1397, by contrast, almost all the masters were graduates, and four had further qualifications. Richard Pede was a doctor of canon law, whilst John Malvern, John Vaughan and his successor, Richard Wycherley, were all doctors of theology. Pede was elected dean in 1463, Wycherley served as suffragan bishop jointly in the Hereford and Worcester dioceses, and three were promoted—or retired—to one of the cathedral's prebends. The 1398 Ordinances were not Prophet's only essay at hospital reform. In 1416 Henry V called on him to enquire into and report on conditions at St Leonard's leper hospital, outside Walmgate Bar in York, founded by Henry's 'royal progenitors', allegedly before the Norman Conquest.[189]

John Malvern

As the first of the new style of master, Prophet recruited an outstanding individual, John Malvern. They knew each other well, for they were both prominent in court circles. Malvern's qualifications were remarkable. As doctor of theology he had been an assessor at the trial of the Lollard, Walter Brut, for heresy at Hereford in 1393. As master of physic, he attended Henry IV, both as earl of Derby and, after 1399, as king. Malvern was not the only royal physician to receive preferment to such a mastership. Another of Henry IV's doctors, Louis Recouches, was appointed Master of St James's leper hospital, Westminster, in 1401 and later Master of the Mint. Richard II had secured first the see of Llandaff and then that of Worcester for his physician, the Cistercian monk, Tideman de Winchcombe, and Nicholas Colnet, who served Henry V at Agincourt, became Warden of St Bartholomew's Hospital, Rye.[190]

Malvern had further qualifications. He was author of *De remediis spiritualibus et corporalibus contra pestilenciam*, a treatise which took issue with current advice on the prevention of plague. Malvern counselled moderation in food and drink but total abstinence from wine, milk and cheese, sweet foods such as figs and honey and 'heating' foods—oats, beans and garlic. Hot baths and undue physical exertion were best avoided. More positively he believed the fragrance of roses and violets and the odour of herbs such as mint, fennel and bay should fill the home. By way of conclusion Malvern admitted that whilst, as a doctor, he could advise flight from the plague, as a theologian he was bound to pose the fundamental question, 'Whither, Lord, shall I flee from Thy Spirit?'[191]

A well-known incident recounted in *The Chronicle of the Reign of Henry IV* illustrates Malvern's dual persona. After an abortive revolt in 1405, Archbishop Scrope and the nineteen-year-old Earl Marshal were being led to execution in the fields outside York. Scrope, in an attempt to raise the failing courage of his young companion, called out cheerily to Malvern, 'I shall need no physic from you now, Master John'. 'For your body perhaps not but for your soul assuredly', Malvern replied. The chronicler's source was in all probability Malvern himself. A different vignette of Malvern's practice and lifestyle is provided by his attendance on Richard Mitford, Bishop of Salisbury, in 1407. Mitford's own physician had been obliged to summon Malvern when the bishop's condition became grave. On 19 April Malvern arrived with six servants but, unable to provide relief, left a week later. His fee for attendance was 53s 4d, plus expenses, for himself, his servants and horses.[192]

Although absentee and pluralist (he was rector of St Dunstan's in the East and held prebends at St Paul's and St George's, Windsor) Malvern nevertheless played an active role at St Katherine's. Bells, like cemeteries, infringed on parochial rights and revenues and thus required a special licence. Before his first year as Master was over, Malvern had obtained a papal indult for a bell to be sounded for divine offices, 'even before the celebration in the (parish) church', and 'to have mass and other offices celebrated in the chapel, solemnly and *alta voce*'. This was no small achievement, for at Ledbury the dangers were evident. In 1386 the chantry chaplains at the parish church had been forbidden by Bishop Gilbert to celebrate mass early. Many parishioners had been attending early masses to free themselves to devote the rest of the day to business and pleasure, thus neglecting High Mass and other parochial services. Of the offerings at St Katherine's Mass three quarters were to go to the hospital and its poor, only a quarter being reserved for the parish church. Malvern's bell was probably replaced by the present bell, cast in 1696 'in memory of 'Dean George Benson, master 1679-92. Malvern also secured a further fourteen acres of woodland at Little Marcle from Margery Wynd in support of 'certain chaplains' to celebrate divine service daily.[193]

The Master's House

At foundation, one of Foliot's fundamental principles had been the observance of the common life by the *familia*, the master and brethren. In its description of their hall and adjacent dormitory the 1316 inventory illustrates well what this meant in practice. It is not known precisely when a master first withdrew permanently to a separate chamber, but this must have taken place before the end of the century, for one certainly cannot envisage Pykesley sharing either the table with the whole community or the dormitory with his brethren. He would have had his own private chamber or chambers within the court. He was not the first master of a hospital to break the rule. As early as 1303 the master of the hospital of St John the Baptist and Mary Magdalene at Ely had to be forbidden from dining in his private room alone and the master of St Giles, Durham, was declared to be exempt from presence at the communal table only when receiving the bishop. By 1336 the master of St Cross, Winchester had his own chambers. As with abbots and priors, the justification for such provision was the need for suitable quarters to receive important guests.[194]

At Ledbury the process was completed when a splendid half-timbered mansion house was built as the master's personal residence. Such change was inevitable. The masters were merely following the example set by the abbots and priors of almost all monasteries. From the late 12th century they usually had their own chamber whilst retaining a bed in the dormitory, but later most moved to separate quarters. Many of these were very grand, the 15th-century Prior's House at Wenlock being a particularly fine local example. Prophet had recognised the need to raise the status of the master but this had implications, not only in terms of the provision of his own demesne. Strong leadership also meant appropriate accommodation. Masters such as Malvern, Pede and Vaughan would expect accommodation comparable at least to the grander of those canonical houses that remained in the cloister at Hereford, such as 20 Church Street and the Canon's House in St John Street. Which master built and first occupied the mansion house cannot yet be determined, for the only date for its construction is a wide-ranging estimate by the Royal Commission of 'the 15th century'. Hopefully dendrochronological evidence will enable us to answer that question in the near future. With the new lifestyle that a 'mansion' provided, not only was the master isolated from his brethren and the poor and needy for whom he was responsible, but inevitably it led to a clash in terms of resources. An increasing proportion of the hospital's income was to be claimed by the masters to support and develop their new lifestyle.

The master's half-timbered late medieval Mansion House still stands encased within the modern brick structure which served until recently as St Katherine's surgery. Despite subsequent remodelling and additions, the key features of its original H-plan can still be detected as one views

Fig 11.1a Mansion House, south façade

110

Fig 11.1b Mansion House: façade from the south-west with major 19th-century south wing

the building from the south (Fig 11.1). The western, left-hand wing, with its projecting gable end with chimney and French windows, should be dismissed for it is of 19th-century construction. The three Georgian sash windows to the left represent the width of the original solar wing. On the first floor would have been the master's Great Chamber, his private accommodation. The heart of the building was a four-bay hall, some 30 by 20 feet, open to the roof. The lack of smoke blackening on the roof timbers indicates that it was heated by a large chimneyed fireplace, in all probability in the north wall. In the western bay would have stood the master's high table, with immediate access to his private quarters in the solar wing beyond. The service wing, where one would expect to find pantry, larder etc, is within the projecting area on the extreme right. Its screens passage, giving access to these services, is marked by the small projecting block, under a separate gable, immediately to the left of the service wing.

Between passage and hall is a spere truss, with two free-standing side posts marking the division between the screens

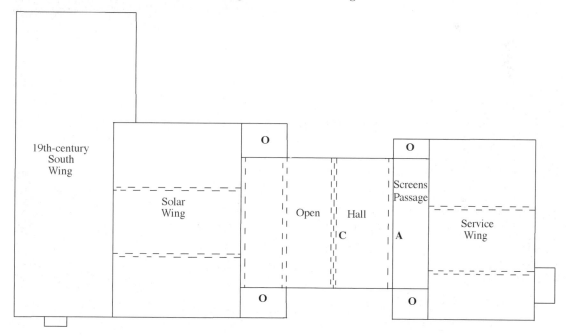

Fig 11.1c Mansion House: Diagramatic plan showing structure of medieval building

passage and hall. These two posts, it has been suggested, are the last vestiges of the arcades of the aisled hall, retained because they had an important function. The two large vertical posts of the spere truss to the east hold the arched tie-beam with its braces below. The arch with its piers was called the spere truss because it provided a place for a removeable screen or spere, that is barrier. This masked the access to the service wing and, to some extent, its noises and smells and the draughts from the external doors at either end of the passage. Access to and from the services was through the minor arches on either side of the spere. Amberley Court, Marden, has a particularly fine example of such a spere truss (Fig 11.2). Spere trusses are open to public view at the Worcester Commandery and at Lower Brockhampton. At the latter, however, it has been considerably modified.

At the Mansion House the roof trusses which divide the hall into four bays are visible above the present first-floor ceiling. Access to its roof space is through a very confined opening. However the effort required is well rewarded, for only in this way is one able at present to see the spere truss which is such a feature of the building. The central truss has an arched collar-beam, with a pair of wide arched braces below (Fig 11.3). Its original tie-beam has been cut and replaced by a pair of timbers. The trusses on either side of the central truss are similar in design from their arched tie-beams upwards, but the eastern is the spere truss dividing the screens passage from the hall. Both have queen posts supporting the collar-beam, between which and the principal rafter is a further pair of posts. These are slightly canted outwards and somewhat crudely cusped internally to form a pair of foiled openings (Fig 11.4). In this respect they represent, in a simplified form, the quatre-foil openings seen, for example, above the hall at Amberley Court where, in addition, the outer sides of the struts, collars and principal rafters have been cut to form pairs of trefoils on either side of the quatrefoil.

Fig 11.2 Amberley Court, diagram of spere truss

Fig 11.3 Mansion House roof, central truss: Arched collar beam with pair of wide arch braces below

Fig 11.4 Mansion House roof, spere truss:
Arched tie-beam with queen posts, collar beam and
canted post above, cusped internally
to form a pair of foiled openings

Fig 11.5 Mansion House roof, spere truss: Two vertical posts with
arched braces supporting tie-beam

The eastern, spere truss differs from that to the west in that, below the arched tie-beam, it has two free-standing, stout vertical timbers supporting it, with braces held by three pegs (Fig 11.5). These are not visible at ground floor level, where originally there would have a removeable screen between them. The purlins at the Mansion House, carrying the roof across the trusses, are supported by pairs of curved braces, as in the infirmary hall, but here the braces are not so finely formed and lack cusping (Fig 11.6).

A comprehensive survey of the medieval fabric of the Master's House, including the detached kitchen (Fig 11.7), commissioned by Herefordshire Council, is anticipated late in 2003. Preliminary results, reported by Richard Morriss, include the discovery of four oriels, contemporary with the structure. From the late middle ages the word 'oriel' was usually applied to windows. However earlier it had a very wide range of applications. It is probably best described as a small structure, of stone or timber, projecting beyond the outer face of a building at ground, first-floor level, or both. An early example occurs at Hereford castle in 1232. Here a chapel 25 feet in length was to be built at the end of the oriel of Henry III's chamber. Other 13th- and 14th-century examples show how wide were the range of uses. Oriels often served as antechambers and were usually glazed. At St Alban's abbey guesthouse the splendid porch was called 'a portico or oriel'. At the former royal castle of Geddington, Northants, a chapel was made 'in the oriol' whilst at Prudhoe, Northumberland, there was 'an oratory chapel'. Locally, at Ashleworth Court, a stone oriel carried a staircase to the Great Chamber. Elsewhere, in both castles and manor houses, oriels served as privies, which term comes from the fact that this was one of the few places where the lord had privacy. In almost all its roles the oriel would have a window or windows (Fig 11.6).[195]

Morriss has identified two oriels on the western side of the

Fig 11.6 Mansion House roof: Purlins supported by pairs of curved braces with vestige of oriel below

Fig 11.7 Mansion House: Timber-framed detached kitchen (left)

hall, at the angles of the north and south where it adjoins the solar wing, and two in similar positions at the eastern end where it meets the service wing. As to their use, he suggests that two may have provided staircases giving access to the upper floors of solar and service wings whilst the others may have served as privies, but would such a facility have been provided for servant use? The provision of additional lighting at the high table end of the hall could well have been a significant factor in the siting of one or both of the western oriels. At the eastern end they could have lit the screens passage or formed porches.[196]

Original accommodation for the exclusive use of the master can be seen at St Cross, Winchester, where it was built as part of the general reconstruction under Cardinal Beaufort's patronage *c*1445. The buildings are around a large quandrangle and the master's quarters are not free standing. They were above the gateway and porter's lodge, providing a commanding view of both quadrangle and entrance court. In the 17th century he moved into more spacious quarters further west in the same north range. At Lord Leycester's Hospital, Warwick, and only a short distance away at St Michael's, Saltisford, founded *c*1135, both master's houses, although free standing, are, as Morriss has pointed out, post medieval. The latter probably dates from refoundation in 1556. Leland, writing 1535-43, tells us St Michael's, once 'an hospital or colledge' with 'master and bretherne', was 'much in ruine and taken for a fre chapell'. Thus St Katherine's Mansion House is very probably unique amongst English medieval hospitals, a free-standing master's house of medieval date.[197]

12   The 15th Century

Chantries

One in five hospitals, it has been calculated, probably disappeared in the half century after the Black Death, and those that remained increasingly placed emphasis on their chantry services and chaplains, at the expense of the poor and needy.[198] The causes are simple. In the later middle ages the Sufferings of Purgatory became 'the focus of Christian fear'. Its horrors are graphically described by Sir Thomas More in his *Supplicacyon of Soulys*. There he speaks of 'ye pain whose fire as far passeth in heat all the fires that ever burned upon earth'; of 'silly souls that lie sleepless, burning and broiling in the dark fire one long night of many days, of many weeks and some of many years together'; of 'keepers (who) are ... despitious enemies and despiteful tormentors, their company more horrible and grievous to us than is the pain itself'. The one consolation was that 'whilst the paynes of helle be eternal the paynes of purgatory have an end'. Hence the ever-growing demand for chaplains to offer up prayers of intercession for both the living and the dead. From the early 14th century St Katherine's had to vie for local funds with chantries established at the parish church—first the Blessed Virgin established by the parishioners in the north chapel by 1323, then the Holy Trinity and finally St Anne in the south chapel in 1384—as well as at other local churches. Indeed by 1369 the Stepultones had established their chantry to the Virgin at St Katherine's church at Weston, where they presented their own chaplains. For Prophet, as for so many others, what Duffy calls his 'post mortem fire insurance', the foundation of chantries, where intercessory prayers would be offered for his good estate during life and his soul after death, became almost obsessive.[199]

By the late 14th century impoverishment, irregularities, maladministration, even proximity to a similar institution, came to account for an increasing number of amalgamations, of hospitals as of chantries. This reduced the number of chaplains, and thus overall expenses. At Ross in 1377 Bishop John Gilbert united the chantry founded in the parish church in 1330 by John de Rosse, Bishop of Carlisle, with a fraternity of the borough as their funds were inadequate for the support of two chaplains. Rather than such a coming together of equals, hospitals were more frequently linked or amalgamated with other, wealthier, and often predatory, religious institutions. In this way the relics of St Bartholomew's, Oxford, had been 'procured and conveyed' to Oriel College's 'owne church' and the fragment of the True Cross from Holy Trinity, Dunwich, appropriated by the Augustinians of St Osyth's.[200]

About 1400 bishop and dean joined forces in a project which could well have proved the doom of St Katherine's. Three years prior to election as dean, Prophet had been presented as one of the two portionists of Ledbury church. Each enjoyed distinct portions of the church's endowments and revenues, the Upper and Lower Hall estates, and each had his own manor house adjacent to the church. In 1311 Bishop Swinfield had sought counsel's opinion on the legal status of the Ledbury portionists and received the firm advice that they did not carry with them the cure of souls, nor did they limit the rights to hold other benefices at the same time. The portionists' sole responsibility was to ensure the provision and adequate payment of a vicar. The fact that the two portions were *sine cure* and could thus be held *in absentia* with other benefices made them highly attractive to both king and pope. Although the bishop was patron, during vacancies of the see and on other occasions, when pressure could be exercised, Crown and papacy were anxious to present their own clerical officers whose income could thereby be supplemented at no charge to themselves. In 1307 Dean John de Aquablanca had enjoyed its income whilst at Rome; a papal nuncio, Itherus de Concreto, was presented in 1335 and William Kelleseye, a royal clerk, in 1349. Prophet himself was presented to the Upper Hall portion by Richard II.[201]

In 1399 Trefnant was granted a royal licence to found a perpetual chantry at the altar of the Virgin in Ledbury parish church. Here a chaplain would celebrate masses for the good estate of the king and the bishop during life and for their souls after death, for which Trefnant was to provide a modest £10 of rents from his Ledbury manor. Prophet grasped what he believed to be a golden opportunity, no doubt without realising the danger to which he would be exposing the St Katherine's community in the long run. By April 1401 he had persuaded Trefnant to embark on a much more ambitious scheme, which also served the interests of Prophet and his fellow portionist, Robert Prees, who held the Lower Hall estate. They would allocate the advowsons, resources, of their two portions, for the foundation of a college of a warden or master, who would be rector of the church, with eight chantry priests to celebrate masses, not only for bishop and king but also for Prophet and Prees. Trefnant had further thoughts, for three months later he reverted to the original proposal, recognising it would be quite improper to take for his own benefit the patronage of the two Ledbury portions which, rightly, he should pass on to his successors. Instead he chose to be buried below the large Perpendicular window which he had had built into the Romanesque south wall of the cathedral's south transept (Fig 12.1).[202]

It was fortunate indeed for St Katherine's that Prophet's scheme came to naught. Ledbury was too small a town to maintain what would in practice have been two colleges of chantry priests: one at the church, with master and eight chaplains; the other at the hospital, with master and five or more. Sooner or later a call for union would have been made. The outcome of the claims of the newly-founded college, located in what has been called the premier (or première) parish church of the county, as opposed to those of St

Fig 12.1 Bishop Trefnant: Tomb in Hereford Cathedral, south transept

116

Fig 12.2 Ringwood Church, Hants: Dean Prophet's brass, from the Gentleman's Magazine 77i (1807) 1001

Katherine's, with merely a humble chapel, would never have been in doubt.

On his collation to the York deanery in 1407 Prophet was obliged to resign the Upper Hall portion. In 1410 he established a chantry chapel with Sir John Berkeley at Ringwood, a church of which he was rector but, thwarted in an attempt to found a chantry chapel at York minster, in 1414 he proposed to build one, dedicated to St John, on the south side of the nave at Hereford Cathedral. He took care to explain that he was motivated by 'his affection for that cathedral church' where he had been prebendary and dean. Now an old man, such was Prophet's haste that he had persuaded Henry V formally to grant that 'Thomas the mason and other stone cutters, fellows and servants of his, to the number of ten persons labouring daily on the work, shall not be taken' for royal works 'before the chapel's completion'. Yet again the scheme came to nought. Two years later Prophet was buried at Ringwood where his brass, virtually life-size, is still to be seen. He wears the canonical cope, a costly vestment used on ceremonial occasions. This is decorated with orphreys, a term derived from the Latin for gold embroidery. The engraving shows these decorated with the figures of eight saints within embattled architectural canopies. The first on his left can be identified as George, with shield, killing his dragon; the third as Peter with his large key; on his right the second may well be Katherine and her wheel, whilst the fourth is certainly Margaret, killing her dragon, with her cross-headed staff in its throat (Fig 12.2).[203]

Masters

John Malvern died in 1422 but the last reference to him as master is in 1409. His successor was Nicholas Lyney who was in office by 1417 when he sought to exchange his mastership for Robert Prees' Lower Hall portion. Prees certainly had the professional qualifications. A civil lawyer presented to the Ledbury portion by the pope in 1389, he had represented St Albans abbey at Rome where, by 1391, he was acting as Richard II's envoy. However, given the parishioners' evidence before Trefnant at the 1397 visitation—of Prees's 'incontinence' with his servant, Alice Smith, and with Maiota Crompe—this was a somewhat surprising proposal. Lyney was master again, probably on Prees's death, for in 1420 he presented John Pope to the vicarage of Weston; yet he retained his Netherhall portion. Despite the failure of the chantry college proposals, and his incontinence, Prees was long remembered in Ledbury. The antiquary, Thomas Dingley, who visited Ledbury in 1677 records that a tablet inlaid with brass under the altar was inscribed: 'Here lyeth Magister Roberde Preece' who 'in his life tyme was counted wyse' together with the request, 'For the love of Peter and St Paul sey a pater noster and ave' for his soul. This is of particular interest as an early abandonment of Latin, the first dated example of such use of the vernacular being the Walsch brass at Wanlip, Leics, of 1393. Prees was kneeling on a cushion, his hands raised in prayer, with the words *miserere mei dominus* on a scroll rising to a representation of the Holy Trinity. He wore a cope, again with orphreys, showing him to be both a dignitary and a man of wealth. This may well represent the vestments in which he was buried. The inclusion of his arms, a chevron, is a further means of emphasising his status (Fig 12.3).[204]

Bishop Spofford was enthroned at Hereford cathedral in 1424. For four years his diocese had, effectively, been without a bishop. During his 26 years' reign Spofford sought to rule a diocese described as 'at the best of times wild'. Henry VI himself was to write to the pope, saying it needed a strong man as ruler. Anarchy was spreading and much of Herefordshire and Salop sank deep into lawlessness. None was more blatant in flouting the law than John, Lord Talbot who, with his fifty retainers at Goodrich castle, terrorised the Archenfield and Wormelow hundreds almost as far as Hereford city. Matters deteriorated even further when Talbot fell out with his former deputy, John Abrahall. Further, Spofford's relations with Dean Baysham and his chapter, at this time just three resident canons, were anything but good.[205]

In 1414 parliament had legislated in an attempt to improve the general condition of the nation's hospitals. Erected 'to sustain impotent men and women, lazars, men out of their wits, poor women with child and to nourish and refresh other poor people', these were now 'decayed

Fig 12.3 Ledbury Parish church: (Lost) Brass to Robert Prees with arms

118

and the goods and profits, by divers persons, as well spiritual as temporal, withdrawn and spent in other use'. On the king's authority the bishops were ordered to 'inquire into (their) governance and estates' and make appropriate 'correction and reformation'. Within a year of his arrival, finding 'transgressions and excesses' at St Katherine's, Spofford threatened to appoint others to visit and reform if dean and chapter failed so to do before Easter. This reflected no credit on Lyney, yet he retained office for four further years—until his collation to the Preston prebend in 1428 when Richard Lye became master.[206]

Richard Pede, doctor of canon law had succeeded Lye as master by 1444. Pede's interests were at Oxford where by 1450 he was principal of the great school of canon law. How often he resided at St Katherine's is not known. Certainly he left the parishioners of the hospital's church at Kempley unserved for the bishop had to present William Lammer in 1448. Bishop Beauchamp nevertheless collated Pede to the Upper Hall portion at Ledbury in 1450 and Boulers, his successor, was also impressed by his qualities. In 1451, with papal dispensation to hold additional and incompatible benefices, Boulers presented Pede to the second portion at Bromyard parish church and a year later to the Hinton prebend and a canonical house in Hereford. Pede took up residence in the city at an unfortunate time. In 1452 Richard, Duke of York, attempted a coup and Sir Walter Devereux, who held York's castle at Weobley and was constable at Wigmore, organised a rising at Hereford. For a time there was a complete breakdown of law and order in the city. On Boulers's translation to the see of Coventry and Lichfield in 1453 Pede followed, serving him for a short time as his vicar general. Boulers's successor, the Carmelite friar John Stanbury, spent little time in his diocese for he was both confessor to Henry VI and a member of the royal council. Its administration was left to Pede as vicar general (1453-73). In 1456 Devereux led a force of some 2,000 men, drawn from the Duke of York's Herefordshire and Radnorshire lands, to seize Carmarthen castle. Ledbury, distant from the lawless Yorkist western parishes, now became a major diocesan centre. Ordination services were reserved to the bishop or his suffragan, the bishop of Kildare. Between 1454 and 1467 only eight services were held in the cathedral and Hereford palace chapel, but there were thirteen at Ledbury and four in the chapel of the episcopal palace at Bosbury.[207]

By May 1459 John Vaughan, rector of Eastnor, was Master, but Pede's subsequent career is of interest for the further light it throws on Ledbury as a growing centre of episcopal administration. On Henry VI's deposition in 1461 Stanbury, who as his confessor had been in constant attendance at court, returned to his overwhelmingly Yorkist diocese. In 1463 he intervened decisively in cathedral affairs. By declaring the election of John ap Richard void on account of 'lay influence and oppression', Stanbury was able to present. Side-stepping James Goldwell, the chapter's choice as dean, he collated Pede, ordering the chapter to instal. Then, leaving the administration in Pede's hands, he devoted himself to the extirpation of Lollardy about Ross and in the Forest. John Vaughan held not only the mastership but the rectory of Hanwell in Middlesex, 1460-74, when he exchanged it for Stoke Lacy which he retained until his death in 1485. After twenty-four years' service, he resigned in 1483 to be collated to the Gorwell prebend.[208]

Richard Wycherley, a Dominican friar and doctor of theology, succeeded. Two years earlier he had represented the English province of his order at their General Chapter in Rome. In 1484 he was consecrated bishop *in partibus Olenensis*, of Olena in the Peloponnese, then part of the Ottoman Empire. In this capacity, without a see, he was able to serve as suffragan bishop not only at Hereford to Myllyng, and in all probability his successors, Audley and Castello, but also to bishops Alcock and Morton and their two Italian successors at Worcester, 1482-1502. Rector of Donnington and administrator of Aylton and Pixley in Hereford diocese, he was also rector of Salwarpe and Powick in Worcester. These parochial responsibilities he combined skilfully with his role as suffragan, which was primarily one of ordination. St Katherine's was an ideal base. Of the twenty ordination services he conducted in this diocese between 1484 and 1492 only five were held at the cathedral. Twelve were at Ledbury church, the remainder in Wycherley's own chapel at St Katherine's. With a master resident much of the time, and Ledbury an ecclesiastical centre, these must have been golden days for the community. Wycherley died in 1502, having requested that he be buried in Worcester Cathedral, next to Richard Wolsey, bishop of Down and Connor, a fellow Dominican and his predecessor as suffragan at Worcester, 1465-79. Whilst most 15th-century masters were non-resident for much of their time, they were generally men of calibre, able to protect St Katherine's from the violence and threats of the years between the accession of the Lancastrian Henry VI in 1422 and of the Tudor Henry VII in 1485.[209]

13 The Chapel's Late Medieval Tiled Pavement

In the chapel are some 500 tiles of *c*1500, of which others remain below the tiled late 19th-century altar platform. They form one of the largest medieval tile collections in the county but it is their quality rather than their quantity which is important. They display patterns derived from at least 27 different dies, of which all but two belong to the so-called Canynges group, described by Elizabeth Eames in the British Museum's *Catalogue of the Medieval Lead-Glazed Earthenware Tiles* as 'the most impressive of the products of the Malvern school (of tilers) in the Museum's collection'. This is confirmed by the dominant position the reconstituted Canynges pavement occupies in the Museum's Medieval Tile and Pottery Room. It was originally laid in the parlour of the Redcliffe Street house of William Canynges, a Bristol merchant, five times mayor, who rebuilt St Mary Redcliffe church. It has now been established that this pavement was laid after his death in 1474 and that its '16-tile patterns had been designed for some other place'. This was probably St David's cathedral where some 3,800 tiles remain of an estimated 13,340—as compared to some 2,000 laid at the Canynges' house and now at the British Museum. The St David's tiles are dated 1496-1504. Smaller numbers have been found at other sites on the south Wales coast. There is another concentration along the Severn and its tributaries. From the distribution of these finds sites it is evident

Fig 13.1 St Katherine's: Non-Canynges designs a) Tudor rose with fleur-de-lys at corners,
b) Beauchamp arms as in (1), smaller, lacking crescent for difference

Fig 13.2 British Museum Canynges Pavement, showing overall pattern

that the tiles were carried from Worcester by river down the Severn to Gloucester and Bristol and then by coastwise trade along the Bristol channel as far as St David's. Others were taken up the Severn deep into Shropshire and along the Avon through Warwickshire as far as Stratford where they were laid in Holy Trinity church.[210] The two non-Canynges tiles are shown in Fig 13.1.

One can be confident as to the original layout from extant pavements at St David's cathedral, the British Museum and elsewhere. These have a carpet of alternating rows of 16- and 4-tile squares, set diagonally, each surrounded by a border of plain dark tiles (Fig 13.2). Such designs of squares of patterned tiles with plain tiles go back to the 13th century. At Worcester cathedral the gallery overlooking the former chapter parlour has a simple pattern of 4-tile diagonal squares, alternating plain and ornamental, but the floors in the lay clerk's vestry and the music room are decorated with squares set diagonally, of 16- and 9-pattern tiles with plain borders. From documentary evidence it is known that these were laid in 1377 but the convention goes back much further. At Lichfield cathedral library alternating four-tile diagonal squares of light patterned and plain dark glazed tiles are dated *c*1300.[211]

The tiles of the Canynges pavement have been classified into 30 design groups: 21 four-tile and nine sixteen-tile patterns.[212] At St Katherine's there is evidence of eight of the four-tile and six of the sixteen-tile patterns (Table 7). The four-tile designs fall into two categories (Rear cover). The

122

St Katherine's: Late Medieval Tiles

4-Tile Designs, giving British Museum Catalogue number

Single-tile (rear cover)

1	1606	On a fesse between six crosses, crosslets a crescent for difference (Beauchamp of Warwick); in each corner foliage
2	2008	A heart within a quatrefoil; in each corner another heart
3	2204	Quatrefoil with 4 fleur-de-lys; in each corner a distorted fleur-de-lys
4	2366	Circular band with annulets, within a 4-petalled flower, each petal cut into 5; in each corner a quarter circle

Quadripartite (rear cover)

5	1442	Square double border band, circular band with 4-fold *dne ihu misere*, within alternating leaf and 3-petalled rose pattern; in each corner trifoliate design
6	2698	Two bands, outer with annulets, inner with pellets, foliate pattern between; at centre sun with rays; in each corner trifoliate leaf
7	2796	2 circles, one arcade design other alternating leaf and 6-petalled rose, at centre 8-petalled rose; in each corner trifoliate pattern
8	NMW[1] 407A	Fourfold fleur-de-lys design within double circle, pair of intertwined leaves; in each corner a 6-petalled rose

16-Tile Designs (Fig 13.3)

9	2421-2	A pair of circular bands with pierced cinquefoils, between four processing **lions**; with the inner circle an 8-petalled rose; in each corner a pair of oak leaves
10	2886-9	A single circular band bearing **deo gratias** four times; within star burst and 4-petalled rosettes; in each corner a pair of **peacocks**
11	2893-6	A single circular band with 5 -petalled rosettes and leaves between intertwines stems; within quatrefoil design with **asymmetrical foliage**; in each corner **Westminster** abbey arms in reverse, between 5 martlets a cross patonce, on either side foliage
12	2973-6	A pair of circular bands with stars between a frieze of **vine leaves** and bunches of grapes; at centre a **sunburst**; in each corner a 5-petalled rose with leaves
13	2990	A pair of circular bands with pellets; between single leaves with 6-petalled roses; at centre **12-petalled flower**; in each corner tripartite leaves
14	2996-8	A pair of circular bands with cable pattern; between **oak leaves**; at centre four hearts; in each corner sunburst with leaves and 6-petalled rose

Non-Canynges Designs (Fig 13.1)

1. Tudor rose crowned on all sides with fleur-de-lys at corners (St David's cathedral)
2. Beauchamp arms as in 1606S but smaller, not centrally placed and lacking crescent for difference

[1] Reference numbers as in British Museum Catalogue and for NMW in J.M. Lewis *The Medieval Tiles of Wales* (1999) 167

Table 7

Fig 13.3 Canynges 16-tile designs 9-14; Godwin replicas at St David's (this page and opposite)

first, (1) to (4), is composed of four of the same tiles, with each a complete design in itself. Thus design (1) is made up of identical shields bearing the Beauchamp arms, a fesse between six crosslets with a crescent for difference. In the second category all four tiles (5-8) are required to make up a quadripartite pattern. Thus in (5) each tile bears a quarter of a circular band, with the text *dne ihu miserere*, 'Lord Jesus have mercy', and in (8) each has one fleur-de-lys within a quarter of a circle. All the 16-tile designs (9-14) are characterized by a strongly drawn, circular band design across the 12 outer tiles. In four cases this band is repeated as an inner circle (9, 12, 13 and 14) (Fig 13.3).

Today the centre of the chapel floor is boarded, the tiles being relaid along the south wall, the east end, with only those in front of the 19th-century tiled altar platform now being visible, and

along the north wall as far as the doorway. At the east end the line of medieval tiles is broken by 19th-century memorial slabs. The crude broken edges along the north and south walls are evidence that the tiles have been reset. All heavily worn tiles, those damaged in the process of being taken up and most plain tiles were rejected. One has only to compare their condition with that of the badly worn tiles about the altar at St David's to realise the selection process at Ledbury was conducted with some rigour. The extant tiles thus represent merely a proportion of the original number, with a serious imbalance in tile patterns.

The Ledbury tilers failed to recover the original layout of the first category of 4-tile designs (1-4), relaying their single components individually. However, they were successful in reconstructing the four quadripartite compositions (5-8) although on occasions they combined tiles of this group with others from the centre of 16-tile designs. The greatest difficulties were encountered of course

with the 16-tile group. The tilers began at the south-west corner. Eight 16-tile designs, I to VIII, were assembled at regular intervals along the three sides (Fig 13.4). I to V are complete examples of (10), with its central starburst, the circular *deo gratias* band and pairs of peacocks at each corner. However with VI, at the north-east corner, the tilers began to find difficulties, using four of the central starburst of (10) with twelve outer tiles of (11). VII and VIII were even more confused. Each is made up of a combination of tiles from three different designs. Thus one has the four central tiles of the 12-petalled flower of (13), at the corners the peacocks of (10), whilst the eight outer tiles come from the circular band of intertwined stems and rosettes of (11). (Figs 13.5) Curiously, there was a distinct surplus of the four asymmetric

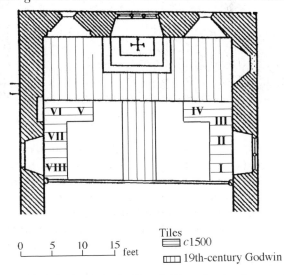

Fig 13.4 St Katherine's Chapel: Plan showing layout of medieval tiles

Fig 13.5 St Katherine's Chapel: Detail of pair of peacocks from corner of tile design 10

foliage tiles, the centrepiece of (11). This, their real position, was never appreciated for the numerous examples all over the pavement are always treated as individual tiles.

The transfer of the four central tiles from one 16-tile design to another can be seen in other places. Even in the British Museum's Canynges pavement there is an example—but, it has been suggested, this was a repair. Certainly the mismatch in such recombination is usually evident to the practiced eye. The central 'sunburst' of (12) appears as a separate 4-tile pattern divorced from its surrounding vine leaves and bunches of grapes. Overall the 16-pattern design, (9), with its anticlockwise procession of lions suffered most during the initial selection process. Its four-part centerpiece of eight-petalled roses was recovered but, of the 12 outer tiles portraying the lions, only one rump has survived.

To produce each of the 16-tile designs four different wooden stamps or dies had to be used four times to impress the pattern on the surface of the red clay. White pipe clay would then be poured on to bring out the pattern. Once this had set each tile would be given a glaze, yellowish in colour but varying in both depth and hue. As most of the Ledbury tiles are well preserved, they retain much of this original rich range of tones. Minor variations in the design of tiles, such as the treatment of the lion's face and tail in (9), sometimes occurred when the short-lived wooden dies were recut and these are valuable in establishing the relationship between the different sites where Canynges-type tiles were used. Thus the fleur-de-lys design (8) at St Katherine's corresponds precisely to that found at St David's, Carew Castle, Carmarthen Grey Friars and Haverfordwest priory, that is National Museum of Wales pattern 407, but not to the Canynges tiles design, for the St Katherine's tile has a double band holding the fleur-de-lys by its neck whereas the Canynges design has a double rope-like band.

Major variations occurred when the die-cutter made his copy directly from a tile, thus producing a mirror image of the original. The coat of arms of Westminster abbey on all the Canynges 14 tiles is such a mirror-image, with the five martlets reversed. The arms of Westminster abbey, commonly believed to have been those of Edward the Confessor, were also those of Westminster's cell at Great Malvern, an important tile-making centre. These were incorporated in designs for the tiles of Abbot Sebroke's pavement, c1450 in the sanctuary of St Peter's abbey, now Gloucester cathedral. Probably due to their popularity, they were copied for use on smaller tiles. One might not be surprised at the laying of tiles bearing the reversed image of the best known of all coats of arms at St Katherine's and smaller churches, but it is hard to understand how they came to be laid over such an extensive area of the cathedral church at St David's. Another reverse image can be seen in design (9). The British Museum pavement shows the lions processing in an anti-clockwise direction, but at Ledbury the haunch, and at St David's cathedral, Gloucester lady chapel and the porch of North Claines church, near Worcester, the lions process clockwise. Here again, as with the fleur-de-lys design, Ledbury's association is with the designs found, not on the Bristol pavement, but at St David's.

Heraldry on medieval tiles, unlike of stained glass, can be misleading for popular designs were reissued over long periods and used in places where they had no connection. Yet the two Ledbury designs bearing coats of arms do give us some indication of their lineage. Eames has shown that the Westminster arms were used in the Sebroke pavement c1450 and then copied again, for use on a smaller scale in the 16-tile Canynges design (11) at St David's, Bristol, Ledbury and many other places. The second heraldic design is the arms of a member of the Beauchamp family, a fesse between six crosslets, with a crescent for difference. This was copied from originals laid c1430 in the Tewkesbury chantry chapel of Richard, earl of Worcester, husband of Isabelle, heiress of the Despensers, and son of William Beauchamp, Lord Abergavenny.

The patron?

Given the St David's dating, 1496-1504, either Richard Wycherley (1483-1502) or Canon Thomas Blundell, who held the mastership from 1503 until his resignation in 1515, was responsible for its construction. Blundell is an unlikely candidate. A local man, from Kempley, he was installed a canon at St John's cathedral, Chester, in 1500, which prebend he retained until his death, 20 years after his resignation as master. Another local man, John Elton of the Hazle, who succeeded him in 1515, presented a George Blundell as vicar of St Katherine's church at Kempley. On George's resignation in 1527 Elton then presented Canon Blundell, the services no doubt being taken by a lowly-paid curate. Yet within a few weeks Elton granted the canon a licence to bargain for a pension. This Thomas claimed on resigning the vicarage two years later. Richard Wycherley, on the other hand, was a man of ability and integrity who had good cause to have the pavement laid. Bishop Myllyng's register shows him holding ordination ceremonies, not only at Ledbury church but also at St Katherine's in 1485, 1486 and 1489. Wycherley continued to act as suffragan in both the Hereford and Worcester dioceses until his death in 1502. As Bishop Audley's register (1492-1502) disappeared during the Civil War, there are no ordination lists for the later period. However, as Wycherley became older and more confident in his role the number and size of ordinations at St Katherine's will no doubt have grown. What could be more natural than to seek to enhance the dignity of such occasions by the laying of a handsome tiled pavement for the chapel and its altar? In many dioceses the high altar of the cathedral church was reserved for the bishop himself. Suffragans had to celebrate at side altars. The temptation to build such a pavement must have been great.[213]

Growth of an antiquarian interest in tiles led in the late 1830s and the 1840s to the production of replicas, first by Chamberlains of Worcester and then by Herbert Minton at Stoke. William Godwin, who had previously managed the Ledbury Brick & Tile Works, moved in 1814 to found his own tilery at Lugwardine. He soon became one of the principal producers of replica medieval tiles, frequently used in the extensive restoration of cathedrals and parish churches being undertaken at the time, on occasions giving them greater similitude by the use of lead glaze and a less uniform treatment of the surface. In 1862, the year prior to the completion of his restoration of Hereford cathedral, George Gilbert Scott was called in to advise on the perilous condition of St David's cathedral. The result was a major reconstruction programme, completed only in 1877. The extensive Canynges pavements on the altar steps Scott retained. However for most of the eastern end of the cathedral, the choir and its aisles, ambulatory and Lady Chapel, he ordered replicas from William Godwin. Scott held the Lugwardine products in high regard, for he pays tribute to Godwin's work in his *Personal and Professional Recollections.* This apparently established a vogue for Godwin's Canynges replicas. Within this diocese they were laid during restoration work at a number of major churches including Ludlow and Madley. Lugwardine tiles were also used for the new altar platform at St Katherine's. Two Canynges designs were included, the central 5-petal rose (9) and the four-tile design (8). These enable us to appreciate more fully the aesthetic qualities of their medieval predecessors.[214]

14   The Age of Plunder: 'the Boiling Flames of Purgatory extinguished'

By 1515 when Wycherley's successor, Thomas Blundell, resigned public criticism was growing of clerical domination, if not exploitation, of existing institutions, and attitudes to hospitals were changing. Anticlericalism was strongest in the large towns. Thus in 1531 St Bartholomew's hospital, Bristol, was converted into a free grammar school. Indeed one hostile commentator, Simon Fish, in his *Supplicacyon for Beggars*, opined that in English hospitals 'the fat of the whole foundation lies on the priests' beards'.[215] By the mid 1530s, under the pressure of Henry VIII's conflict with the pope over the divorce of Catherine of Aragon, his ever-increasing need for more money and the break between the Lutheran German princes and Rome, the pace of change accelerated rapidly.

It was enacted in 1531 that 'the King's Grace be authorised Supreme Head' of the church. This was confirmed by the act of supremacy in December. Annates, the first year's revenue of all benefices together with one-third of the annual income, formerly paid to Rome, and a tenth of the income in succeeding years, were now appropriated to the Crown. A new survey of all benefices was conducted, hospitals being included for the first time, and full details of the valuations published in the *Valor Ecclesiasticus* of 1535. Although the heading, St Katherine's, is no longer legible, the text establishes that a number of entries refer to the hospital and its churches. The pension, of 40s due annually to dean and chapter, is recorded and the total value assessed at £22 5s. This was confirmed the following year in the bishop's certificate of the annual value of all benefices within the diocese. No longer was St Katherine's an institution exempt from clerical taxation.[216]

The Monasteries

The dissolution of the monasteries, houses valued at under £200 in 1536 and the remainder shortly after, raised ominous questions about the future of hospitals, especially those linked to monastic houses. When the last monastery fell in March 1540 'a great many hospitals had fallen in their wake'. At Worcester in 1534 Henry VIII had appointed John Bell, his chaplain and a principal agent in his divorce proceedings, master of St Wulstan's. Elected to the see in 1539, Bell then surrendered the hospital, valued at £79 12s 6d, to the Crown. St Leonard's, York, probably the greatest of England's medieval hospitals, fell to the Crown in 1540, becoming the Royal Mint for the North.[217]

In November 1538 Henry VIII 'stopped the Reformation dead' but repercussions of measures already taken continued. The plundering of monastic shrines spread to secular cathedrals. From the minsters of York, Ripon and Beverley and the abbeys of Durham and Wenlock Henry received 24,000 oz of silver. His act to suppress chantries, 1545, was not based on principle but arose from his virtual bankruptcy. In the event it amounted to little. Indeed, in his will the king pleaded for the intercession of the Virgin and the saints, leaving 1,000 marks for a chantry at St George's chapel, Windsor, and another 1,000 for the poor to pray for his soul.[218]

Fig 14.1a York, St Leonard's Hospital

The Chantries

The accession of Henry's young son as Edward VI and the protectorship of the Duke of Somerset provided Archbishop Cranmer and the reformers with a second chance. It is doubtful if any chantry was dissolved as a result of Henry VIII's first chantry act. Dissolution came with the second chantry act, of 1547. This was prefaced by a forthright attack on intercessory prayers: 'a great part of superstition and errors in Christian religion hath been brought into the minds and estimations of Men by reason of the ignorance of their very true and perfect salvation through the death of Jesus Christ, and by devising and phantasying vain opinions of purgatory and masses satisfactory to be done for them which be departed ... upholden by the abuse of trentals and chantries'. 'The boiling flames of purgatory' were now being extinguished. Hospitals were not included under the terms of the act but, given that many had major chantry functions, they were very vulnerable. Land granted for the reciting of masses provided such hospitals with a considerable portion of their annual revenue. Many private individuals recognised this as 'the last dish of the last course' and that 'after chantries, as after cheese, nothing was to be expected'.[219]

At Ledbury Foliot's original foundation charter had estab-

Fig 14.1b York, St Leonard's Hospital: Undercroft

lished one chaplain to celebrate mass, 'in perpetuity', for the bishop's 'own soul, those of his predecessor and successors, the canons of Hereford and all faithful'; but he had expressed his hope that there would be a second chaplain to celebrate for 'all benefactors'. This second chaplaincy was founded by William of Ockeridge who by 1234 had granted 60 selions in *Peseden, Twyseledway* and West fields, hayland and a small wood specifically for prayers 'for the souls of himself and his wife'. John de Stanford's grant of rents at the Hyde, Cradley was debt repayment but his charter insists, and he well believed, that they were for 'the salvation of his own soul and that of his wife'. Bishop John de Grandison had refurbished St Katherine's chapel to serve as a chantry for his father and mother. By the 1360s, when the Esegar family granted 480 acres of arable at Hill Farm and Orlham to establish a further chaplaincy, there is evidence of at least five chaplains. In 1398 Prophet had sought to restore the status of these chaplains by placing them under the supervision of dean and chapter and by allocating them a stated annual stipend and money for their vestments. In 1407, when Margery Wynd granted fourteen acres of wood at Tyrells Frith, Little Marcle, she specified that 'certain chaplains' were to 'celebrate divine service daily'. Such grants represent an important part of St Katherine's land holdings. In 1836 out of a total income of £1,114 from St Katherine's general estate Orlham and the Hyde farms provided £458 .[220]

The 1547 act authorised royal commissioners to determine the annual value of all lands and possessions, including ornaments, jewels, plate, goods and chattels, belonging to 'all chantries and hospitals yet undisssolved'. For each a formal Chantry certificate had to be completed. The result was the dissolution not only of chantries and free chapels but also of 110 hospitals. Half the hospitals valued at over £50, that is twice the valuation of St Katherine's, were dissolved by one means or another at this time. In the provinces the proportion was slightly higher, 16 out of 30, in London somewhat lower, three out of eight, but there Sir Richard Gresham, Lord Mayor, and the corporation exerted considerable pressure on the Crown to save some and place them under the City's control.[221]

St Katherine's, at £22 5s, was by far the most affluent of the Herefordshire hospitals; St Ethelbert's, Hereford was valued at only £10 1s 10d. Although smaller hospitals suffered less at the hands of the Crown, they were frequently dissolved by patrons 'graspingly indifferent to the state of their forebears in purgatory' or by men of influence in the locality. The fate of St John's, Ludlow, founded in 1221 by Peter Undergod near Teme Bridge, is fairly typical. The master persuaded the remaining almsmen to agree to the granting of a 99-year lease of their estates to William Foxe, a local oligarch who served as high bailiff on six occasions. At Hereford in 1525 Bishop Charles Booth (1517-35) united St Ethelbert's and its revenues with the cathedral treasurership. A century later its property was 'let at very small rents to the great injury of the poor'. Booth's predecessor, Richard Mayhew, 1504-16, had set a clear precedent. As President of Magdelen, he had annexed the hospitals of St John and St James at Aynho and Brackley and the leper house at Romney to his college in the 1480s.[222]

That St Katherine's survived unscathed was due to a number of factors. The most important was that political control of the borough and the area it served was now in the hands of a small group of lay families, closely linked by blood and economic interests: some, such as the Eltons and Skynners, were local; others, such as the Skyppes and Willisons, were outsiders. This they achieved by a web of complex transactions. Indeed Bishop Scory was, with some truth, able to describe the hospital in 1559 as 'converted to the uses of certain private men of sufficient wealth'.[223]

From his presentation as Master of St Katherine's in 1515 to his death in 1547, Canon John Elton was at the centre of this group. The eldest son of William Elton and Sibill Wylse of Dymock, he rose under the patronage of Edmund Audley, the former bishop of Hereford who became bishop of Salisbury in 1502. There Elton was collated first to the rectories of St Peter's, Marlbourgh and Sherston and then to a prebend at the cathedral in 1512. In 1515 he obtained a prebend at Hereford and succeeded Blundell as Master. In 1517 Bishop Booth presented Elton to the Lower

Hall portion in Ledbury parish church. For Edward, one of his brother William's younger sons, Elton then secured a Salisbury prebend and in 1520, as portionist, presented him to the Ledbury vicarage. From 1544 to his death in 1547 Elton served as Chancellor of the cathedral. The *Register*, described as 'begun and collected by the venerable man John Elton', he compiled as a cartulary of all the medieval records he could find relating to the St Katherine's estates. Its numerous deeds, some 80 court rolls plus rentals, are discussed in earlier chapters. Given his close relationship with Booth, his even closer relationship with Bishop Skyppe (1539-52) and his position within the cathedral hierarchy, Elton was well placed to defend what he considered his own interests.[224]

St Katherine's estates were saved but its chantry priests had to go. A number will have moved on to serve as parish priests elsewhere. John Potter, former chaplain of the chantry of the Virgin Mary in the parish church, held the benefice of Tedstone Wafre. Other chaplains served as schoolmasters. Under the mastership of Edward Baskerville, the character of St Katherine's appears to have changed. A former Franciscan friar who assisted in the dissolution of friaries, he had gained a prebend at the cathedral in 1540 and served as chancellor from 1555 to 1567. Some of the hospital accommodation intended for the poor and needy was now being granted to members of the clergy. A deed of November 1550 was witnessed not only by Baskerville as Master but also by 'William Hyler, clerk and Thomas Kylling, clerk'. Of the latter further details are provided by a list of pensions to former chantry priests of April 1554, the first year of Mary Tudor's reign. There he is described as 'a former chaplain of St Anne's chantry in Ledbury, of honest conversation, aged 80 years old and receiving an annual pension of £4 6s 8d'. When he was buried, in Ledbury churchyard in 1558, the burial register tells us he was a 'priest of the hospital'. Next year the register contains a further entry for 'Gryffyn Fouler, sometime Chauntry Priest and after Priest of the Hospital' who, according to the pension list of 1554, when he was aged 53, was also a former chaplain of St Anne's chantry. Of Hyler nothing further is known. In his case we probably have the internal reappointment of a chaplain, similar to that of Robert Grynsell at Hereford, who had been chaplain at Foliot's chantry of St Katherine in the episcopal chapel. In the 1554 list Grynsell had a pension of £4 11s 9d, and a stipend of £3 0s 10d as a vicar choral of the cathedral.[225]

Objects of Idolatry and Superstition

Henry VIII's injunctions of 1538 had launched a vigorous attack on 'offerings of money, candles or tapers to images or relics or kissing or licking the same' as 'tending to idolatry and superstition which of all other offences God doth most detest and abhor'. Payments for candles ceased but, for the moment, images remained. No longer were country folk, such as Adam le Strete, able to ensure that their candles, funded from small rents, in his case 5d and 1d from *Clerkennesfelde* and *Baystefelde* in Ledbury foreign, would 'burn before God, the Virgin, the Blessed Katherine in the church of the Blessed Katherine' for their own souls and those of their parents.[226]

In February 1541 Henry himself ordered the removal of relics and shrines but it was only after Edward VI's accession that the shrine of St Thomas and all relics were removed from Hereford cathedral. In 1548 his royal council issued a third set of injunctions, ordering the removal of all images and prohibiting all religious processions. In the north and the southwest of the country there was stout resistance to the reforms, but in the dioceses of Hereford and Chester opposition was passive. Senior members of the chapter must have decided to take pre-emptive action, for some of Cantilupe's bones were removed from the shrine and secreted nearby. Later, possibly in 1610, his relics were even carried in procession around the city. That was not all. In 1841 carved alabaster fragments of a 'very gorgeous elaborate mid 14th-century shrine', evidently that of Cantilupe, were found hidden in the groin of the central tower of the cathedral. With them was a fine processional cross, 2 feet high, with Christ crucified on the head and symbols of the evangelists on a blue enamel background on the arms and the base of the cross, and also two or three small crosses (Fig.14.3).

As late as 1560 Bishop Scory refers to dean and vicars choral still observing the canonical hours and celebrating private masses.[227]

At Ledbury St Katherine's impressive collection of relics, including such treasures as the fragment of the 'cross of (Our) Lord', 'small parts' of the vestments of the Virgin and the 'oils' and a 'piece of the tunic' of St Thomas (Cantilupe), as well as 'items of the blood, hair and vestments of Thomas (Becket) the martyr', will have been taken from the security of its aumbry to be disposed of. Additionally the oft-mentioned and much favoured images of the Blessed Virgin and St Katherine, with all others, were removed. Whether, as with Cantilupe's relics, some were rescued and found their way, at least temporarily, to safe-keeping in the homes of the faithful will have depended on the character of Elton's successors. Of John Lord (1547-50) little is known but the general tenor of events in the town suggests that the ruling

Fig 14.3 Hereford Cathedral: Processional Cross found on the belfry floor in 1841

oligarchy, with their overriding interest in speculation in lands formerly held by the church, had little if any concern for such things.

Images were not the only objects of attack. Pictures of the world of the blessed and the damned also caused grave offence to those who, holding the doctrine of justification by faith, denied the efficacy of good works and ceremonies in salvation. The Rood and the Doom were swept away. Christ crucified was replaced by the royal coat of arms, symbol of royal supremacy. The Doom, the Last Judgment, was painted over so that texts, such as the Ten Commandments, the Lord's Prayer and the Beatitudes, could be displayed. At Kempley the master and brethren as rectors must have been responsible for taking down the carved Rood over the chancel arch and whitewashing over the accompanying frescoes of the Virgin and St John, together with the 'Glories of Heaven' in the chancel. At Pixley the 14th-century screen with rood beam remains and it is notable that the only place in the county where any trace of the Doom can be seen is at Madley, a church granted by Bishop Giles de Braose to the canons of Hereford about 1200. At St Katherine's, after the departure of the chantry chaplains, weekly services were conducted by a resident chaplain and, although the arch between hall and chapel would have remained open, the Doom would have been painted over and the Rood replaced by the royal arms. In the 19th century dark brown painted timber partitioning closed off the chapel from the hall it was built to serve, and the fundamental relationship between chapel and hall was destroyed.

Edward VI's injunctions also ordered the destruction of all images of a superstitious character in glass windows. These Elizabeth reissued in 1559 but countermanded the following year. Such images in glass could now be removed only with the express consent of the bishop. Writing in 1577, William Harrison explains: 'Onelie stories in glasse windows are excepted (from destruction) for want of sufficient store of newe stuff and the extreame charge' of inserting plain glass. The extraordinary quantity of medieval stained glass preserved at Great Malvern and Tewkesbury suggests that the Grandison glazing programme was in all probability a victim, not of the reformers, but of subsequent neglect. It is ironic that one of the few remnants of St Katherine's medieval painted glass is the key of St Peter, symbol of papal power.[228]

The replacement of the medieval altars, with their five consecration crosses signifying Christ's five wounds, by timber communion tables was the work of the reforming bishops. These included Skyppe who, prior to nomination as bishop of Hereford, had been chaplain to Queen Anne Boleyn and earlier, it is believed, temporarily abbot of Wigmore. In 1551 the altar of St Laurence's, Ludlow, was removed and the stones carefully set into the paving in case of future need. At St Katherine's any trace of the stone altar has been overlaid by the mid-19th-century altar platform with its Godwin glazed encaustic tiles. The present communion table, with its moulded rails, small brackets and turned legs, is of the early 17th century. As few medieval stone altars still remain in the county, as at Pipe and Lyde and Stretton Sugwas, it is possible that St Katherine's was not removed until that time.[229]

During the tumult of the Reformation much was lost, especially the mystery of religion and sense of community which had played such an important part in sustaining Bishop Hugh Foliot's 'poor and needy' in their distress. Although St Katherine's managed to retain its lands, the historic role of its chaplains, the offering up of prayers for the swift passage of the souls of benefactors through purgatory, had to be abandoned. Foliot had founded St Katherine's for the care of souls. Now its primary role became one of care for the bodies, not the souls, of the 'poor and needy'.

Appendix 1

An inventory of all the goods, movable and immovable, chattels, books, letters, chargers, instruments, relics, and other ecclesiastical ornaments belonging to the Hospital of the blessed Katherine of Ledbury made on Tuesday after the Festival of the Conversion of St Paul, Apostle, A.D. 1315 (27 January 1315/16) by Robert de Byford, vicar in the (cathedral) Church of Hereford, the Venerable Men ... the Dean and Chapter of Hereford ... by special commission on the entry of Brother Philip de Chaddesleye, *custos* of the aforesaid hospital appointed by the said ... Dean and Chapter.

(1) Books
Firstly there were found there two mass books and the Canon, separately.
Two antiphoners with notes. One legendary (book of acts of the saints) bound in two volumes.
One bound psalter in which is contained a martyrology with the Rule of the house.
Item one bound psalter in which is contained a hymnary and a certain part of an antiphoner.
Item one bound psalter with a hymnary and services for saints days without notes.
Item one bound portiphorium without notes for the master of the house.
Item two bound graduals, with notes, one containing a troper.
Item one bound troper with notes.
Item one bound ordinal.
Item one unbound book of placebo (vespers for the dead), old.
Item one unbound troper, old and worn.
Item one book in French which begins '*Coment Sapientes ...*'

(2) Ornaments
Item there were found there two silver gilt chalices with patens.
One pair of vestments for solemn feasts, viz an alb with silk parure, a stole and maniple of rich material with an amice embroidered with gold, and a chasuble of brocade, one striped tunic of silk.
Item one Sunday alb with apparel and a chasuble of cloth of Tars.
Item four week-day albs with three chasubles of fustian.
Item 9 embroidered altar cloths.
Item three towels.
Item four surplices for the brothers, two rochets.
Three pewter cruets.
Two chests for books and ecclesiastical vestments to be put in.

3) Relics

One phylactery in which is contained a small part of the vestment of blessed Mary with other unknown relics.

Item another phylactery in which is contained part of the vestment of St Mary and of the vestment of St Thomas, and certain other relics.

Item (a fragment) from the cross of (our) lord (and) from the cross of St Andrew.

A certain small silver cross.

Item another larger silver cross with small silver images.

Item another cross, of latten, old.

Item a silver pyx in which is contained oils of St Thomas with other minute items.

Item one silk purse in which are the relics of St Stephen, pope, with certain other minute (items).

Item another purse in which are contained the bones of Saints Symon and St Stephen and certain other relics, that is part of a wax candle kindled with celestial fire on the vigil of Easter.

Item another purse, white, in which is contained items of the blood, hair and vestment of the blessed Thomas the martyr.

Item another purse in which are contained tiny stones.

Item another purse of red muslin containing a small piece of the chasuble of the blessed Denis.

Item another purse, black, containing a certain small bone of the blessed Andrew and a certain piece of wood of the cross of St Andrew and a certain piece of the tunic of St Thomas.

Item a little ivory box in which is contained the common seal of the house of which the keys (are held by) the master of the house and the brethren.

(4) Writings

In the sacristy in one large deed box 68 deeds and writings for tenements in Ledebury borough and Ledebury foreign and 44 writings of John Garsant of tenements at Ledebury.

Item in another deed box 2 deeds of title of the house and 1 papal bull, 20 letters of various indulgences for benefactors of the said house by divers episcopal grants.

Item in one chest 22 writings for tenements in Estenore and 23 for tenements in Storchintone.

Item in one deed box 8 writings and 2 feet of fines levied for tenements in Kempeley.

Item in one deed box 18 writings for tenements in Westone and Yarchull, Hyda and Berga.

Item in one deed box 20 writings for tenements in Donyntone.

Item in one deed box 24 writings for tenements in Alkrugg, Masnoton and Colewelle.

Item in one deed box 8 writings for tenements in Walynton and ... at Estenor.

(5) Lands and Rents (at Ledbury with Eastnor, Cradley and Berrow)

Item there are there in the lands held by the said hospital 4 burgages.

Item for rents of assize in Ledbury 66s.

Item at la Hyde in the parish of Credely 38s 6d.

Item at la Berwe 24s.

Item for arable land at Ledebury 180 acres of land and it is worth 60s 8d per annum viz 4d per acre. And $9^{1}/_{2}$ acres of meadow land which are worth 9s 6d at 1s per acre.

Item 31 acres of pasture worth 10s 4d at 4d per acre.

Item 4 acres of underwood worth 12d per acre.

Item there are in another place 5 acres of underwood and moreland worth 20d per annum at 4d per acre.

Item a certain water mill at Malmespole valued at 4 loads of corn, each load worth 4s (16s per annum) ... which mill is worn out and almost collapsed.

(6) Tables and Utensils (at Ledbury)

Item in the hall 4 tables with trestles, 2 long benches and 3 other short ones, 1 bench cover of pales, 2 andirons of iron with iron forks, 1 basin with a cauldron for washing.

Item in the cellar 1 brewhouse, 4 large bins for malt, 4 barrels, 2 casks, 10 barrels, 1 tankard, 6 wooden cups, 18 silver spoons, 1 store for holding bread, 1 pewter salt-cellar, 6 table cloths, 4 towels.

In the kitchen 1 large bronze ale measure of 12 gallons, 2 small ale measures, 3 other small measures and 6 other small measures called posnets, 1 cup and 1 lead cauldron, 11 pewter dishes with 11 saucers of the same metal, 1 stone mill for salt, 2 mortars with pestles.

In the washhouse 1 big trough divided for the brethren and the community, 1 table for bread-making.

In the larder 4 ox carcasses and 20 salt bacons.

In the dormitory a bed for the master and for 5 of the brethren of the said house, 1 large chest and 2 smaller ones with a double set of clothing for each brother.

(7) Animals (at Ledbury)

Item in the stable 2 draught animals (horses) for the cart, 1 cart bound with iron (*careta*) and decayed with trace and harness.

In the cattle shed 12 oxen, 2 wagons bound with iron (*plaustra*), 2 ploughs with trappings, 2 hoes of iron, 2 ropes for the wagon, 2 forks, 2 spades, 4 shovels, 2 mattocks, 2 bills.

In the byre 120 sheep with *creckes* (cratch, a rack, manger or cradle for feeding beasts) and hurdles for pens.

In the piggery 1 boar, 4 sows, 16 hoggetts, 19 piglets with 3 troughs for feeding.

Item in the barn by estimation 12 loads of corn, 8 of oats, 6 of peas and beans and 4 wagon-loads of hay.

(8) Kempeleye

Item at Kempeleye the church is in our own use and is worth £8 per annum at farm.

Item of rents of assize 15s 6d.

Item 247$^{1}/_{2}$ acres of land worth £4 2s 6d per annum at 4d per acre and 10 acres of meadow worth 10s per annum at 12d per acre and 3$^{1}/_{2}$ acres of more worth 2s per annum.

Item from livestock 2 draught animals (carthorses) and 12 oxen.

Item in the store 1 cart bound with iron (*careta*) with harness, 2 wagons bound with iron (plaustra) with harness, 2 ploughs with trappings, 2 iron hoes, 1 bronze ale measure, 1 tripod, 1 pail, 2 shovels, 2 bills, 1 mattock.

Item there are in the barn by estimation 20 loads of corn from the demesne land, 12 loads of oats, 6 loads of peas and beans.

(9) Westone

Item at Westone the church is in our own use which is estimated at £4 per year and fines there 10s 4d. Of rents of assize ...

Item 96$^{1}/_{2}$ acres of arable land worth 48s 3d per annum at 6d per acre.

Item 7 acres of meadow land worth 14s per annum at 2s an acre.

Item 1$^{1}/_{2}$ acres of pasture worth 2s 3d per annum.

Item 2 acres of more worth 11d (?) per annum.

Item from livestock 1 draught animal (horse), 6 oxen, 1 bull, 10 cows, 8 bullocks, 6 heifers, 7 calves.

Item from dead stock 1 wagon bound with iron with harness, 1 plough with trappings, 1 iron mattock, 1 sieve.

Item 1 bronze measure, 1 tripod, 1 table with trestles, 1 cheese mould.

Item in the barn by estimation 16 loads of grain, 10 of oats, 10 of peas and beans.

Item hay stored in sacks.

(10) Yarchull

Item the church of Yarchull in our own use which is estimated at 106s 8d and 3 acres of land worth 18d per annum and ... acre of pasture worth 7s.

Item at la Hyde 17s rents from tenements there.

Item 1 acre of meadow ground at 18d.

Item in the barn there at Yarchull by estimation 12 loads of grain, 3 of oats and 3 of peas and beans.

(11) Memorandum

The said house is charged each year with payment of 12s 7d to the lord bishop of Hereford.

Item 3d to Robert de Masinton.

Item to John Saff ... and 1lb of cumin.

Item 6d to the hospital of Dunemor.

Item for the mill of Malmespol 1d.

Item to the lord of Kempeley 1 pair of spurs of ungilt silver and 1lb of pepper.

Suits

For various suits of court 7s 8d.

(12) Pensions

Item the said house pays to the lords, the dean and chapter, 40s per annum and to the prior of Hereford 10s for the church ...

Item to the vicar of Marcle 20s.

Item to the lord archdeacon of Hereford for procuration and synod of the church of Weston 6s 8d.

Item for the procuration and synod of the church of Kempeley 7s 8d.

Item to dom. Nicholas, chaplain, when he stays at the said hospital, 3s for shoe money.

(13 Debts)

These are the debts of the house of St Katherine of Ledbury on the day of the Conversion of St Paul the Apostle AD 1315.

To Richard Bras of Studdley £10.

To Robert Joye of Ledbury 10s.

To William Miller 18s.

To Thomas Vigerous 40s.

Total £13 8s.

These are the debts owing to the aforesaid house on the day and year aforesaid.

Executors of Master Walter of Ludwardine £6 4s 8d.

Emeritus (Emeric) Pancefot 13s 4d.

Item from various debtors by particulars of rents unpaid 40s.

Total £8 18s.

HD&CA 1658a

Appendix 2

St Katherine's Hospital, Ledbury: List of Masters, 1239-1562?

(earliest and latest records)

1239-50	William[1]
nd	Adam Beyvin[2]
1259-72	Adam de Putley[3]
nd	John de Marcle[4]
nd	Richard de Evesham[5]
d1316?	John de Wynyard[6]
1316-28	Philip de Chaddesley[7]
1333-37	Stephen le Yong[8]
1339-49	Gilbert de Middleton[9]
1350	Richard[10]
1350-51	Thomas de Ledbury[11]
1351-53	Thomas de Bradewardyn[12]
1354-62	William le Brut[13]
1362-68	Hugh Cradock[14]
1368-73	John Wynd[15]
1384-97	William Pykesley[16]
1398-1409	John Malvern[17]
-1417	Nicholas Lyney[18]
1417-	Robert Prees[19]
1420-29	Nicholas Lyney[20]
1429-	Richard Lye[21]
1443-51	Richard Pede[22]
1459-83	John Vaughan[23]
1483-1502	Richard Wycherley[24]
1502-15	Thomas Blundell[25]
1515-47	John Elton alias Baker[26]
1547-50	John Lorde[27]
1550-62	Edward Baskerville[28]

Note

There are three masters for whom only undated charter evidence survives. The ten Hereford cathedral charters in which he appears show that Adam Beyvin (Beyvyn) was successor to Brother William, first master.[29] In the last two he is identified as keeper or preceptor of St Katherine's. In HD&CA 616, a charter of Juliana, daughter of Alan *de Walintone*, concerning a tenement in

Walintone, the witnesses include such local worthies as Roger *de Berwe* (Berrow), Walter *Marescall* and Hugh *de Furches*. With Alan they witnessed a number of the charters in which Brother William appears. The witnesses to HD&CA 1889, relating to a messuage and 6 acres of arable at *More* in *Estenoure*, include William Chamberlain, another member of that group, whilst Walter *Marescall* is a witness again in HD&CA 3701 where Adam Beyvin, now canon of Hereford cathedral, grants an annual rent of 8s to St Katherine's, one half for the 'sustenance' of brothers and sisters, the other to the 'pittancer' for the 'infirm lying in the hospital'. A further 2s was to sustain 'a lamp burning by night'. This complements the evidence brought forward by Julia Barrow in *Fasti Ecclesiae Anglicanae: 1066-1300* (2002) and that of the Patent rolls that Beyvin went on to become a canon by August 1263. He should not be confused with Adam de Ledbury, 'seneschal of our hospital' prior to August 1234.

John de Little Marcle is Master in three undated charters.[30] Again witness lists provide evidence as to date. In a charter relating to lands at *Berga*, Berrow, they include Robert *de Furches* and Absalon, the clerk. Both were important local officials. In 1286 men who had entered the bishop's chase at Colwall with bows, arrows and hounds and shot a deer appeared before William Mortimer, Swinfield's seneschal, and Robert *de Furches* as bailiff. Robert had been appointed bailiff of Whitbourne by Cantilupe but under Swinfield assumed a wider role.[31] He appears seven times between 1283 and 1289 in Swinfield's register and was responsible for the local entries in the *Red Book*.[32] This date of the 1280s is confirmed by what is known about Absalon the clerk, for he appears in the same register as clerk to the sheriff or sub-sheriff in 1281 and 1286.[33]

For Richard de Evesham the evidence is much less helpful. The only secure dating is as a contemporary of Reginald de Grey during the long period Grey was lord of Kempley manor, 1266-1308.[34]

1. HD&CA 1791; 7018/1/3/119-20.
2. HD&CA 7018/1/3/48-9 & 49.
3. *TB&GAS* 36 (1913) 137; HD&CA 1757.
4. HD&CA 1167; 3729; 3708a; 70181/1/3/9, 39 & 133.
5. HD&CA 7018/1/3/6, 27 & 116; 3703.
6. 'Once Master 1316', Kempley Court Roll 6 May 1316.
7. HD&CA 1658a; 3276.
8. HD&CA 1723; 1729; 3292.
9. HD&CA 3293; *Reg Trillek* 376.
10. HD&CA 7018/1/3/140.
11. *Reg Trillek* 505; HD&CA 3299.
12. HD&CA 3299, 1730. Resigned 2 Dec 1351.
13. Appointment HD&CA 1730; Kempley Court Roll 1362.
14. HD&CA 7018/1/3/12, 12-13.
15. *Reg Lewis de Charlton* 69; HD&CA 7018/1/3/146.
16. *Reg Gilbert* 61 & 122; HD&CA 1779 fxii.
17. *Cal Papal L* v, 263; *Reg Mascall* 184; died 1422.
18. *Reg Lacy* 120.
19. *Reg Lacy* 120.
20. *Reg Lacy* 116; *Reg Spofford* 354; HD&CA 1226, 1796.
21. HD&CA 1796.
22. HD&CA 3742; *Reg Boulers* 22, 23. Canon of Hinton, house in Hereford 1452.
23. HD&CA 1638; 7031/1 f175r; *Reg Stanbury* 175.
24. HD&CA 3749; 7031/1 f175r-v; *Berrow Court Roll* 1483.
25. HD&CA 7031/1 f175r-v; 3749.
26. HD&CA 7031/1 f213v; 1840.
27. HD&CA 7031/1 f103r-v; 1992.
28. HD&CA 7031/1 ff103r-v, 169r; 1994.
29. HD&CA 616, 625, 752, 865, 912, 1889, 2461, 3701, 7018/1/3/48-9 & /49.
30. HD&CA 3708, 3709, 7081/1/3/133.
31. *Reg Cantilupe* 108; *Reg Swinfield* 112.
32. *Reg Swinfield* 93, 112, 127, 128, 138, 147, 216.
33. *Reg Swinfield* 40, 95.
34. Baddeley, see n11 in main text.

References

Abbreviations

CPL	*Calendar of Entries in Papal Registers (Letters)* ed W.H.Bliss, PRO 13 vols (1893-1995)	NS	New Series
CPR	*Calendar of Patent Rolls*	Reg	*Reg Cantilupe - Reg Bothe*: Registers of the bishops of Hereford, 1282-1539 (Cantilupe Soc, 1906-21; Canterbury & York Soc, 1907-21)
HD&CA	Hereford Dean & Chapter Archives		
HCRO	Hereford County Record Office	RS	Rolls Series
J	Journal	TWNFC	*Transactions: Woolhope Naturalists Field Club*

1. HD&CA 2175, 1389; *English Episcopal Acta VII: Hereford 1079-1234* ed J.Barrow (1993) nos 348, 342; *Charters and Records of Hereford Cathedral ed W.W.Capes (1908) 68-71. The death of* dean Thomas de Bosbury, 29 Sept 1231, provides *terminus ad quem* for the foundation charter. Barrow, 304-5. HD&CA 3701 has *ad opus infirmorum*.

2. M.Carlin, 'Medieval English hospitals' in *The Hospital in History* ed L.Granshaw & R.Porter (1989) 29-31; R.Gilchrist *Contemplation and Action: The Other Monasticism* (1995) 32-8; *A Roll of the Household Expenses of Richard de Swinfield* I & II, ed J.Webb, Camden Soc OS 59 & 62 (1853 & 1855) 140, 152, cxxxii.

3. R.M.Clay *The Mediaeval Hospitals of England* (1909) 158-62; N.Orme & M.Webster *The English Hospital, 1070-1570* (1995) 50-53. For the role of charity R.M.Swanson *Religion and Devotion in Europe c1215-c1515* (1995) 206-12. The best recent introduction to the subject of purgatory is E.Duffy *The Stripping of the Altars* (1992) 338-76. HD&CA 3696. For Thomas Foliot see Barrow, see n1, xlix, 306, nos 341, 355, 360, 367.

4. HD&CA 7018/1/3/32-3.

5. See p131. *The Cartulary of God's House, Southampton* i, ed J.M.Kaye, Southampton Record Series 20 (1976) xxxiii-iv; HD&CA 3735. Five chaplains are named in HD&CA 7018/1/3/102, 106-7; 760, 3307, 3309, 3310b but six are named in 3733 and in *CPR* 1405-8, 318.

6. Capes, see n1, 61; H.Wharton *Anglia Sacra* ii (1691) 310-11; J.Hillaby, 'The saint that never slept: Robert de Bethune, bishop of Hereford 1131-48' *Friends of Hereford Cathedral: Annual Report* 46 (1980) 21-42; M.Rubin *Charity and Community in Medieval Cambridge* (1987) 58-70 and B.Tierney, 'The Decretists and the "Deserving Poor"' *Comparative Studies in Society and History* i (1958-9) 360-73. examine contemporary views on charity.

7. HD&CA 2175.

8. J.Hillaby *Ledbury: A Medieval Borough* (2nd ed, 1997) 9-18, 25-42, map on 24.

9. For Walter II de Lacy J.Hillaby, 'Hereford Gold, Part 2: The Clients of the Jewish Community at Hereford, 1179-1253: Four Case Studies' *TWNFC* 45(i) (1985) 195-239; J.Hillaby, 'A magnate amongst the marchers: Hamo of Hereford, his family and clients 1218-1253' *Jewish Historical Studies* 31 (1988-90) 23-82. For de Lacy manors in the Frome valley W.E.Wightman *The Lacy Family in England and Wales, 1066-1194* (1966) 118-19.

10. J.Hillaby, 'Colonisation, crisis-management and debt: Walter de Lacy and the lordship of Meath, 1189-1241' *Ríocht na Mídhe* viii(4) (1992/3) 1-50.

11. Barrow, see n1, no.348; Capes, see n1, 68-70. For valuations of the three churches Record Commission: *Taxatio Ecclesiastica c. AD 129*1 (1802) 158, 160-1. W.StClair Baddeley, 'The History of Kempley Manor and Church, Gloucestershire' *Bristol & Gloucs Archaeol Soc Trans* 36 (1913) 130-9.

12. Hillaby 'Hereford Gold 2' (1985) 228-30, 233-7; *Monasticon* vi, 1035-6; C.Hutchison *The Hermit Monks of Grandmont* (1989) 94, n2 quoting Christ's College Cambridge MS, God's House Drawer C; *Reg Bothe* 185-7; R.W.Eyton *Antiquities of Shropshire* v (1854) 296-9; *Reg Gilbert* 65-6; M.Faraday *Ludlow 1085 - 1660: A Social, Economic and Political History* (1991) 64-9; D.Lloyd *Broad Street: its houses and residents through eight centuries* Ludlow Research Paper 3 (1979) 10, plan facing p1, figs 18a&b.

13. A.Gwynn & R.N.Hadcock *Medieval Religious Houses of Ireland* (repr Dublin, 1988) 313, 128, 106; *Calendar of Documents relating to Ireland* ed H.S.Sweetman (1875) nos 1909, 2295, 2302; *Calendar of Charter Rolls* (1235) 215; *Irish Cartularies of Llanthony Prima & Secunda* ed E.StJ.Brooks (Dublin, 1953) 81-4, 101.

14. *The Golden Legend* trans W.G.Ryan, II (1993) 334-41.

15. For the cult's adoption V.Ortenberg *The English Church and the Continent in the Tenth and Eleventh Centuries* (1992) 256-8; K.J.Lewis, *The Cult of St Katherine of Alexandria in Late Medieval England* (2000) 45-110; C.Jamison *The History of the Royal Hospital of St Katherine by the Tower of London* (1952); Ryan, see n14, 339.

16. Barrow, see n1, no 343; Bodleian MS Top Gen d.13 reproduced in N.Drinkwater, 'Hereford Cathedral: The Bishop's Chapel of St Katherine and St Mary Magdalene' *Archaeol Jnl* 111 (1954) 129-37; idem *TWNFC* (1957) 256-60; HD&CA 2098; *Valor Ecclesiasticus* Record Commission, 6 vols (1810-24) III, 13; *Reg Bothe* 273; F.Mugnier *Les Savoyards en Angleterre au XIIIe siecle et Pierre d'Aigueblanche, eveque d'Hereford* (Chambery, 1890); a copy of Aquablanca's will, pp308-16, is in Hereford Cathedral Library. Barrow points out that Aquablanca's college was dedicated also to St Mary Magdalen.

17. See p105.

18. HD&CA 3754, 3575, 4248, 3564: 'An Act ... to rebuild the Almshouse of St Katherine's Hospital for the Better Regulation of the Affairs of that Charity', 59 GIII c22.

19. HD&CA 1658a; 7018/1/3/26a, 27, 29, 33, 91-2, 140, 141, 141-2, 147, 152, 153, 154, 154-5, 160; *Reg Swinfield* 536; *Reg Orleton* 386, 388; *Reg Trilleck* 376; *Reg Lewis Charlton* 69; *Reg Gilbert* 122; F.C.& P.E.Morgan *A Concise List of Seals belonging to the Dean and Chapter of Hereford Cathedral* (1966) 6.

20. J.C.Dickinson *The Origins of the Austin Canons and their Introduction into England* (1950) 145; Orme & Webster, see n3, 69-75.

21. For the infirmary-hall plan and subsequent architectural development of the English hospital and almshouse W.H.Godfrey *The English Almshouse* (1955) 20-6 *et seq*; E.Prescott *The English Medieval Hospital, 1050-1640* (1992) 5-22 *et seq*; Clay, see n3, 112-25 and Orme & Webster, see n3, 85-92.

22. Dickinson, see n20, 145. The Dudston regulations are in the *Registrum Magnum* of Lanthony Secunda, Gloucester, PRO

C115/K2/6683 microfilm in Gloucestershire County Record Office. C.A.Swainson, 'The Hospital of Saint Mary, in Chichester' *Sussex Archaeol Coll* 24 (1872) 41-62; P.H.Cullum, 'St Leonard's Hospital, York: the spatial and social analysis of an Augustinian hospital' *Advance in Monastic Archaeology* ed R.Gilchrist *et al*, BAR British S 227 (1993) 11-18. For other regulations Orme & Webster, see n3, 293-5.

23. HD&CA 1658a. The 1316 Ledbury inventory should be compared with the 1303 inventory of St Bartholomew's, Bristol, Glos CRO D340a/T143 translated in *Trans Bristol & Gloucs Archaeol Soc* 74 (1955) 181-4 and that of the rooms, buildings, lands and tenements of St Mary of Ospringe in 1561, G.H.Smith, 'The Excavations of the Hospital of St Mary of Ospringe commonly called Maison Dieu' *Archaeol Cantiana* 95 (1979) 90-107.

24. For the books listed see C.Wordsworth & H.Littlehales *The Old Service-Books of the English Church* (1904) and for inventories of books at God's House in 1362 & 1414-15 Kaye, see n5, I, xci-xcii.

25. HD&CA 7018/1/3/68-9, 3681.

26. Swainson, see n22, 47; *Cartulary of St Mark's Hospital, Bristol* ed C.D.Ross, Bristol Record Soc 21 (1959) 9. For *familia* and *hospitalis* Kaye see n5, I, xxxii-iii.

27. Godfrey, see n21, 28-9, 34.

28. HD&CA 7018/6/19/14; F.C.Morgan, 'The Accounts of St Katherine's Hospital, Ledbury 1584-1595' *TWNFC* 34 (1952) 88-132.

29. Swainson, see n22, 46-7; Dudston Statutes 2 & 23 in E.J.Kealey Medieval Medicus: *A Social History of Anglo-Norman Medicine* (1981) 108-9, 200-1.

30. HD&CA 1791, 3722.

31. HD&CA 3659, 3664, 3666, 3668, 3679, 3685, 3722.

32. For brethren and sisters Swainson, see n22, 44-7; S.E.Rigold, 'The Hospital of St Mary, Ospringe' *Archaeol Cantiana* 30 (1914) 34; C.Thomas, B.Sloane & C.Phillpotts *Excavations at the Priory and Hospital of St Mary Spital, London* (1997) 36-7, 43-4, 52-3, 71-3, 79, 83-4; Clay, see n3, 145-7, 152-6; Orme & Webster, see n3, 80-3. For Brother Roger see p61. Sisters, women and medicine in medieval society are discussed by C.Rawcliffe *Medicine and Society in Later Medieval England* (1995) 204-13.

33. For hospital precincts, water supply and drains C.J.Bond, 'Water management in the urban monastery' in *Advances in Monastic Archaeology* ed R.A.Gilchrist & H.Mytum, BAR 227 (1993) 43-78; R.A.Gilchrist, 'Christian bodies and souls: archaeology of life and death in later medieval hospitals' in *Death in Towns* ed S.Basset (1992) 101-18; Ross, see n26, xxxiv, 75-6; G.H.Smith, see n23, 83, 86-7, figs 2 & 3; Thomas *et al*, see n32, 18-19, 45-6, 50-1, 54, 63, 94, 98-100; R.Price & M.Ponsford *St Bartholomew's Hospital, Bristol: The Excavations of a Medieval Hospital, 1976-8* (1998) 84, 108, 110, 125, 222-3; B.Durham, 'The Infirmary and Hall of the Medieval Hospital of St John the Baptist at Oxford' *Oxoniensia* 56 (1991) 29-34, 66-70. For water supply etc at Ledbury J.Lydiard's *Plan of Ledbury, 1788; Ledbury Tithe Map, 1841; Ledbury Enclosure Act, 1813*; HCRO K13/17: Ledbury Improvement Trustees, *Letter to Subscribers, Nov 1820*.

34. For cemeteries and burial Thomas et al, see n32, 115-24; Price & Ponsford, see n33, 81, 107-8, 119, figs 35-7; G.H.Smith, see n23, 81, 91, fig 2; Clay, see n3, 199-200; Orme & Webster, see n3, 106, pl 16.

35. *The Registers of Ledbury: 1. Baptisms, Marriages & Burials, 1556-1576* (1899) 113, 118.

36. A.T.Bannister in his 'Descriptive Catalogue of Manuscripts dealing with St Katherine's, Ledbury' *TWNFC* (1923) 231-53 lists169 of both original deeds and those transcribed into Elton's *Register*. In this, 232, he gives 2 Edward I, 1273-4, as the date for the inspection and confirmation of Foliot's charter and the seven sets of deeds and the Hereford City Library copy of W.Dugdale *Monasticon Anglicanum* ed J.Caley (2nd ed, 1846) V, 685-6 has an ink amendment (by Bannister?) to that date. However *CPR 1327-30*, 245 confirms Dugdale's *Monasticon*, that the date was 2 Edward III, 25 Jan 1328-24 Jan 1329. Elton's *Register* is HD&CA 7018/1. The separate paginations are 7018/1/1-3. The first series is 52 pages, the second, of court rolls and some rentals, is 106 pages and the third, of deeds etc, is 170.

37. See p34.

38. R.H.Hilton *A Medieval Society* (1966) 115; Webb I, see n2, 7, 38.

39. HD&CA 1658a.

40. H.L.Somers-Cocks *Eastnor and its Malvern Hills* (1923) 83.

41. HD&CA 7018/1/3/35.

42. B.Coplestone-Crow *Herefordshire Place-Names* BAR British Series 214 (1989) 78.

43. HD&CA 7018/1/3/36; P.Sawyer *Anglo-Saxon Charters* (1968) no 1306; H.P.R.Finberg *The Early Charters of the West Midlands* (1972) no 108; E.Ekwall *English River Names* (1968) 181.

44. HD&CA 3659, 3677. Other transactions include 1728, 1741, 3664, 3678, 3682. R.E.Zupko *British Weights and Measures* (Madison, 1977) 18.

45. HD&CA 1728, 7018/1/3/119-20.

46. HD&CA 3666.

47. HD&CA 1744, 3702, 3703.

48. HD&CA 7018/1/3/32-3, /42-3.

49. M.Bowden, 'English Heritage: Malvern Hills Archaeological Survey' *Worcestershire Recorder* 63 (Spring, 2001) 8-9.

50. HD&CA 1888.

51. HD&CA 7018/1/3/1; *Lay Subsidy Roll for the County of Worcestershire c1280* ed J.W.Willis Bund & I.Amphlett, Worcs Hist Soc 1 (1893) 44; *Thomas Habington: A Survey of Worcestershire 1* Worcs Hist Soc 5 (1895) 125, 131.

52. P.H.Sawyer *Anglo-Saxon Charters* (1968) nos 216, 786; D.Hooke *Worcestershire Anglo-Saxon Charter-Bounds* (1990) 199-203; B.Grundy, 'Saxon Charters of Worcestershire I' *Birmingham Archaeol Soc Trans* 52 (1927) 172-5.

53. D.Hooke *Anglo-Saxon Landscapes* (1985) 180-3; *Compotus Rolls of the Priory of Worcester of the XIV and XV Centuries* ed S.G.Hamilton, Worcs Hist Soc, 26 (1910) 15, 23; *The State of the Bishopric of Worcester 1728-1808* ed M.Ransome, Worcs Hist Soc, NS 6 (1968) 116; HCRO HE/1/133677 *Red Book* pa 124, 127.

54. HD&CA 7018/1/3/1.

55. HD&CA 7018/1/3/155-6, 156-7.

56. For Hamo and Manasser J.Hillaby, 'Hereford Gold:Irish, Welsh and English Land. The Jewish Community at Hereford and its Clients, 1179-1253. Part 1' (1984) 358-419; idem (1988-90) see n9, 23-82.

57. HD&CA 7018/1/3/155-6; J.Hillaby, 'The Worcester Jewry, 1158-1290: Portrait of a Lost Community' *Trans Worcs Archaeol Soc* 3S 12 (1990) 101-6; M.Rubin, 'Development and change in English Hospitals, 1100-1500' in *The Hospital in History* ed L.Granshaw & R.Porter (1989) 48; Rubin (1987) see n6, 218-26.

58. HD&CA 2098, 2013.

59. HD&CA 7018/1/3/157-8.

60. HD&CA 3724, 3725, 3731. For other examples of 'great

necessity' etc see HD&CA 3671, 3698 & 3723.

61. HD&CA 7018/1/3/91; H.G.Richardson *The English Jewry under the Angevin Kings* (1960) 86-100; M.Rubin, 'Development and Change in English Medieval Hospitals, 1100-1500' in *The Hospital in History* ed L.Grimshaw & R.Porter (1989) 48.

62. HD&CA 3700.

63. HD&CA 7018/1/3/165; T.H.Lloyd *The English Wool Trade in the Middle Ages* (1977) 299; W.R.Williams *The Parliamentary History of the County of Hereford, 1213-1896* (1896) 74-5, 79.

64. *Reg Cantilupe* xli, 38-9; A.T.Bannister, 'A Lost Cartulary of Hereford Cathedral' (BL Harleian MS 6203) *TWNFC* (1917) 274 refers to goods left by Foliot to St Katherine's in his will; HD&CA 1401 & 2778.

65. HD&CA 1658a, 3695; A.T.Bannister, 'A Transcript of "The Red Book": A detailed account of the Hereford bishopric estates in the 13th century' in *Camden Miscellany* 15, Camden Soc 3S 41 (1929) 22.

66. Coplestone-Crow, see n42, 72, 120-1; *Reg Swinfield* 404; HD&CA 1658a, 7018/1/3/33-8, 53-9, 62; F.Pollock & F.W.Maitland *History of English Law before the time of Edward I* 2 vols (2nd ed, 1898) I, 560-9, 605-34.

67. H.L.Gray *English Field Systems* (repr 1969) 146-8, 150, 153; J.A.Sheppard *Origins and evolution of field and settlement patterns in the parish of Marden* (1979) HCL LC333.7; J.Hillaby, 'Early Christian and Pre-Conquest Leominster' *TWNFC* XLV(iii) (1987) 594-60.

68. M.Kirk *Silent Spaces: The Last of the Great Aisled Barns* (1994) 54, 59. For granges and their economy: C.Platt *The Monastic Grange in Medieval England* (1969); D.H. Williams *The Welsh Cirstercians* ii 91984). For a European viewpoint D.H. Williams *The Cistercians in the Early Middle Ages* (1998) 258-384.

69. Bannister (1929) see n65, 20-1.

70. For sale price of major grains 1165/6-1355/6 and 1350/1-1499/1500 see *The Agrarian History of England and Wales II, 1042-1350* ed H.E.Hallam (1988) 787-95 and *The Agrarian History of England and Wales III, 1348-1500* ed E.Miller (1991) 502-5. For the single harvest in 1369-70 the price was marginally higher. See also I.Kershaw, 'The Great Famine and Agrarian Crisis in England, 1315-22' *Past and Present* 59 (May 1973) 3-50; M.M.Postan & J.Titow, 'Heriots and Prices on Winchester Manors' *Ec Hist R* 11 (1959) 407, graph 1; J.Titow, 'Evidence of Weather in the Account Rolls of the Bishopric of Winchester, 1209-1350' *Ec Hist R* 2S 12 (1960) 384-7; B.F.Harvey, 'The "Crisis" of the Early Fourteenth Century' in B.M.S.Campbell *Before the Black Death* (1991) 1-24.

71. J.Langdon *Horses, Oxen and Technological Innovation* (1986) 127-41.

72. *Walter of Henley and other Treatises on Estate Management and Accounting* ed D.Oschinsky (1971) 318-19; Langdon (1986) see n71, 158-212; J.Langdon, 'Agricultural Equipment' in *The Countryside of Medieval England* ed G.Astill & A.Grant (1988) 86-107, fig 513.

73. Langdon (1986), see n71, 142-56, 224; *Fitzherbert's Book of Husbandry* ed W.W.Skeat, Eng Dialect Soc 37 (1882) 138

74. See Ch 10; HD&CA 3566.

75. HD&CA 3700, 1991; *Reg Lewis Charlton* 70; P.H.Sawyer *Anglo-Saxon Charters* (1968) no 1264; H.P.R.Finberg *Early Charters of the West Midlands* (1972) no 413; A.T.Bannister *Place-Names of Herefordshire* (1916) 203.

76. Oschinsky see n72, 332-3, 282-5; HD&CA 3271. Also see p60.

77. Ch 5 For bounds in 1277 BL Harley MS 6726, in 1394 *Reg Trefnant* 169, in 1575-80 HCRO HE/1 *Swithun Butterfield's Survey*. For bounds of Ledbury Chase see map in Hillaby (1997) see n8, 72. For Malvern Chase B.S.Smith *A History of Malvern* (1964) 13-34.

78. Webb I & II, see n2, 10, 93, 140, 168, xlix-l; HD&CA 7018/1/3/1, 13, 23, 24-5; *Reg Cantilupe* 43.

79. HD&CA 1888, 3665; *Reg Cantilupe* 96; *The Domesday Geography of Midland England* ed H.C.Darby & I.B Terrett (2nd ed, 1971) 75, 106; Bannister (1929), see n65, 18, 20. For *Rudyng* see pp28-29 & n48.

80. HD&CA R1204. For the 3-storey gatehouse of God's House, Southampton Kaye, see n5, figs 2&5.

81. See p28.

82. HD&CA 3264, 3270.

83. Oschinsky, see n72, 338-9; E.Power *The Wool Trade in Medieval England* (repr 1969) 24-8.

84. Oschinsky, see n72, 334-5, 176-7, 188-9; Webb, see n2, I & II, 176, 188-9, clxx.

85. M.L.Ryder *Sheep and Man* (1983) 679-711.

86. HD&CA 1904, 3258, 3259, 3260; 7018/1/3/33 & 36.

87. J.Price *An Historical and Topographical Account of Leominster* (1795) 150-79; Hillaby (1987) see n67, 594-8 discusses the demesne of the four Leominster priory herneys.

88. HD&CA1899. Prentout is not found in P.H.Reaney *The Origin of English Surnames* (1967) or P.Hanks & F.Hodges (Oxford) *Dictionary of Surnames* (1988) but is listed in P.H.Reaney & R.M.Wilson *A Dictionary of English Surnames* (3rd ed, 1991) 361.

89. HD&CA 1658a; O.Rackham *Trees and Woodland in the British Landscape* (1981) 20, 23, 72-3.

90. *Historic Environment Today* 4i (2001) 2.

91. Hillaby (1997) see n8, 7-8.

92. HD&CA 3575, 7018/1/3/91, R1204, 3575.

93. For Elton see p132. The court rolls for Berrow are HD&CA 7018/1/2/1-47; for Kempley /45-61, /97-9; for Weston /71-6, /95-6; for the Hyde, /77-8; and for Ledbury /91-4. As the rolls are in chronological order no individual referencing is made when dates are given in the text.

94. HD&CA R889, 1110, the rolls for Norton, Clehonger, Marden, Holme Lacy, Eggleton and Ploughfield Hundred all commence in 1273. *Select pleas in memorial and other seigneurial courts* ed F.W.Maitland, Seldon Soc 2 (1889); W.J.Hone *The Manor and Manorial Records* (1906) Appendix 1, 243-301.

95. HD&CA 1991, 3536 i, iii, xxxviii.

96. HD&CA 1991, 3475 i-viii.

97. HD&CA 3536 ii & viii. There had been an earlier lease to Wootton in 1558.

98. *Lay subsidy roll for the county of Worcester c1280* ed J.W.Willis Bund & J.Amphlett, Worcs Hist Soc 1 (1893) 44.

99. Pollock & Maitland, see n66, I, 372-3; R.H.Hilton T*he English Peasantry in the Later Middle Ages* (1975) 58 for rates.

100. F.R.H.du Boulay *An Age of Ambition* (1971) 108.

101. Hilton (1975) see n99, 98-100.

102. See p32.

103. HD&CA 3679, 1643, 7018/1/3/27. For 'Netherton mount' see also 1763, 7018/1/3/17-18.

104. Pollock & Maitland, see n66, II, 416-20.

105. See pp30-3; HD&CA 3505, 3509, 3510.

106. HD&CA 3566.

107. S.R.Bassett, 'A Probably Mercian Royal Mausoleum at Winchcombe, Gloucestershire' *Antiq J* 65 (1988) 82-100; J.Hillaby, 'St Oswald and the Revival of Monasticism in the late Anglo-Saxon and Norman Diocese of Worcester' *Trans Worcs Archaeol Soc* 3S 16 (1998) 97-8, 103-5; Oxford, Bodleian MS Hatton 113, ffvr & vi; Cambridge, Corpus

Christi College MS 9, pp7 & 9; J.C.Wall *Shrines of British Saints* (1905) 209-10.

108. J.Bolton, '"The World Upside Down"; Plague as an Agent of Economic and Social Change' in *The Black Death in England* ed M.Ormrod & P.Lindley (1996).

109. *Reg Lacy* 67-81.

110. HD&CA 3697; Capes, see n1, 73.

111. R.A.R.Hartridge *A History of Vicarages in the Middle Ages* (1930, repr 1968) 20-1 quoting Lateran Council IV canon 32; *Reg Spofford* 368; *Reg Stanbury* 187; *Reg Myllyng* 189.

112. *Reg Swinfield* 534, 536; *Reg Orleton* 388; *Reg Trillek* 376; *Reg Lewis Charlton* 69; *Reg Gilbert* 122.

113. Baddeley, see n11, 136-9, 142; *Reg Cantilupe* 245; *Reg Orleton* 82; *Reg Spofford* 368; *Reg Stanbury* 175, 179, 187; *Reg Mylling* 189, 193.

114. David Crouch, quoting PRO Just I/615 m46d, points to a dispute as early as 1253 over the advowson of Yarkhill church when it was claimed that these had been granted by Walter de Lacy to Ralph de Toeny on his marriage to Walter's daughter, Petronilla. However at his death Walter had but two heiresses, his daughters Matilda and Margaret. *Taxatio*, see n11, 158; R.Graham, 'The Taxation of Pope Nicholas IV' in *English Ecclesiastical Studies* (1929) 271-301; M.J.Franklin, 'The Assessment of Benefices for Taxation in 13th-Century Bucks' *Nottingham Med Studies* 29 (1985) 73-85.

115. HD&CA 1316; Barrow, see n1, nos 7, 21, 22, 204, 260. No. 155, like no 7, is spurious. *History and Cartulary of St Peter's, Gloucester* ed W.H.Hart, 1 (1863) 73, 84. For Price see A.T.Bannister, 'The Possessions of St Guthlac's Priory, Hereford' *TWNFC* (1918) 39-41 quoting St Guthlac's Priory Rental, now in HCRO.

116. Hartridge, see n111, 38

117. *Oxford English Dictionary* Rectory 2: 'consisted of tithes alone, reserving a rent'.

118. HD&CA 3333, R1204

119. HD&CA 7018/1/3/50; see pp63, 73 & n1

120. HD&CA 1980, 3553 i, iii, viii, 1321

121. E.W.Tristram *English Medieval Wall Painting: the Twelfth Century* (1944, repr 1988) 42-4, 134-6

122. B.M.Morley, 'The Nave Roof of the Church of St Mary, Kempley, Gloucestershire' *Antiq J* 65 (1985) 101-11; B.M.Morley & D.W.H.Miles, 'The Nave Roof and other Timber Work at the Church of St Mary, Kempley, Gloucestershire: Dendrochronological Dating' *Antiq J* 80 (2000) 294-6

123. *Reg Stanbury* 112

124. R.H.Morris, 'The Local Influence of Hereford Cathedral in the Decorated Period' *TWNFC* 41i (1973) 61-5

125. *Reg Lewis Charlton* 66, 70; *Reg Courtenay* 11; *History and Antiquities of the County of Hereford in Continuation of Duncumb's History: Hundred of Radlow* ed M.G.Watkins (1902) 159.

126. For Bishop John de Grandison see pp 85, 94-5, Fig 8.7.

127. *Reg Spofford* 359, 365; *Reg Stanbury* 175, 177; C.J.Robinson *Mansions and Manors of Herefordshire* (1873) 257; *Reg Mayew* 286; *Reg Bothe* 337; *Reg Foxe* 377; F.C.&P.E.Morgan, 'Some nuns, ex-religious and former chantry priests living in the diocese of Hereford c1554' *TWNFC* 37(ii) (1962) 140; *Valor* see n16, III 36.

128. HD&CA 3536(ii), 3566.

129. HD&CA 1779 fi, x, xi, xii in A.T.Bannister, 'Visitation Returns of the Diocese of Hereford in 1397', Parts I-IV *Eng Hist Rev* 44 (1929) 279-89, 445-53; 45 (1930) 92-101, 444-63. A revised edition of the text by C.&M.Whittick

and translation and further notes by P.E.H.Hair has been deposited in the Herefordshire County Record Office.

130. *Reg Trefnant* 182.

131. *Reg Gilbert* 123.

132. Clay, see n3, 248-9, 191-3.

133. *Anthony Wood: Survey of the Antiquities of the City of Oxford* I ed A.Clark, Oxford Hist Soc 15 (1889) 516-7; Clay, see n3, 190.

134. The *Roman Martyrology in accordance with the reforms of Pope Pius X* (1923) 299; *The Golden Legend* trans W.G.Ryan, 1 (1993) 29-35.

135. I.Barrett, 'The Relics of St Thomas Cantilupe' in *St Thomas Cantilupe, Bishop of Hereford* ed M.Jancey (1982) 181; Lewis, see n15, 52, 60; I.Peña *The Christian Art of Byzantine Syria* (1996) 132-3.

136. E.W.Kemp *Canonisation and Authority in the Western Church* (1948) 56-108.

137. P.H.Daly, 'The Process of canonization in the thirteenth and early fourteenth centuries' and R.C.Finucane, 'Cantilupe as Thaumaturge: Pilgrims and their "Miracles"' in Jancey, see n136, 125-44; A.T.Bannister *The Cathedral Church of Hereford. Its History and Constitution* (1924) 167-75.

138. HD&CA 3156; Capes, see n1, 246-8.

139. D.E.O'Connor in *Age of Chivalry* ed J.Alexander & P.Binski (1987) 212 and Peter Newton's note in N.Pevsner *Herefordshire* (1963) 108.

140. *Reg Swinfield* 230; *Reg Orleton* 76, 77.

141. E.Bond *The Chancel of English Churches* (1916) 204-14.

142. R.Shoesmith, 'St Katherine's Chapel, Ledbury: An Archaeological Investigation of the Blocked Locker in the North Wall' (Report to the Dean & Chapter, 2001).

143. J.Hillaby, 'The Buried Evidence: the Opus Dei', S.Harrison, 'The loose architectural detail' and J.Hillaby, 'Cults, Patrons and Sepulture' in *Dore Abbey* ed R.Shoesmith & R.Richardson (1997) 41, 63-72, 97-8; F.Rose-Troup, 'Bishop Grandisson: Student and Art Lover' *Trans Devon Ass* 60 (1928) 257.

144. *Calendar of Ancient Correspondence concerning Wales* ed J.G.Edwards (1935) 118-21, 135, 159.

145. C.L.Kingsford, 'Sir Otho de Grandison, 1238?-1328' *Trans Ryl Hist Soc* 3 (1909) 150-8; G.E.C.(okayne) *Complete Peerage* 6 (1926) 60-5, 69-73. For Otto and William de Grandison see *The History of the King's Works* I (1963) 244, 370-1 & ns4&1, 377 and for Hugh and Walter, 141, 358, 373, 379.

146. H.E.Mayer *The Crusades* (2nd edn, 1988) 74-5, 135, 146, 191, 203, 224.

147. *CPL* i, 505-9, 530, 579, 594, 599; Kingsford, see n145, 150-8.

148. For the manor of Earley: *Reg Cantilupe* 113, 118, 121-3, 141-2, 154, 185, 211, 213, 217-18, 225-6, 236, 242, 245, 262-3, 267, 283.

149. *Annales Monastici* 4, ed H.R.Luard, RS 36 (1869) 483, 493. See R.C.Finucane, 'Cantilupe as Thaumatuge: Pilgrims and their Miracles' and I.Barrett, 'The Relics of St Thomas Cantilupe' in Jancey, see n136, 142 & 181.

150. HD&CA 1822; Capes, see n1, 199.

151. *CPL* ii, 5, 100, 101, 161, 178, 224, 226, 254, 265, 417, 481; *The Register of John de Grandison 1327-1369* III (1899) 1521. For John's chantry foundation at Ottery see J.Dalton *The Collegiate Church of Ottery St Mary being the Ordinancio et Statuta* (1917).

152. *Reg Cantilupe* xxii-vi; A.L.Moir *The Deans of Hereford* (1968) 16-20.

153. HD&CA 3390.

154. A.G.Vince & T.Wilmott, 'A Lost Tile Pavement at

Tewkesbury Abbey and an Early Fourteenth-Century Tile Factory' *Antiq J* 71 (1991) 158-9 quoting J.P.Brooke-Little *Boutell's Heraldry* (rev ed, 1970) 112; T. Wilmott, 'An early Grandison difference' *Coat of Arms* NS 7 (1988) 112-14..

155. *The Golden Legend* I trans W.G.Ryan (1993) 368-70.

156. P.A.Newton, 'Schools of Glass Painting in the Midlands 1275-1430', unpub London Univ PhD thesis (1961); R.Marks *Stained Glass in England during the Middle Ages* (1993) 161-5; M.Archer, S.Crewe, P.Cormack *English Heritage on Stained Glass: Oxford* (1988) 12, 14; P.A.Newton 'Stained Glass at Oxford' in J.Sherwood & N.Pevsner *Oxfordshire* (1974) 79.

157. Matthew 16:18, 19.

158. R.K.Morris, 'The Gothic Mouldings of the Latin and Lady Chapels' in *Saint Frideswide's Monastery at Oxford: Archaeological and Architectural Studies* ed J.Blair (1990) 182.

159. For the papal indult of 1327 CPL ii, 265. *Les vitraux du chœur de l'église Saint-Ouen de Rouen* I, Corpus Vitrearum Medii Aevi France IV-2/1, ed J.Lafond (Paris, 1970) 21-4, 46-9, pls iii, iv; S.Brown *Stained Glass: An Illustrated History* (1992) 71-2.

160. HD&CA 3390; *Reg Trilleck* 373-84; C.Harper-Bill, 'The English Church and English Religion after the Black Death' in Ormrod & Lindley, see n108, 85-6 & n22, relying on F.A.Gasquet *The Black Death of 1348 and 1349* (2nd ed, 1908) 165, gives 175; Hillaby (1997), see n8, 41-2. Figures for the diocese in W.J.Dohar *Black Death and Pastoral Leadership: the Diocese of Hereford in the Fourteenth Century* (1995) Table 2.1; G.G.Coulton *Medieval Panorama* (1938) 495-9 using J.Lunn's unpublished 1930 Cambridge University PhD thesis. The most recent discussion as to the reliability of the bishops' registers is J.Aberth, 'The Black Death in the Diocese of Ely: the Evidence of the bishop's register' *J Med Hist* 21 (1995) 275-87.

161. *Reg Trillek* 376-83; Dohar, see n160, 52; Ormrod & Lindley, see n108, 26-33; CPL iv, 390

162. Bannister (1924) see n137, 156-7; Capes, see n1, 226-9.

163. C.Dyer *Lords and Peasants in a Changing Society, the Estates of the Bishopric of Worcester, 680-540* (1980) 145-9, 209-11, 236-9; Capes, see n1, ix-xi, 168-9; HD&CA Kempley Court Rolls 7018/1/2/52-4; E.B.Fryde, 'The tenants of the bishops of Coventry and Lichfield and Worcester after the plague of 1348-49' in *Medieval Legal Records Edited in Memory of C.A.F.Meekings* ed R.F.Hunnisett & J.B.Post (1978) 228-32, 242-57; idem *Peasants and Landlords in Later Medieval England* (1996) chs 4 & 5; B.Harvey *Westminster Abbey and its Estates in the Middle Ages* (1977) 148-51; *Agrarian History of England & Wales, III, 1348-1500* ed E.Miller (1991) 444-5, Table 5.1 & Appendix D, 502-4.

164. HD&CA 1789.

165. HD&CA 1787; *Reg Trefnant* 163. For Devereux's *Plan* and 'Bishop's Palace' Hillaby (1997) see n8, 33, 36. Royal Commission on Historic Monuments *Inventory of Historical Monuments in Herefordshire* II (1932) 113, no 74 & pl 22.

166. *Reg Trillek* 503-27; G.Williams *The Welsh Church from Conquest to Reformation* (1962) 147-8.

167. *Henry Knighton: Chronicon* ed J.R.Lumby, RS 92 (1895) II, 63.

168. *Reg Trillek* 505, 514, 524; HD&CA 3299, 3304, 1932.

169. HD&CA 1932, 3304, 3299, 1730; *Reg Trillek* 196-7.

170. *Reg Trillek* 240, 481, 486, 491, 496; HD&CA 7018/1/3/12, 13.

171. Orme & Webster, see n3, 129; see p2 & 104 and n5.

172. HD&CA 3256; CPR 1321-4, 79; *Calendar of the Records of the Corporation of Gloucester* comp W.H.Stevenson (1893) nos 755, 782, 795, 803, 805, 807, 865, 866; *Victoria County History: Gloucestershire* xi (1972) 287.

173. HD&CA 3257, 7018/1/3/67-8 & 102-4.

174. HD&CA 7018/1/3/98 & 100-101, 3307.

175. *Reg Lewis Charlton* 14-17; HD&CA 3308, 1804, 7018/1/3/108-9.

176. HD&CA 1804. Hospital corrodies are discussed in P.H.Cullum *Cremetts and Corrodies: Care of the Poor and Sick at St Leonard's Hospital, York, in the Middle Ages* Borthwick Paper 79 (1991).

177. *Reg Lewis Charlton* 1-2, 43-5, 71; *Reg Courtenay* 3-4; HD&CA 3307, 3317, 3735; Jakeman & Carver's *Directory and Gazeteer of Herefordshire* (1890) 467; Kelly's *Directory of Herefordshire* (1937) 120.

178. HD&CA 3315; *Reg Lewis Charlton* 14-17.

179. HD&CA 3308, 3309, 3310B, 3311, 3312, 3313, 3315; *Reg Lewis Charlton* 14-17.

180. *Reg Bothe* viii; *Valor* see n16, III, 13; G.Marshall *Hereford Cathedral: Its Evolution and Growth* (1951) 89, 163-4.

181. HD&CA 3564, 3754, 4248; see pp32-3, 102-3, 105.

182. *Reg Lewis Charlton* 69; *Reg Gilbert* 61 122; HD&CA 1807, 2220.

183. HD&CA 1807, 3333; 1779 fxir in Bannister, see n129 (1930); *CPR 1330-34*, 333.

184. *CPR 1377-81*, 577-8; Clay, see n3, 223.

185. *Reg Trefnant* 56-8, 138-40; A.B.Emden *A Biographical Register of the University of Oxford to AD 1500* 3 vols (1957-9) 1521-3; J.F.Baldwin *The King's Council in England during the Middle Ages* (repr 1969) 149-52, 364-5, 389-91 with the text of Prophet's *Register* 489-504; Tout *Chapters in Administrative History* iii, 466-7, 471-3; J.H.Wylie *History of England under Henry IV* (4 vols, 1884-98) ii, 484 n4, 5 & 6.

186. Emden *Biog Reg to 1500*, see n185, 1522; *CPR 1381-5*, 490; *1388-92*, 308; *1401-5*, 327; *Reg Trefnant* 178, 186; J.Hillaby, 'Early Christian and pre-Conquest Leominster' *TWNFC* 45iii (1987) 648-9 for details and maps of St Tyrioc's isle.

187. HD&CA 3333. At St Cross, Winchester c1136 bishop Henry de Blois directed that the thirteen poor men have daily 'a good loaf of wheaten bread' and 'drink of good stuff' (strong not small beer). P.Hopewell *St Cross: England's Oldest Almshouse* (1995) 3.

188. *Valor*, see n16, III, 46 '*Terr' dñical' jac cuce hospital*'; HD&CA 4248, 3564, 3754; 23 Elizabeth I, c14 (private act).

189. *CPR 1413-16*, 410.

190. Emden *Biog Reg to 1500*, see n185, 1211; *Reg Trefnant* 360; Wylie, see n185, iii, 231; iv, 153, 171; C.H.Talbot & E.A.Hammond *The Medical Practitioners in Medieval England* (1965) 204-5, 220-1; W.A.Pantin *The English Church in the Fourteenth Century* (1955) 24.

191. T.Tanner *Bibliotheca Britannico-Hibernica* (1748) 505; C.H.Talbot *Medicine in Medieval England* (1967) 168; Wharton *Anglia Sacra* i (1691) 536.

192. *Incerti Scriptoris Chronicon Angliae de Regnis trium Regum Lancastrensium* ed J.A.Giles (1848) iv, 46; *Chronica monasterii S.Albani: Annales ... Ricardo II et Henrico IV* ed H.T.Riley, RS 28c iv (1866) 409-10; *Chronicle of Adam of Usk, 1377-1421* ed & trans C.Given-Wilson (1997) 203; C.L.Kinsford *English Historical Literature in the Fifteenth Century* (1913, repr 1962) 23-7; Wylie, see n185, ii, 237-9; *Household Accounts from Medieval England* i, ed C.M.Woolgar, Records of Social and Economic History, NS 17 (1992) 373-7, 424.

193. *Reg Trefnant* 360; *Reg Mascall* 171, 184; Emden *Biog Reg to 1500*, see n185, 1211; Wylie, see n185, ii, 238-9; iii, 231; iv, 153, 171; *CPR 1405-8*, 111, 318-9, 343, 461; *1408-13*, 56; Clay, see n3, 198; *CPL* v , 263; *Reg Gilbert* 90-1.

194. Prescott, see n21, 38; Godfrey, see n21, 45-7

195. H.Lloyd *A History of the English House* (repr 1975) 44-5; L.Salzman *Building in England down to 1540: a Documentary History* (1952) 94-5; M.Wood *The English Medieval House* (repr 1990) 99-121.

196. R.K.Morriss *The Master's House, Ledbury: An Archaeological and Architectural Analysis for Herefordshire Council* (2002) 6, 12-14.

197. For plan of St Cross Hospital see Godfrey, see n21, 46; Morriss, see n196, 18; *The Itinerary of John Leland* V ed L.Toulmin Smith (repr 1964) 154; Prescott, see n21, 166-7.

198. Orme & Webster, see n3, 129-31.

199. M.Rubin, 'Imagining Medieval Hospitals: Considerations on the cultural meaning of institutional change' in *Medicine and Charity before the Welfare State* ed J.Barry & C.Jones (1991) 14-25; Rubin (1987) see n6 72-4, 182-3; idem (1989) see n57 52-3; Orme & Webster, see n3, 127-36. For a critique of these views A.D.Brown *Popular Piety in Late Medieval England: The Diocese of Salisbury, 1250-1550* (1995) 181-90; *Reg Orleton* 388; *Reg Gilbert* 48-54; *CPR 1549-51*, 27-30; Duffy, see n3, 302, 341-2.

200. *Reg Thomas Charlton* 76; *Reg Gilbert* 2-3; see p75.

201. *Reg Swinfield* 464-7. For origins and background of portionists A.Hamilton Thompson *The English Clergy and their Organisation in the Later Middle Ages* (1947) 85-7; at Ledbury, Hillaby *Ledbury* (1997) 2-4; *CPL* i, 533; ii, 23, 227, 327; iii, 313, 314, 523, 566, 569; *CPR 1343-5*, 209; *1348-50*, 297, 501, 545; *1399-1401*, 489; *1413-16*, 226; *Monasticon* vi, 1398-9; *Reg Trefnant* 138-40, 175; *Reg Gilbert* 60-1. The myth that Ledbury, and Bromyard, were collegiate churches dies hard. Raised unsuccessfully under the 1547 Chantries Act by, in bishop Scory's words, 'certain lewd persons, being clerks of the exchequer' in 1559 and 1574 it is revived by John Blair in *The Church and the Medieval Town* ed T.R.Slater & G.Rosser (1998) 278 & fig 12.3. H.W.Phillott *Diocesan Histories: Hereford* (1888) 183-4; A.J.Winnington-Ingram, 'The Constitution of the Church of Ledbury' *TWNFC* (1942) 70-4; *Bromyard: A Local History* ed J.Hillaby & E.Pearson (1970) 10-11.

202. *CPR 1399-1401*, 62, 489.

203. *Reg Mascall* 170; *CPR 1408-13*, 168; *1413-16*, 226; *Gentlemans' Magazine* 77i (1807) 1001 .

204. Emden *Biog Reg to 1500*, see n185, 1515; *CPL* iv, 196-7; vii 263; *Reg Lacy* 113, 116, 120, 204; *Reg Spofford* 355; HD&CA, 1796; George Skyppe *MS Diary, 1668-90* WNFC Library, HCL Strong Room; T.Dingley *History from Marble* 2 vols, Camden Soc OS 94 & 97 (1867-8) II, ccxlvii.

205. *Rotuli parliamentorum* 6 vols (Record Commission, 1783) 253-60, 275, 345-6; *Cal Close Rolls 1442-30* 317-18.

206. *Statutes of the Realm* 2 Henry V, c.1; *Reg Spofford* iii-iv, 60-61, 354; HD&CA 1796.

207. Emden *Biog Reg to 1500* see n185, 1449-50; *Reg Spofford* 365; *Reg Beauchamp* 15; *Reg Boulers* 22, 23; *CPL* x, 15; R.L.Storey *The End of the House of Lancaster* (1986) 179, 228-301.

208. Emden *Biog Reg to 1500* see n185, 1941; *Reg Stanbury* 175, 191, 192; *Reg Myllyng* 193, 194. As *Fasti Ecclesiae Anglicanae 1300-1541: II Hereford Diocese* comp J.M.Horn (1962) 25 explains, *Reg Mylling* 193 prints Richard rather than John Vaughan in error.

209. Emden *Biog Reg to 1500* see n185, 2102-3; HD&CA 7031/1/175; *Reg Myllyng* iii & n11, 169-83, 193, 197.

210. E.Eames, 'The Canynges Pavement' *J Brit Archaeol Ass* 3S 14 (1951) 33-48; E.Eames *Catalogue of Medieval Lead Glazed Earthenware Tiles in the British Museum*, 2 vols (1980) I, 239-54; J.M.Lewis *The Medieval Tiles of Wales* (1999) 57-68, 160-

73. For dating see Eames (1980) I, 247 and more precisely A.C.Fryer, 'The Encaustic Tiles in St David's Cathedral' *Archaeol Cambrensis* 6S 3 (1903) 177-9; W.B.J.&E.A. Freeman *The History and Antiquities of St David's* (1856) 93. B.Williams, 'Late Medieval Floor Tiles from Acton Court, Iron Acton, Avon, 1974' in *Rescue Archaeology in the Bristol Area, 1* ed N.Thomas (1979) 61-76; P.B.Chatwin, 'The Medieval Patterned Tiles of Warwickshire' *Trans Birm & Midland Archaeol Soc* 40 (1936) fig 33 nos 2, 3 & 6.

211. Eames (1951) see n210, 34; Eames (1980) see n210, 240; L.Keen, 'The Medieval Decorated Tile Pavements at Worcester' in *Medieval Art and Architecture at Worcester Cathedral* Brit Archaeol Ass Conf Trans 1 (1978) 144-60.

212. Eames (1951) plates XXIV-XXVI and (1980) fig 14

213. HD&CA 3749; Emden *Biog Reg to 1500*, see n185, 2102-3; *Reg Mayhew* 283; *Reg Bothe* 340, 346; *Reg Myllyng* 171-82.

214. B.Greene, 'The Godwins of Hereford' *J Tiles & Architectural Ceramics Soc* I (1982) 10-16.

215. HD&CA 7031/1/175r&v; *Ancient Deeds* iii, D488, D801; Orme & Webster, see n3, 148-50; S.Fish *Supplicacyon for the Beggars ...* ed J.M.Cowper (1871) & see A.Kreider *English Chantries: The Road to Dissolution* (1979) 64.

216. *Valor*, see n16, III, 46; *Reg Foxe* 367.

217. Clay, see n3, 232-4. For survival and change Orme & Webster, see n3, 155-6. *Letters &Papers of Henry VIII* 23 vols (PRO 1862-1932) vi, nos 317, 661, vii no.1121(59), xv nos 695, 831(64), xiv(ii) nos 113(2)(6)(13), 264(29), 400(140); A.B.Emden *Biographical Register of the University of Oxford, 1501-1540* (1974) 38-9; *Victoria County History: Worcestershire* ii (1906) 176.

218. C.Haigh *English Reformations: Religion, Society and Politics under the Tudors* (1993) 152-67; 37 Henry VIII c4; B.Nilson *Cathedral Shrines of Medieval England* (1998) 192.

219. 1 Edward VI, c14; Kreider, see n215, 186-208; Haigh, see n218, 171-2; G.H.Cooke *Medieval Chantries and Chantry Chapels* (1947) 60.

220. See p105 and n5. *Charity Commissioners Reports: Herefordshire* (1819-37) 116-17.

221. Orme & Webster, see n3, 161-2.

222. *Valor*, see n16, III, 8; *Reg Bothe* 171-4; *Reg Foxe* 367; Kreider, see n215, 55; Faraday, see n12, 68-9, 191; *The Statutes of the Cathedral Church of Hereford, promulgated AD 1637* (1862) 141-9; Clay, see n3, 226, 253-4.

223. Hillaby *Ledbury* (1997) ch10.

224. A.B.Emden *Biographical Register of the University of Cambridge to 1500* (1963) 211; C.H.Mayo *A Genealogical Account of the Mayo and Elton Families* (1908) 9-18; HD&CA 1163, 7018/1/3/2; *Reg Bothe* 331, 339-41, 346; *Fasti Ecclesiae Anglicanae III: Salisbury Diocese* comp J.M.Horn (1962) 55, 57, 58, 31; HD&CA 7018/1. See especially p53.

225. *The Registers of Ledbury Pt 1. Baptisms, marriages and Burials 1556-1576* ed G.H.Piper (1899) 118; F.C.&P.E.Morgan, 'Some nuns, ex-religious and former chantry priests living in the diocese of Hereford (c1554)' *TWNFC* 37ii (1962) 135-48.

226. Haigh, see n218, 156-8; HD&CA 7018/1/3/68-9, 94; 3670, 3681, 3683, 3727.

227. Haigh, see n218, 170; Barrett in Jancey, see n136, 181-5; F.Havergal *Fasti Herefordenses* (1869) 147, pl xii; Phillott, see n201, 181.

228. *William Harrison: Description of England in Shakspere's Youth* ed F.J.Furnivall (1877) 31.

229. Haigh, see n218, 177.

Index

150

151